W9-CPC-139

Long Distance Love

1855-1870

257 Letters
from a
Pioneer
Homestead

Jodie Sewall

Long Distance Love
1855 – 1870
257 Letters from a Pioneer Homestead
ISBN 978-0-578-02683-1
All Rights Reserved
Printed in the United States of America

Long Distance Love

1855-1870

257 Letters from a Pioneer Homestead

Contents

Acknowledgement

I would like to thank Dave Taghon, president of the Empire Heritage Group for believing in me and allowing me to undertake this project. Your interest in the project and your encouragement along the way were vital to the completion of this project.

The Empire Area Museum shared their large collection of letters and memorabilia with me which enabled me to read and transcribe each letter in its original state, the result of which is this book with all 257 letters from the Boizards. I would also like to thank Grace Johnson for the personal tour that she gave to my family when we visited Glen Arbor in August 2006.

I am also thankful for my family who persevered through the endless days of my *working on the book*. I really did eventually finish it, although I know there were many days when you doubted that I would.

I am most grateful to my parents, Jack and Michele Pattan for my upbringing and for the love of family history that I learned from them.

I would also like to thank Edwin Fisher. His commitment to preserving local and family history spurred me on many times when the task seemed overwhelming and out of reach. Without his help and knowledge along the way we would never have seen a book printed that reunited both sets of Boizard letters.

Jodie Sewall

2009

Introduction Part I

The House Had a Story to Tell

Time had marched like an enemy, for over a hundred years, against the old gray house as it languished forgotten in the hidden glen. It stood with aged dignity beneath the protective shadows of towering oak trees. Those ancient trees poised tall and straight like age-old sentries guarding the house and protecting the memories of those who had once lived there.

The driveway to the aged house was just off the main street of the village of Glen Arbor, but as it gently wound its way through dense trees and underbrush, one instantly felt isolated from the hubbub of the present time and transported back to a simpler time when this house was younger and it's door swung open and shut with life.

For thirty year old Michele, this was the first glimpse of her great grandmother's house in over 15 years. Just the sight of the old gray house, brought back faded memories of Great Grandma Todd, walking around her yard with her cane carefully tending to her flowers.

While growing up, Michele and her mother Jessie had made annual trips to Glen Arbor on Memorial Day to drive Grandma Todd to the Maple City cemetery. Grandma Todd had always carefully and thoughtfully brought flowers for the graves of each of her loved ones. Each flower was tenderly placed like a tribute to the lives of those who had passed on before her.

 For Michele, this visit to Great Grandma Todd's house was her tribute; her way of remembering and giving honor to her great grandmother. This would be Michele's final opportunity to visit the house that had belonged in her family for over 100 years and most recently to her great grandmother.

Michele's mom, Jessie, had urged this occasion, by encouraging Michele to "Stop by and see if there is anything left in the house that you would be special to you."

The house had sat vacant for sixteen years, and its dilapidated condition had, for safety reasons, warranted its destruction. This demolition would take place within a week or two, so this visit would be the one and only opportunity to remember and to look around.

The thick layer of leaves on the porch bore testimony to the many seasons that had passed since anyone had come or gone from the house. As the key was turned in the rusty lock, the door heaved as if it had been holding its breath for this day. The musty odor from being closed up was pungent and overwhelming.

The last activity in the house had been a sale of the contents of the house. The piles of stuff that had been left were considered valueless. Michele and her husband Jack, and their family of five children began the slow process of sifting through the piles of clothes and papers that were strewn about the rooms. Within just a few minutes of sorting through piles a thick cloud of dust filled the air.

Many 'treasures' were unearthed as they dug around: wooden marbles, hand sewn baby gowns, a hand carved bed frame, a pencil box, a few tattered china dolls, a small cast-iron toy train, an old iron toy car, hand carved canes and many other things. Some of the more unusual finds were bags of hair saved from hairbrushes, false teeth, a glass eye, a hardened old sandwich wrapped in paper, and a shoe box containing a dead parakeet.

As Michele and her family searched through the piles from one room to another, one common thing drew Michele's attention, the stacks of letters, cards, envelopes and tax papers strewn about as if they had been dumped out of bureau drawers. Curious as to what they were, Michele picked up an old tin bucket and stuffed it full of the interesting looking papers.

The visit to the old homestead only lasted an hour or two due to the thick dust being stirred up by their searching. Any other 'treasures' would remain hidden and lost forever with the destruction of the house.

When Michele, got back home, she began to organize and clean up all of the things they had collected from Great Grandma Todd's house. She began to sort the papers and the letters that she had picked up and as she began to read the letters, she was instantly drawn into the lives of relatives that she had never 'met' before. Their devotion to one another and the struggles they endured with long absences from each other brought about a sincere appreciation of her amazing heritage.

These letters became a valuable link to her past and became her window to the past. On occasion, regret crept in her mind when she would think about the other 'letters and papers' that had been left behind in the house, but she also knew that nothing could be done about that now, as the house had been demolished, so pushing aside the regret she treasured the letters that she had and the family history they preserved. She took this knowledge of her heritage and introduced her children to their Great Great Great Great Grandparents, Oliver and Eleanor Boizard.

Introduction Part II

The year was 1974 and the old house, known to the local residents as the 'Westcott' house, behind the Glen Arbor Town Hall in Leelanau County, Michigan, was being torn down. Its' last resident, Etta May Fisher Westcott Todd, had died in 1958 and the building was in a state of disrepair having sat vacant for the past 16 years, when Julia Dickinson & Jo Bolton learned about it. All the furniture had been sold at auction and uneven floorboards; plaster and lath littered the floor of the old building. They didn't know if they would find anything of historical interest.

Closer searching, however, revealed old newspapers, old magazines, and best of all old letters scattered throughout the house. There were names that were familiar to them such as Fisher and Westcott, and there were names that were unfamiliar, such as Boizard and Dow.

Julia and Jo gathered every letter whether they were tattered or whole until they had found over one hundred letters. When it came time to sort the letters they had collected, they sorted them chronologically in order to have some continuity. The letters told the story of a pioneer family, John Oliver Boizard and his wife, Eleanor. The letters described

5

firsthand the hardships involved with settling new lands and the worries and sorrows and joy they experienced along the way.

A dream began to form in the hearts of Julia Dickinson & Jo Bolton to transcribe the letters that they had and print them in book form in order that their rich history be preserved in such a way that many people could read these detailed and personal accounts of pioneer life in the mid 1800's. In 1993, their dream became reality, with the printing of "The Boizard Letters, Letters from a Pioneer Homestead."[1]

Introduction Part III

What an Amazing Discovery!

My mother, Michele Pattan, has been the custodian of our family 'treasure' ever since she discovered the Boizard letters in her Great Grandma Todd's house in 1974. During the summer of 2005, I asked my mom if I could bring the letters to my home in New York State. I wanted to organize and transcribe them so that all the members of my family could have their own personal copy of our family treasure.

In the process of organizing the letters, I out of curiosity, did a simple online search for the name "Boizard." Much to my surprise and shock a book came up entitled The Boizard Letters. There wasn't much information listed about the book in the item description, but I bought the book on the spot. I wondered how it was possible that it was the same family, but I also wondered with the unusual name of "Boizard" how it could *not* be the same family? Waiting for that book to come in the mail was equivalent to a small child waiting for Christmas to come.

The day the book arrived I immediately sat down and thumbed through it and I knew in an instant that it was indeed the 'missing' letters. The fact

---

[1] Dickinson & Bolton, *The Boizard Letters, Letters from a Pioneer Homestead,* Empire Heritage Group, 1993 page ix

that they had been preserved and eventually printed into a book was something that I could hardly believe. Calling my mother to tell her of my discovery was one of the highlights of my life. She was just as amazed and thrilled as I was.

My family certainly rejoices in the discovery of the 'missing' letters and I know the Glen Arbor historians also celebrated finding the 'missing' letters, but in fact, neither set of letters was ever actually 'lost.' Each set was highly valued and treasured by their respective owners. This new book which contains all of the letters might also be called 'The Boizard Letters - reunited.'

My personal connection to this project is vibrant and real and it is my earnest desire to preserve with integrity and accuracy each of the 257 letters that represent my grandparents' life.

Reading the letters that comprise this collection was both a joy and a difficult task. I loved the discovery of information that each letter brought, but learning to decipher the writing styles of each writer took considerable effort. Oliver's letters were probably the easiest to read as his penmanship was beautiful and he used punctuation. Eleanor however, did not write her own letters and in the early years she had several different writers, many of whom were barely literate themselves. When their daughter Marietta grew old enough to write, she took over the task of writing for her mother. The most difficult letters in the collection to decipher were those written to Marietta by a childhood friend named Emma Bridges.

It was my decision as the editor to transcribe all of the letters as closely to the original as possible. I have kept the misspelled words and the incorrect capitalization and punctuation, because I believe that is a true representation of the people and the times in which they lived.

If I thought that a word might need additional explanation I have added in brackets an italicized word that will help the reader to understand what the writer was trying to say. If I could not decipher a word you will see an italicized question mark in brackets and possibly a guess as to what the word might be.

Because very few of these writers used punctuation, I have added extra spacing in between sentences or where a new thought begins. This extra space is designed to keep the sentences from running together and it provides a 'break' for the eyes of the reader.

The words that are underlined throughout the book are words that were underlined by the original writers for emphasis.

Some of the words and/or names that they used are words/names that we are not familiar with today, so I have bolded those words and included a definition or explanation of the word in the glossary at the back of the book.

My desire is that you will enjoy this amazing treasury of letters which will introduce you to ordinary people who faced the challenge of settling a new land with very few resources because they believed that they could create a better life for themselves and in turn for their neighbors. These great pioneering spirits established communities and those communities are their lasting gift to us.

Jodie

Principal Characters

This portion of the book is designed to put 'skin' on the people mentioned in the letters. By rehearsing the personal information that is known about each person, my hope is that as you 'meet' them in the letters, you will recognize each character as a real flesh and blood person, with sorrows and joys, struggles and accomplishments just like you and I.

Eleanor Melvina McGill Magill Boizard: Eleanor Melvina McGill was born January 19, 1828, in Wheeling, WV. A scrap piece of paper within the collection of "Boizard" papers indicates that Eleanor's mother, Sarah McGill died in 1832. This note also mentions that her father's name was Charles McGill and that Eleanor went to live with a Quaker family in western PA.

In 1851 at the age of 23, Eleanor married James Magill. Their daughter, Marietta Magill was born March 18, 1852. (This information is taken from the flyleaf of a Bible that belonged to Eleanor.) There is never another mention of James Magill and it can be assumed that he died prior to Eleanor's marriage to John Oliver Boizard, July 16, 1855.

The oldest letter in the entire collection is a letter written to Eleanor shortly after her marriage to Oliver in 1855, the letter addressed Eleanor as 'sister' and spoke about her father as still living and farming. The name that was signed on the letter is E. Hudson. It is possible that this "E. Hudson" is the sister that Eleanor writes about on occasion and whom she often wished to visit. Oliver makes mention of Eleanor and Marietta visiting "Aunt Lizzy." This could be a nickname for a sister named "Elizabeth."

Details gleaned from within the collection of letters indicate that Eleanor was not able to write her own letters, and that she solicited help from various people to take her dictation. Many of these 'writers' were barely literate themselves. When Marietta became old enough to write, she became the chief 'writer' for her mother. Later census records indicate that Eleanor did learn to read and write before she died. Eleanor died in Glen Arbor Michigan in 1911, at the age of 83.

John Oliver Boizard: From census records, we are able to determine that "Oliver" was born in Canada, approximately 1820. He was fluent in French & English. His penmanship was beautiful and his command of the English language exemplary. At times, Oliver was fondly referred to as "Bus." This nickname sounds like a shortened version of his last name. He married Eleanor Magill, when he was 35 years old.

The exact date that Oliver first enlisted in the Army has not yet been determined. Eleanor's obituary stated that her husband Oliver had fought in the Mexican War, the Indian War and the Civil War. It also stated that he had served the U.S. Army for twenty-five years. Using this information, we can speculate that his initial enlistment occurred around 1838, which interestingly, is the same year that John Fisher enlisted.

Oliver served with the 4th Artillery, Company "K", during 1856 and 1857 in the Seminole Indian Wars in Florida, and also in 1858 and 1859 on his tour of duty to the Nebraska Territory. It appears from the contents of his letters that initially, Oliver may have been assigned field duties, such as helping to build roads through the Florida swamp. In time it appears that he began to take on the responsibility of writing for some officers and later we learn that his principal assignment in the army is in the Quartermasters Department, filling out the muster rolls.

In 1859, Oliver received either a furlough or a discharge from the army and he moved his family to the forty-acre piece of property that he had bought in the Glen Arbor area. After a short time of living in Glen Arbor, they sold their property. It appears that Oliver re-enlisted in 1861 to serve in the Civil war. He and his family moved to Newport, KY.

The contents of the letters suggest that in 1864 when Oliver's three year term was up, that he moved to Chicago where he was employed as a civilian for Capt. Pomeroy in the Quartermaster's Department. Probably due to Eleanor's health problems, she and Marietta moved back to Glen Arbor, purchased property and built a small log home. Oliver sent money and supplies to his wife and daughter in Michigan and they kept in contact through correspondence and occasional visits.

Oliver died in Chicago, in 1870, at the age of 50. The cause of his death is unknown; however, there is a reference to paralysis, in a letter written by a military doctor, in response to a letter sent to him by Marietta. In the letter Marietta had sent to him she had apparently requested his help in securing military compensation. It does not appear like this compensation was ever received.

Marietta Magill Boizard: Marietta was born March 18, 1852. She was affectionately known as "Ettie" throughout her life. Ettie, attended school sporadically growing up, but she was able to both read and write. When she became 'of age' to write, she became the primary 'writer' for her mother. There are many times in the course of taking dictation from her mother that Ettie slipped into first person and wrote directly to her father and then reverted back to the dictation of her mother. In January 1870 just shy of her 18th birthday, Marietta married the neighbor boy, Charles Fisher. She and Charlie had three children, John Edward, Etta May & Charles Frederick. Ettie died in 1935 at the age of 83.

Catherine Boizard: *Possibly*, Oliver's mother. The 1860 census shows a record for a Catherine Boizard, in the city of Philadelphia. She was born approximately 1786. This date fits closely with Oliver's mom's age, which is mentioned in the letters. This Catherine Boizard was born in Ireland, and could not read or write. She died April 25, 1871 at the age of 85. She is buried in Old Chester Cemetery, PA, Section M, Lot 147 grave 5. She is buried next to Elizabeth Boizard, probably her daughter, "Libby".

Elizabeth Boizard: Oliver's sister, affectionately called "Libby." From the cemetery record in Old Chester, it appears like Libby was never married and that she is buried next to her mom in lot 147, grave 4. Her date of death was October 7, 1871; she was 60 years old.

Jacob Boizard: Jacob was Oliver's oldest brother. Census records point to his birth as being in 1809 and that he resided in Philadelphia.

Mary (Boizard): Oliver's sister, Mary traveled to California in a covered wagon around 1856. She settled in the Sacramento area. Initially she and her husband ran a successful boarding house for California's former governor, John Bigler and his staff. Communications ceased coming from Mary in 1858 and the family surmised that she had probably died.

Lewis Pierre Boizard: Oliver's brother, Pierre was known as "Pete" and also by the nickname "Zarty." This nickname was a word play off of his last name. Pete was born in 1815. Pete was referred to as a day policeman and also a shoemaker. He was married to Caroline (b. 1813) and they had a daughter named Caroline, nicknamed "Cally" (b.1849) and a son named Charles, referred to as "Charley" (b.1850). Charley grew up to be an accomplished early American artist.

Emma Bridges: Emma Bridges was a childhood friend of Marietta Boizard. It appears that they met while their fathers were both stationed at Newport Barracks, KY during the years of 1861-1864. In the 1860 census, there is a record that lists an Emma F. Bridges as living with a Catherine Johnson in Indiana. This Emma was born in Ohio and was nine years old. That would make her one-year-older than Marietta. In our letters, Emma is referred to as staying some nights with a Mrs. Johnson. If indeed the Emma in the 1860 census is the same as our Emma, it seems reasonable to assume that Emma's family moved to Newport Barracks, KY about the same time as the Boizards, 1861.

From the collection of letters, we know that Emma's father, William Bridges, had a drinking problem and references are made that would suggest that Oliver Boizard may have had a drinking problem as well. William Bridges re-enlisted when his term was up and he was sent to the Arizona Territory. Emma's mother's name was Eliza, and there appears to have been a very close friendship between her and Eleanor Boizard.

Emma Bridges was married December 27, 1866, to Edwin A. Brown, a soldier in the army. In a family photo album there is a picture of a Mr. Brown with the following note, "married cousin Eleanor Boizard." Research has not uncovered that family relationship yet. The note written on Mr. Brown's photo also mentions that Edwin and Emma were both killed by Indians on their way to California.

William & Evelena Brown: Not much is known about this family. His letters indicate that he was the principal musician with the 15th Infantry. He was stationed at Fort Adams, RI. He wrote to Oliver and he asked about Wm. Bridges. This leads to speculation that at one time, William Brown's regiment may have been stationed at Newport Barracks and then transferred to Fort Adams, RI. The Browns and the Boizards appear to have been very good friends as there was talk about coming and visiting each other and their desire to move close so that they could be neighbors.

John & Elizabeth Dorsey: There is a detailed account of John and Elizabeth Dorsey's life in James Tozer's book, <u>Glen Arbor Pioneers</u>. This paragraph contains very basic information, for the purpose of introducing to the Dorsey family. The Boizards first became acquainted with the Dorsey's, when the Boizards moved to the Glen Arbor area in 1859. When Eleanor and Marietta moved back to Glen Arbor in 1864, they ate a meal with the Dorsey's and then went to stay with the Fisher's. Many references are made about the Dorsey's in this collection of letters. They were true friends to the Boizard family.

Kate Boizard Dow: Kate was Oliver's sister. She was born December 2, 1830. She resided in the Philadelphia area and was married to C.C. (Christopher) Dow. They had one son, Phineas.

Charles Fisher: Charlie was the first son of John and Harriet Fisher. He was born in Fond du Lac, Wisconsin in 1849. The 1870 & 1880 census records listed Charlie as a farmer. He was also involved as a commercial fisherman and in selling, pigeons, fish, apples and other products to companies in Chicago & Traverse City. Charlie's public service career included county surveyor, school board member, county supervisor and Justice of the Peace.[2] In January 1870, Charlie married Marietta Boizard. Charlie obituary lists his death as 1909 at the age of 60.

Harriet Maria McCarty Fisher: Harriet McCarty was born on March 2, 1826, in West Martinsburg, Lewis County, New York. Her parents migrated to Wisconsin in 1841. Harriet McCarty married John E. Fisher, April 23, 1843. Harriet and John had two sons, Charles Andrew born August 29, 1849 and Francis born July 3, 1851. As a family they moved to Glen Arbor in 1854.[3]

In 1857, Harriet Fisher's brother, Charles C. McCarty also followed the Fisher's to Glen Arbor. He built an Inn in 1858 and a dock for ships in 1865. Harriet's sister, Sarah McCarty King and her family moved to Glen Arbor around 1867. Harriet died in 1914 at the age of 88.[4]

John E. Fisher: John E Fisher was born in Salem, NY in 1818. He enlisted in the army in 1838 and was in Co. F, Eighth Infantry. It is believed that it was during this time in the army that John Fisher became acquainted with John Oliver Boizard. In 1841, Fisher mustered out of the army in Brooke, Florida and John and Harriet moved to Fond Du Lac, Wisconsin. In 1854 the Fishers sold their Wisconsin property and moved to the Glen Arbor area in Michigan. John and Harriet acquired many land grants in the Glen Arbor area, and John became one of the 'founding fathers' of Glen Arbor. John built a sawmill and was also active in many areas of public service i.e. Justice of the Peace, Judge of Probate, County Clerk etc. [5]

---

[2] Edwin Fisher, *Sawmills and Family Trees*, 2006 page 26

[3] James R. Tozer, *Glen Arbor Pioneers*, Glen Arbor, MI Leelanau Press, 2003 pages 32-33

[4] Edwin Fisher, *Sawmills and Family Trees*, 2006 pages 10-11, 25

[5] Edwin Fisher, *Sawmills and Family Trees*, 2006 page 26

John's enthusiasm for the beautiful land in Glen Arbor was influential in bringing many new settlers to the area.

John's sister Elizabeth, her husband Bishop Wilson Tucker and their three-year-old daughter Sarah moved to Glen Arbor in 1854 also. There are many references to the 'Tuckers' in the letters.

In 1855 the *US Saginaw*, chartered by George Ray, brought 14 settlers to Glen Arbor. Among those settlers would be another of John Fisher's sisters, Margaret Fisher Coggeshall. Margaret with her husband William, and their three daughters, Elizabeth Clark (Nov. 28, 1840), Margaret Mariah (Oct 18, 1846), and Sarah Jeanette (May 10, 1851) As the passengers were disembarking from the steamer, John Dorsey, one of the founding fathers of Glen Arbor, stated his intent to marry Elizabeth Coggeshall. He did marry her one-year later on September 18, 1856.[6]

John Fisher wrote several letters to Oliver during Oliver's service in the Civil War. John's letters read like speeches and are some of the most eloquent letters in the entire collection. He staunchly opposed slavery and was in strong favor of fighting to preserve the Union.

When Eleanor & Marietta moved back to Glen Arbor in 1864, they purchased 10 acres from John Fisher. This property adjoined the Fishers and that close proximity played an important role in the eventual courtship and marriage of Marietta Boizard, to Charlie Fisher on January 19, 1870.

More information about John & Harriet Fisher and genealogy charts can be found in the highly recommended books. Glen Arbor Pioneers, by James R. Tozer, and Sawmills & Family Trees, by Edwin Fisher.

---

[6]Robert Rader, Beautiful Glen Arbor Township (Traverse City, MI: Village Press 1983) page 21

Austin Newman: From census records we can determine that Austin Newman was born in New York around 1836. He remained single at least through the 1900 census. In letters written to Marietta Boizard from Emma Bridges she mentioned an "oscar newman" who left Newport Barracks in 1864, and that he had left a picture of himself for Marietta. It is possible with Emma's poor spelling that this "Oscar" is actually Austin, or that they had nicknamed Austin, "Oscar." Austin Newman did serve in the army during the Civil War, so he may have become friends with Oliver at that time. Austin seemed to show up quite often in the Boizard's life. It appears like he was actually waiting for Marietta to grow up, so that he could court her. He would have been approximately 16 years older than Marietta.

Aunt Tourison: Catherine Boizard's only sister. When Aunt Tourison died in 1858 her daughters, Margaret and Elizabeth, withheld some important Canadian documents from Catherine Boizard. Mrs. Tourison was buried in St. Mary's Cemetery next to her husband.

I hope that by the time you finish this book you will have come to recognize all of these people with their pioneering spirits and their stalwart courage as 'relatives' of your own.

Florida – Seminole Indian War
1855-1857

Rev. John Henderson married Eleanor Melvina McGill to James Magill in Pittsburgh, PA on June 4, 1851. Marietta Magill was born March 18, 1852. Nothing more is known of James Magill and it is assumed that he died. Eleanor M. Magill married John Oliver Boizard on July 16, 1855.[7] Oliver was 35 years old when he married 27-year -old Eleanor.

The very first letters in this collection primarily introduce us to Eleanor and Oliver's family members. Comments are made about Eleanor and Oliver's recent marriage and their desire to meet the spouse. Names of siblings and friends are frequently mentioned.

Exactly where Eleanor & Oliver lived during the first year of their marriage is unknown. There is a letter that refers to their living in Pittsburgh in 1855.

Oliver was a Sergeant Major with the 4th Artillery, in the U.S. Army at the time they were married. During the years of 1851-1856, the Regiment Headquarters for the 4th Artillery was in Fort Hamilton, New York. Its individual companies were distributed to Fort Hamilton as well as Forts Lafayette, Mifflin (PA), Washington and some of the companies were disbursed to forts along the Great Lakes.[8]

Oliver made a reference about having his mail forwarded to him in Florida from a Sergeant Bates in Brownsville. There is a Brownsville, PA which is near Pittsburgh and McClellandtown (the small town that Eleanor was raised in). There is also an old military fort in that town, but

---

[7] This information is written in the flyleaf of Eleanor's little black Bible, which now belongs to Michele Pattan.

[8] The timeline of events for the 4th Artillery was gleaned from a website article http://www.usregulars.com/usartillery/4us_art.html

I have not been able to determine if a company from the 4th Artillery occupied it during the years around 1855.

How Eleanor and Oliver met and where they lived during their first year of marriage remains a mystery at this point in time. We do know that in the fall of 1856 the 4th Artillery was sent to Florida, to engage the Seminole Indians and that Eleanor accompanied him to Florida.

In January of 1857, Oliver's Company K was sent on a mission to Fort McRae, on the eastern side of Lake Okeechobee. Eleanor remained at Fort Myers, and corresponded with Oliver for six months until she was able to join him at Fort McRae as a cook and laundress.

New Salem
20 1855 August

Dear Sister

I received your letter on the 18th of this month and was glad to hear from you as it is the first we have heard from you for a long time   we having wrote three letters to you in the last year without recieving an answer we are as well as usual this time   all your relations is well as far as we know   we would be very glad to see you but it is not likely we will come down to pittsburgh   so you must come up and see us and bring your Sargent along as we would like very much to see him and hope that you will have all the happiness that mortals can enjoy   we have left **McClellandtown** and live near **New Salem** in the same hous that we used to live in on Wobley's farm   your father lives on the same farm and has raiset *{raised}* over 1 thousand bushels of oats and has a large crop of corn in which looks very promising   but I must close for the presant   pleas answer this letter soon   yours as ever

E Hudson

From Caroline Boizard, sister-in-law, to Oliver

Philadelphia
April 27 /56

Dear Major,

I was requested to answer your last letter, at the time we received it Kate was very sick and your mother was there attending on her, we do not wish you to think you are forgotten by not writing to you or acknoledgeing the amount sent to your Mother, it was received and greatfully to. for you know money never comes *{?}* with her, and always cheers her spirits when cast down. Mother is as well as usual and is much obliged to you for thinking of her in your absence, may none of us forget her while she is spared to us. we know not how long it will be. I was much surprised when I looked at the date of your last letter, I was not aware so much time had elapsed since you wrote, but "<u>time</u> and <u>Tide</u> wait for <u>no man</u>" Your brother Pete has been promoted to day Paliece *{police}* which is much better, he gets so tired when he gets home at night he is fit for nothing but goes to bed. I have been waiting for him to

19

write but begin to think we will wate in vain. I hope you will be able to make this out, I am in a great hury. Kate is much better, than when your letter came, Christopher, also and Phin, my mother & father and sisters are well as usual. we have not herd from Elizabeth lately but are in hopes she is well. Jakob has left the City and gone to Baltimore to see if he can get along any better he is a teacher and willing to work but he could get nothing to do, he could get hardly enough to keep his teeth a going. Your Mother and all the Family send there best wishes to your wife and little Daughter and hope this will find them in better health than when you wrote last, we all like the likeness you sent very much. when will you send some more. I have wrote all that is nessary and more and hope you will answer this as soon as commencement. I believe you owe us one letter already, give us all the particulars of your family and office we all feel interested in your wellfare you know you have allways been so punctual in answering our letters that we did not know what to think of your not writing to us, we did not know but what something was said in the last letter to offend you, we are glad to lern that you are promoted, I hope you will remain there for many years, do you think you will be able to come to P. this Summer with your little Family. tell us if you think there is any prospect of coming I would like to see you all very much indeed the children often speak of you, and say they want to see Uncle Oliver

This from your affectionate friends and <u>Sister in law,Caroline</u>
C.M. Boizard
No 18 Marian Street

{Written on the bottom of Caroline's letter}

<u>To John O. Boizard</u>

Sargt Major

Brother Olly,
I congratulate you on your good fortune of being promoted. And I hope you will continue to aspire. We have received a letter from Mary 2 or 3 weeks ago She states they had a very hard time of it in crossing the Plains they where attacked twice by the Indians and lost two wagons and four horses in the affair and narrowly escaped with their lives. there was in company with them a man and his wife which were killed. they

left two small children the youngest five weeks old which Mary took in her arms and Doctor the other and escaped to the woods with them   they finally arrived in Sacramento and set up Boarding house and had **Governer Bigler** and Lady and the upper ten boarding with them and was making out well. but the lady they rented the house from thought they was doing so well she would try her fortune at it. consequently she ordered Doc. and Mary out   they now live about ten miles out in a valley private   with the expectation of visiting Phila. ere long. No More at present My love to your wife and family
 yours Pierre Boizard

From Kate Dow to brother Oliver

Phila
Aug 29th /56

Brother Oly
Mom has been waiting for an answer to my leter   we thought you might be sick or left where you were   mom say she has great need of your assistance you know the amount she recivs *{receives}* from Zarty is limited   she would like you to rite as soon as possible   she is not very well this summer the heat has been so great   how do you do this warm weather   how is Elenor and little girl   all the family is pretty well   Zarty and family are well   we received a leter from sister mary a week ago she is well sends her love to you and say she hope <u>pa</u> words will come true that you will be the support of mom old age as your young day you enjoyed to yourself with the care of mom   she say Oly be kind to mom and God will reward you tenfold   a dying fathers words must come to pass   these are your sister Mary words   she say how she wold like to see you   she say she hope to see us all in two years the furthest   if she live   dear Oly rite soon and direct your letter to me   the last leter you sent mom was in feb or March and mom did not get it for a week after Zarty received it   send the answer to me and I will answer it immediately   rite soon   very soon   mom and all the famly send their love to you   Phineas send his love to uncle Oly   Excuse this short leter as I am righting *{writing}* for mom   Brother Oly rite as soon as possible good by from sister   Kate

From Oliver to Eleanor

Fort McRae, Fla
January 28th 1857

My Dear <u>Eleanor</u>
Your few lines Came to hand this Evening, and did not come an hour to soon, as you and Etty had hardly for a moment been out of my thoughts. I thought you would suffer at night with the cold, and I hope that you will be as Comfortable as a <u>tent</u> will admit of. We are working constantly on this road across the Swamp and when it is completed it will be nothing but a foot path. What they intend to do after, it is hard to tell. The Paymaster came to **Fort Center** and paid off Company "D" but our company with the Exception of a few of us, was left at Fort Center Consequently we could not be paid off as our Rolls, were with the Company. I must manage Somehow or other to send you some money before 10 days as I know you must be in need of it. I am on Extra duty in the **Subsistence Deptmt**. And do the duties of the **Quarter Masters Deptmt.** Lt. Hudson is the quarter Master, and Commissary and appears to be a good sort of <u>fellow</u> He wished me to wait upon him, and I thought I would not refuse, as it may <u>pay.</u>
And now <u>Dear</u> dont be uneasy for I will use my Endeavor to remit you a small sum of money as soon as possible. I hope the child is well kiss her for me and don't let her forget me. It is now midnight and the Musquitos are giving me **<u>Jessee</u>** Don't forget to Enquire at the Post office for my letters from Philadelphia by way of **Brownsville**, if old Bates Ever Sends them to me and now Eleanor a long good night. Answer this as soon as you can PS Tell Mrs Bowman her husband is on guard and is well and I suppose he will write to her this mail and now once more Farewell
Your Husband John O. Boizard

From Oliver to Eleanor

Fort McRae, Fla
February 1st 1857

Dear Wife

Friend Wood who is discharged will hand you 5 Doll's. (in gold) which I got from the Captain the sum is rather small but I thought there might be others wanting money, and Every body must have a chance of such favors. Don't be backward in letting me know what you require as I will contrive to get it for you. If you want Coffee or Sugar and cant get it out of the Commissary store let me know in your answer, and I will speak to Lieut. Hudson and either send it or the order. I am busy now making out my monthly papers for the Subsistence Dept'mt. My white shirts are all torn and rotten I have 2 Flannel shirts which will do me for the present. I wish I had 2 strong check shirts for the woods, and if I had taken <u>your advice</u> I should have them now. Dear <u>Eleanor</u> don't forget to go to the Post Office and see about my letters and have them forwarded to me. I cant tell you how soon you can join me but I hope very soon as the Company is 79 strong and there would be more work than you would like to do   Keep up a strong constitution and don't be lonely, for <u>He</u> that's above soothes the Wanderer. Kiss the young one for me and receive my Blessings. Your Husband Oliver

<u>From Eleanor to Oliver</u>

February 11th 1857

My Dear Husband
 i received your kind and welcome Letter and 5 Dollars with Wood on the 9th of this Month   with respect to Marietta i transfered the Kisses and you can do the same if you please to this letter   the money was verry usefull as i was near out   i bought you 2 shirts because they was nothing to buy to make them   i have sent you the likeness as we can not come ourselfs Mrs Bereman as {*has*} left and living with Mrs Best   Mrs Paterson will leave soon   i would like for you to have me come up to you   the Black thread is for {*Cannada ?*}   the towel is yours   with respect to provisions we can not get extra rations   sugar and Coffee is not out but candles is scarce and there is none in the setters {***sutlers***} store   i have got Browns washing this Day and was surprised to know that he was here   i was at the letter office for to see but they was none come   you send word wether i shall rite to your Mother or not   Wood expects to Leave here to Morrow for New Orleans please rite by return Mail God Bless you.   E.M.B.
Mrs Paterson and children are all well

23

<u>From Oliver to Eleanor</u>

Fort McRae, Fla.
February 15, 1857

My Dear Wife

Enclosed you will please find a 5 dollar gold piece   the mail had just come in and I seize this opportunity of answering your letter. The Company has gone on a Scout with Companies "E" and "H" 4th artillery and 2 companies of volunteers. They expect to be gone 20 days. I received a letter from Philadelphia from Mother, it came from Brownsville as I recognized Serg't Bates handwriting forwarding it, the other letter that the Post Master wrote about I have not received. Mother and all the family is well and send her love to you, and Etty. Kate says that Mother prays for us every day and says that <u>God</u> will bless us, Kate tells me that Elizabeth met with a heavy loss, she came up to shop for the winter and somebody Robbed her in the Market house. Some of her own money and a Bill of Mr. Little's. It will take a year for her to make it up. <u>Dearest Eleanor</u> you spoke of joining me   I had a talk with Capt. Roberts and he tells me that we will not occupy this place longer than 2 or 3 months as the rain will then commence, we will likely go over to the Atlantic Side to **Fort Jupiter**, or **Fort Lauderdale**, and very likely we may pass the summer at **Fort Myers**. I have been more busy here than any other post. For I had to issue to Seven Companies, Lt. Hudson has gone with the Company. Capt. Ireland is sick, Lieut Weed relieved Lt. Hudson as Commissary and Quartermaster. Lieut. Hudson paid me my Extra pay and gave me <u>Five</u> $5 dollars for taking care of his things. I will be obliged to write hard all this month to close his papers and Lieutenant Weed's. I have now Eleven dollars still in my possession and I wish you had it. I think some of the Sick from "K" Company is coming down to **Fort Myers**, and then I will be able to send you some more. You spoke of the likeness and the thread and towel. I suppose I shall get it in a few days. Dear Ellen don't be uneasy we may meet again this Summer. The End of the Month I will have 59 dolls Coming to me, and if I can collect what they owe you it will amount with my Extra pay, near 100 dollars, that looks like a start don't it. I am afraid the likeness might get broke. Give my Etty a big Grissley hug for me and Dear Ellen receive my Blessing. Your Husband, Oliver

Please answer this letter as soon as possible as I am anxious also send me some letter stamps. J.O.B.

<u>From Eleanor to Oliver</u>

Fort meres *{Myers}* Florada
February 26, 1857

My Dear Husband
 I received your welcom Letter two days ago   in said Letter I was glad to
hear that you enjoy good health as this leaves Hety and I and feel
thankfull to the Lord for preserving both you and us and I also got the 5
dollars you enclosed in it   my dear Husband Brown of our cp
{company} is dead on the 8th of said month and you better put in his
wash bill as I wash hear *{here}* for him since he came back   I am having
to make struggle hear *{here}* as well as I can   when ever I can get
washing or sewing there is not much chance for there is too many
woman hear and all idle   but however I wish you would wright to you
mother and send her some money if you can   for she will expect it and it
may be that the winter is hard in the north   please to go to the Sergent
Dean for a bottle of pickels and a pare *{pair}* of drawers i sent to you
his wife was sending him a box   it would hold nothing more   Let me
know if you stand in need of any over halls *{overalls}* and perhaps I
might get some other chance to send them to you or any thing else
Hetty tells you kiss her likeness for her and send her word when can we
both kiss you   no more at present but i bid you an affectionate fare well
and ever   remain your loving and Affectionate wife untill death
Elinor Buszard

Lett sergent patterson know the 2nd artilary will be leaving hear *{here}* on
the 20 of March and she wants to know if he will able to go home with
the Company as it would save a good deal of money for him or if not Let
him wright *{write}* and let Mrs patterson know if he would let herself and
the children to go on before him. Wright soon good by

<u>From Oliver to Eleanor</u>

Fort McRae, Fla
March 4th 1857

Dear Eleanor,
Serg't Dean has just handed me a Bottle of Pickles, and a pair of
drawers, which I needed very much. I do not Know whether you
received 5 dollars Enclosed in a letter or not, which I Sent you, Since

25

Wood's letter. I am very anxious about such matters. You will please find Enclosed in this 7 ½ dollars more, and be particular in acknowledging the receipt of it. I am well but I have So much to do at present, I have not had time to wash this week, and I got McLaughlin to wash me 5 or 6 pieces. I hope you are well also the girl. I have a new tin plate for her with the initials of her name on it. I sent you Brown's Bill in case you do not get it I think I can get it at the next pay day. Dear Eleanor be not uneasy but Keep a good heart I feel lonely Enough myself, and I miss the good cakes & coffee, we used to have. This is a poor place for fresh Provisions we have had since we have been here about one day, Fresh Pork, and about Venison Enough for one meal. We occasionally get Pickles & molasses, but I miss my Beef Soup very much. I suppose, you get enough to get along, slowly, for I suppose there is not much to do at **Fort Myers**, but try to get along as well as you can, and I will try to send you money at Every opportunity. I will in about a week try to send you some Coffee, and Etty's tin plate in a little box, you will not forget to send me some letter stamps say about 6 or 8 if you can get them. It is getting late and I will close my letter, Give my Etty a long kiss for me, and please receive my fondest wishes for your future wellfare. Your Husband Oliver

From Eleanor to Oliver

Fort Myers
march 5th 1857

Dear husband

I received your letter and I was glad to hear - that you are well as this leaves Hetty and me   I am sending you a small box of notions and half of the tobacco is for patterson half the cheese sugar coffee   norman lost his knapsack coming from **fort denaud** and the parcel you give him and candles is very scarce and I can't get one. I would write more but I am in hurry No more at present but remains your loving wife EMB

26

<u>From Eleanor to Oliver</u>

Fort Myers
march 8th 1857

Dear husband
I received your letter and the money and I was very glad to hear that you
was well and I received your other letter and the money   you wished to
know how I was getting along   I am doing very well and has plenty of
work now and you need not be uneasy about me   you wanted to know
how I am getting along in the tent   it does very well in dry weather but it
is very disagreeable wet   I had a small box all ready packed to send you
when donaldson was here but he did not like it   I sent that bill of Browns
the day after I got the letter but is wasnt take until next day   there is not
letter stamps to be had here but I have 2 that I will send you   I wish you
would send me some candles if you can   there has been quite a massacre
in fort keys *{Fort Keis}* Friday 6th 15 killed and wounded   four taken
prisoner one drummer and 3 fifers and we have one squaw and a child in
the guard house   you wanted me to kiss Etty   I did so and she is
growing a big girl and want to see her papa   No more at present
from your loving wife E M B
tell patterson that his wife and children are well

<u>From Oliver to Eleanor</u>

Fort McRae, Fla
March 13th 1857

Dear Wife
I received your <u>Box</u> last night, which contained 3 Pairs overalls & one
<u>shirt</u> (all Blue) and also some <u>Tobacco</u>, Coffee, sugar & cheese which I
divided with Sergeant Patterson. I also discover that there is 1 Box
Lobsters, 2 pairs of Stockings, & 2 pairs Drawers, 1 Bottle of <u>Tea</u> which
is really more than I can carry, should we be ordered off – However I can
sell most of them. I wish you would let me know if the shirt &
pantaloons that was wrapped up in a <u>newspaper</u> (a Glasgow paper) is not
for Sergt. Ford of "D" Comp'y the other two pair I suppose is mine   I
found in my uncovering them a paper with <u>Serg't</u> Fords name on it,
which I supposed was put in the box to let me know they were his. You
mentioned that you send me some notions but did not specify all the
articles, which causes me to be doubtful whether they all belong to me or
not. I wrote to my Mother the other day and told her how we were

27

situated, also told her as soon as I could spare the money I would send her some. The Company is still on the Scout and Comp'y "D" has gone to Establish a Post near **Fort Jupiter** I have not heard of them since Sergt. Dean desired me to write to his wife about his whereabouts and told me when he started that he would write to her, after he got settled. I sent you a small Box with Roach which contained some articles you may require. I am sorry that Norman lost them Candles as there are scarcely any here as "D" Comp'y took 2 Boxes with them.

I see by your letter that you are very busy, at present, that is better than doing nothing, I expect there is a great excitement about **Fort Myers**, about those men being killed I hope the next news we get, that the Indians will get their dose In answering this letter please tell me exactly what belongs to me and what belongs to Serg't Ford I will let the overalls and shirt remain as they are, before I can make any use of them, until I receive your instructions.

Dear Eleanor Please not send me any more untill I tell you as my stock increases in Clothing and I will have too much to carry, in case we should be ordered off, we expect the Company here in about 7 or 8 days then there will be some further news. The Musquitoes are awful, I put up the Bar but it don't do much good Please answer this as soon as possible, and Believe me to be yours with sincerity. Oliver

From Oliver to Eleanor

Fort McRae, Fla
March 24th 1857

My Dear Wife
This night the Boats have arrived from **Fort Center**, but they bring no news from **Fort Myers**, I have not news to communicate, with the exception of the Company returned, and they being paid off. I collected 28 dollars of your wash money, there are 4 men who still owes you, which is Roach (4 doll's) Poor Brown who is dead 4 doll's Meier 3 ½ dolls and Douglass 75 cents they say they will pay me at the first chance. Dieckman who is discharged will give you 15 dollars, for me and let me know whether you are in want of any more and I will send you some more with Leary who will leave us in a few days. You may if you please sell Deickman or Leary those 3 shirts of mine for $1.50 cents each, as I may not want them. I have written to my Mother and sent her 10 dollars,

and I have 20 dollars in gold left for another <u>remittance</u> besides paying the <u>Captain</u> 10 doll's which I owed him and paying 2 doll's which I owed Lieut. Weed. There is now 7 months pay nearly due me, and I don't owe a cent to any body. Since your letter dated March 8th we have had no news from **Fort Myers**. I sold one pair of them Overalls you sent me for 3 doll's. I wear the other pair. I still have <u>one</u> <u>shirt</u> and <u>overalls</u> which I suppose belongs to Serg't <u>Ford</u> which is near **Fort Jupiter**, but we have sent them nothing as we have no transportation. Dear <u>Eleanor</u> I never was so <u>home</u> <u>sick</u> in my life. I know we cant stop here more than 2 months longer, but whether we will go down to **Fort Myers**, or **Fort Jupiter** I cant tell. Try to Keep up a good <u>heart</u> I hope you and my big girl Keep your healths, when you get this letter from <u>Dieckman</u> get him to answer it immediately, for this is a lonely place, especially if you don't give us any news, so I beg of you to write the same day you get it, and tell me all the particulars and how you get along. It in now <u>one</u> o'clock and yet I must not <u>sleep</u> until 2 more Boats arrive with **Forage**. I am well enough in health, but I want to See you and <u>Etty</u>. You need not send me any <u>more</u> <u>clothes</u> as I have too much to carry now. I drank <u>some</u> of the <u>tea</u> and sold the rest, and the <u>coffee</u> and cheese, Pickles and Tobacco. I believe if I had a small portion of <u>Tobacco</u> I could sell it, but if you do get a chance to send me some up, let me know who much you pay for it. And now <u>Dearest</u> I will close this shortly, by wishing you a good night and pleasant dreams, give my girl a long kiss for me and receive my Blessing. Don't forget to mention whether <u>Roach</u> gave you the little <u>Box</u> with the candles plate & c. Once more good night your Husband Oliver

<u>From Eleanor to Oliver</u>

Fort Miris {*Myers*}
March 25th 1857

My Dear Husband

I received your welcome letter a few days ago and was glad to hear that you enjoy good health as this leaves Hety {*Ettie*} and I at present   thank god for it   we have great reason to bless the Lord for his kindness to us and so many dying and sick with diarear {*diarrhea*}   poor norman was buried today   I washed for him this last month   I want you to arrange that for me   I got the box from roach and all the things candles and coffy

29

{coffee} and a plate for hety *{Ettie}* it was as good as a play to be
looking at her she felt so glad when she hurd you sent is to self Mrs
ford and I settled for the things she was sending to her Husband I want
you to dispose of them as well as you can or if you need any of them you
may have them also I paid her what they cost her here miss patterson
and the childrin is well also I now conclude by sending you my best
Love and ever remains your wife until death Elinor obvrard *{Boizard}*

wright soon hety *{Ettie}* send you a ciss *{kiss}* for her papa

From Eleanor to Oliver

Fort Myers
the 30 March 1857

Dear Husband
I received your letter on the eighth from W. Dieckman with the amount
of $15. and I am glad to hear that you are in good health. I am not in
want of anything and in very good health. the 2nd Art. is about to go
from here and I will not have anything to do after they have left and
therefore if you think that we will not meet together before next May I
shall prepare to go North and it will be also better for Ette to go North for
the purpose of going to school. because she is not learning anything here
if you want me to send you anything let me know and I will send it to
you I am going to write to my sister and I will go and seek her if you let
me go North I am sending you three letter stamps there being no other
news therefore I remain yours E.M. Boizard.

*This note was written at the bottom of the letter, apparently William
Dieckman was taking dictation from Eleanor and he added his own
postscript.*

Between you and me if you take my word from what I heard and seen
it would be better to send your Wife away from here because she will not
than she has already a bad name by being so close to Missus Patterson
I do not belief what I heard and I would take a solemn oath upon myself
to be the truth but as afore said take her away from here as soon as
possible. It was her own wish to write this to you. Mss. Ptt. has a great

deal of company with men but your Wife is innocent of everything. Your Friend, William Dieckman

<u>From Oliver to Eleanor</u>

Fort McRae Fla
April 3rd 1857

My Dear Wife
Your letter dated the 25th of March, 1857, Came to hand last. I am glad that you and the girl enjoy good health. You mention <u>Norman's</u> Burial Please let me know how long you washed for him, the number of days & c. And I will have it put on the Muster Rolls. Be particular as regards the number of days. I sent by Dieckman on the 25th of March 1857, 15 dollars which I hope you got. It takes about 10 days before any answer from your letters reaches me – Should you get any chance of Buying Tobacco send me up some. That is a reasonable quantity, say 10 pounds. Try to send the amount of Norman's Bill - before the last of this month. Yours with Sincerity Your husband Oliver

Write soon and direct your letter's thus
John. O. Boizard
Compy "K" 4th Art.
Fort McRae Fla
N.B. I have no news of any importance If you want any money tell me J.O.B. Tell me the Price you pay for the tobacco

<u>From Eleanor to Oliver</u>

Fort Myers
April 11th 1857

Dear husband
I received your letter on the tenth of this month and by it i am glad to hear you are in good helth as this leves me at present and the child Dear husband this note will tell all about Norman Mrs Dyer wants to know did Corporal weber got that boxes she sent up Dear husband if Mrs Patterson is going North i will not go i have got some tobacco at 50 cts per pound and as soon as i will get a chance i will send it up Mrs

31

Patterson is getting better   Dear husband if you make up your mind to send me North i would like you would come down to see me before i would go   there is good chance in May   if you would get a chance to send some money down   you may but i do not want money very bade {*bad*} Nor more at present from your Effectionate Wife and Daughter E.M Boizard

From Oliver to Eleanor

Fort McRae Fla
April 14th 1857

My Dearest Eleanor
I received a letter written by <u>Dieckman</u> which stated that you had received 15 doll's. and I was rejoiced to hear that you was in good health, and also that you are not in want of anything. I am indifferently well at present, and rather melancholy, at present, to think I cant be with you. <u>Dieckmans</u> <u>letter</u> gave me great uneasiness. I would to <u>Heaven </u>that we were together, and I think before the 1st June, we shall meet at **Fort Myers.** However write to your <u>sister</u> and try to hold on untill the 1st <u>June</u> 1857 and place your trust in <u>Him</u> that never deserts the <u>honest </u>and <u>virtuous.</u> It is now nearly 8 months, since we have been paid off, and as soon as I receive my Money, I will have it all for you and a sum besides, which will enable you to go to the north. I know the Child requires <u>Schooling</u>   We received a letter from Mrs <u>Dean</u> that Mrs. Patterson was dangerously ill   the letter was dated April 3rd and Patterson asked the Captain to go down, but the Capt. told him that there was a general order to let nobody go during the war. It seems strange that she got so suddenly ill. I have had a touch of the <u>Fever</u> but I am much better. I still attend to my duties. There is one thing which I fear of you going to the <u>north</u> alone, perhaps you cant get along without reasonable sum of money, but I hope you will be able to hold out another 2 months, which will give you the opportunity to get an answer from your <u>sister</u> after you write to her, and then by that time, we may be together. There is all probability that we will leave here in about a month, and it's the <u>impression</u> that we will go to **Fort Myers.** Dear Wife be not backward, in telling me whether you want money or not. I am devoting my whole time for your future welfare and trying to save Every Cent, so that I can have you go to your Sisters. I have not spend 1 Dollar foolishly since I

left you. Poor Etty, how I would like to see her. We had a great <u>Blow</u> on <u>Sunday</u> and <u>Monday</u> and it is a blowing hard this day. I will be able with Saving up to the End of this month, my <u>extra pay</u> and my <u>monthly</u> pay for 8 months, it will amount to about 130 Dollars, and then <u>Dear</u> perhaps that will carry you through. This letter of <u>Dieckman's</u> has been 15 days Coming, and you may think how i feel in regard of you   Keep up a good heart and be persevering and things will turn out right yet. Enclosed you will please find <u>7 ½ Dollars</u>, and I have 30 dollars, more at your disposal, if you wish it dear. If the 2nd Art'y. Goes, why we may come down there ourselves. I know you must be greatly harassed, with Children, and waiting on other people from what I can understand., but be <u>firm</u> and <u>resolute</u> and may the <u>Lord</u> who is ever Kind to all never <u>desert</u> <u>you</u>. I have just been looking at your likeness, it fills me with <u>pain</u> and <u>pleasure</u>, Poor Etty, looks so natural. But let me change this theme which grows sad. If you have not written to your Sister yet, get some trusty person to write to her and by the time you get an answer, maybe I will be with. Kiss the girl for me and believe me to be your Husband in Sincerity John Oliver Boizard

Recollect what old Sally told you about the slander of other people but don't mind them. J.O.B.

Capt. Ireland thinks you had better stay until about the month of June and then likely we will meet   yours J.O.B.

<u>From Kate (Boizard) Dow to brother Oliver</u>

My love to Eleanor and child

Phila
April 14th

Brother Olly,
I recieved with ten dollers in and it came very actable *{acceptable}* we wher *{were}* glad to hear from you as we read of the indians   we felt as if you might be near them but I am glad to hear you have no orderly duties and that you are well and you have sutch a kind wife and so industerious   Oly be kind to her as a good wife is as precious as gold   I am pleased to hear that she sent you the word of God to cheer you up trust in God and he will protect you throu your troubles. Elisabeth was

33

heare when your leter came and was glad to hear from you and send her
love to you and wife and child   Dear Oly you want to know about Zarty
he is well and working at his trade   shoe making is very good now   it
never was as good   Cally and children are well at present they have a
nice house in Vane street between 9th street and washington and wallace
mom monthly dues has stoped since September last Everything
agreeable   Caley is as pleaset *{pleased or pleasant ?}* as a kitten since
then but you Lib and myself has not stoped. *{stopped}* Fin dow sends
{there is a rip in the paper and there are some words missing.}   you
want to know about Jacob   he is as you left   getting a long for him *{?}*
he is very well   hearty *{?}* a Buck   Dear Oly Tourinson are well sends
their love to you all   Mom health is good except rumatism *{rheumatism}*
she dont sew   her sight is so poor   she prefers to live a lone as she likes
her church so mutch   lent is over   mom sends her love to you and God
bless you as a dutiful son mom love to Elenor   Cris sends his love to
you and says take care of yourself Old Boy   take care of the ingines
*{injuns} {the next paragraph is badly soiled and only a few words can be
distinguished. The words that can be read are as follows:* We have no
news. . . Federal street. . .between seventh and 8th street . . . No 700 . . .
no 704 . . . south. . . has removed his shop . . . from house} I was very
happy to leave but the walk was to long for Cris   Good By   God Bless
you   rite soon and please let me know a bout *{Cris Mathew ?}*as *{?}* is
so ancious *{anxious}* to hear from your sister Kate Dow   rite very
soon

From Oliver to Eleanor

Fort McRae, Fla.
April 24th 1857

My Dear Wife
I received your Kind letter dated the 11th of April, and was rejoiced to
hear that you was in good health, also my little Etty. I will give
norman's account to the Captain and he will put it on the muster & Pay
Roll, also Brown's   I wrote you a letter Since the one that Deickman
conveyed to you with 15 dolls. in it, and on the 14th, I send you another
letter with 7 ½ dollars in it, and I expect to get that answer next mail, I
now send you (10) dollars more, in this letter Saved up by Kennedy. The
whole which I have sent you, is the 471/2 Doll's. and I hope you have
received it all. My Dear Wife, I am not in very good health at present I

34

have Every now and then that heavy feeling about the head, Something like the <u>Fever</u> I have been taking **Quinine Pills**. I wrote to you about going to the north in a letter, and Dearest <u>Eleanor</u> do not think of going away without Seeing me. If you only Knew the <u>distress</u> it gives me, you Certainly would give up the notion. I could not rest. my happiness would be at an End, and then think of it a <u>Lone</u> <u>Woman</u> travelling without means in a Strange <u>City</u> or <u>town</u> without a <u>Protector</u>, Subject to the rude treatment, of every <u>Ruffian</u>, Oh, do give up the notion   I shall be able probably to see you about next June   The Company is on a scout for 20 days, they left here on the 18th of April, as for me coming down before the Compy. It is impossible, as **General Harney** has issued orders to give no leave of absence, to any body, during the campaign. It is the general impression, this will be the last Scout, have patience until I see you, and the <u>Lord </u>will protect you. I console myself by reading in your little <u>Bible</u>, and looking at your likenesses. I expect you will hear that a letter from <u>Philadelphia</u> for me will be in the Post office, as soon as it comes, Please forward it as soon as you can. No more at present, but remain yours with sincerity. <u>Oliver</u>

Mrs. E. M. Boizard
Laundress K Co.
Fort Myers, Fla

Tell Mrs. Dwyer, that Corpl. Weber has received no box, nor did he write for any so he says.

Give Etty a hug, and don't let her forget me in her growing up so fast
JOB

*The previous letter actually has the date of April 24, **1856** on it, but it is an answer to the April 11, 1857 letter that Eleanor wrote to Oliver. I have placed it here, where it fits chronologically.*

From Eleanor to Oliver

My Dear Husband
I Received your letter yesterday morning and by it i am sorry to hear that
you have the fever but i hope it will be nothing me and the child are in
good health at present   Dear O it was not my intention to go North until
i see you and therefore do not be uneasy for i will not go   I hope the next
letter i will get from you better news about the Company comming to
fort myers i have four boarders   they are giveing me four dollars a
month and their rations each   three Clerks and the post butcher there all
in the quartermaster employment   i thought it was easyer then to wash
for i could not hall *{haul}* water Enough   it is so hard to get it here, i
rote to my sister a week ago I got letter from your mother and i opened
it   but before opened i thought it was for me and i put another envelope
on it and sent it up to you   i also Sent you box with the train Burdick
went up in   Please tell Corporal Weber to send to **fort Center** for his
Box   Mrs Duyer says it is there   Cornell got his discharge he is going to
Tampa in the morning   he did not get a red cent of pay   Roche is still
lame in left leg   But the doctor says he will send Jimmy Hasy up to the
company again   My Dear O i have got fifty dollars yet and can give
account for thirty, Burdick owes me twelve if he gets paid up there i
have received all the money you sent me that makes 47 ½ dollars correct
No more at Present From your Effectionante Wife and Daughter
 E M Boizard

From Oliver to Eleanor

My Dear <u>Eleanor</u>
The Box came to hand yesterday, and you don't Know how grateful I
feel for you, for your Kindness, the tobacco I sold for 50 cents per plug,
the cheese which was a little damaged, I got one dollar for it, part of the
Ham I retained, the other I got 50 cents for it, the **Hickory Shirts** you
send me I have sold them all. I got $1.50 for the last one, I wear nothing
but <u>flannel</u> as it suits my health better. The <u>Tea</u> will come good some

Evening before I go to bed. The flannel shirt you send me was very acceptable however I have made a trade for 2 new ones, about one month ago, which leaves me 3 good ones and one old one. I also managed to trade for 2 pairs of good drawers, as the old ones are worn out. I was highly gratified to hear that you and <u>my **Cosey**</u> was in good health and that you had got somewhat out of the notion of going north before I see you. there is a rumour that the troops will be moved soon, where, I know not, but as our Company property is at **Fort Myers**, likely we shall come there   if not you may be able to join me elsewhere, but I think you will not be long before you see me. Any other place but this and no doubt, but you could be with me. The fleas, Blowflies, an Musquitoes are Intolerable. I am well at present, as the <u>dumb</u> **ague** has left me. I relished those lobsters you send me with a <u>Zest</u> fit for an **Epicurean.** I am anxiously awaiting a letter from my Mother. You did not mention whether you wrote to your Sister or not. I am so glad that you are doing well. I am straining every nerve to get along, as I have something in view, if this <u>war</u> closes, however when we meet, I will tell you all, "and then we will <u>smile</u>" I send you since Dieckman gave you that letter, 2 letters one contained 7 ½ dolls, the other 10 dollars (17 ½ dolls in both) which I hope you have got. Burdick tells me he owes you 12 ½ dolls, which he says, he will pay me at the first pay day. I must close this letter as the Company has just returned from 20 days scout, and I will have plenty to do. So no more at present. But remains yours with Sincerity. Your husband "Oliver"

have patience dear, don't be uneasy, the child is 5 years old this month Kiss her for me, and try to learn her letters, and also Keep up her good behaviour, your's J.O.B.

<u>From Eleanor to Oliver</u>

Fort Myers
May 12th 1857

My Dear Husband
I Recived your letter on the 9th wich gives me great Plesure to hear that you are well of the dum egeu {*dumb ague*} as this leves me with a great head ached for the last week   Dear O we had a great Ball here and me and Mereatta was there   were {*where*} we enjoyed ourselvs very happy let me Know if there is any talk of the company moving or comming to F

Myers   there was none of the men in the hospital musterd {*mustered*}
so i canot collect that Bill of Jimmy hasy   tell Corporal McCarthy there
is none of them will get paid here as i here {*hear*} the Pay master has not
come here yet for to pay the last two months pay Pendergast and Koler
is here   they are going up as soon is the boat will come here from tampa
Mrs Patterson and the children are all well and in good helth {*health*}.
Plese give this note to Corporal weber it is from Mrs Deen.   Mereatta is
well and getting a very big girl   she is longing to see you
No More at Present From your Effectionate {*affectionate*} Wife and
Daughter E M Boizard

From Oliver to Eleanor

Fort McRae, Fla
May 13th 1857

My <u>Dear Wife</u>
The mail came here last Evening and I received three letters, one from
Kate, the other two was from yourself. I have not heard any news about
our going out of this place yet, but is was generally supposed that we
would leave **Fort McRae** as it is very unpleasant here and not a fit place,
for any body to live in much longer any how. I never was so troubled
with fleas and other insects as I am here. I feel better than I was, but now
and then I feel like the **<u>Ague</u>**. I am glad to hear that you are doing well,
without washing so hard, it would be better for you not to work so <u>hard</u>,
for the weather is getting so hot you will get sick. The news from
Philadelphia is cheerfull enough. Since the mail arrived I hear the
<u>Indians</u> is been giving the volunteers a <u>brush</u> and I fear that will prolong
our stay in <u>Florida</u> Try to Keep the girl in <u>check</u> and use all your
energies to learn her to spell & c. Try to Keep up her behaviour and you
will find it usefull some future day. Should the Paymaster come up here
I will collect Brown's 4 dolls, <u>Normans</u> 75 cts, and Burdicks $12. It was
thought by the officers of this Post, that we would be removed from this
post, but what this <u>mail</u> has brought, I know not. Should there be any
news that would be cheering to you I will let you Know at the Earliest
Convenience I receivd from **Fort Center** Some Bread and **Forage** in
the Boat, which we cannot well do without, all other provisions we have
plenty. You may <u>Bless</u> your <u>stars</u> that you are at **Fort Myers**. I believe
you could not live here, particulary at night for the insects. I will close
this letter as I have nothing of importance to Communicate to you

further. And now My Dear Wife, give the Child a long Kiss for me, and Tell her I will buy her something nice when I see her. I hope you read Kate's Letter it would afford me great pleasure for you to read all the letters from Philada. Farewell and God Bless You Your husband Oliver

Invitation to Cotillion party

Fort Myers
May 14 '57

The honor of your presence is requested at a **Cotillion** party to be given this evening in the **Garrison.**

Very Respectfully
Jos. Miller
L. G. Murphey
Managers
To Mrs Boizard
Present

From Oliver to Eleanor

Please send me a Bottle of good Claret wine and pack it So it won't Break. J.O.B

Fort McRae Fla
May 20th 1857

Dear Eleanor,
I received your letter with Corporal Weber's letter enclosed on the 19th of May'57 and was sorry to hear that you had a Bad Head Ache, I am well aware what you suffer while you have it. My Dear Wife I am not Exactly well yet, although I am doing duty. I took Medicine yesterday. I do not believe I can Keep my health here, we have about 20 men on the Doctor's list. As regards our moving, I really Cannot tell you when or where, we shall move, but as soon as I can get any word to that Effect, I

39

will let you Know immediately. There is one sure thing that we can stop here not much longer than the month of May. Wherever we will go in all probability, you will join the Company. I am glad to hear that you and the girl Enjoyed yourselves at the <u>Ball</u>, as it was a nights <u>recreation</u> for you. Although it used to be a <u>rather-unusual</u> thing for Ball among <u>Soldiers</u> to be a genteel affair, as some <u>fellows</u> were sure to get drunk and Kick up a <u>Row</u>, or be insulting.

Dear Wife, by the time this letter reaches you I hope you will be in good health and still Sooner. I thought about you getting me a pair of <u>Soldiers overalls</u>, to have them ready. I don't care if you can get 2 pair reasonable, about no. 3's and also Boots about no. 8, I do not know that it is worth while to send me up any thing to Eat Except a little tea, as I Eat very little at present. Dear Eleanor, do not work too hard, this approaching hot <u>weather</u>. Better make less money and not Kill your self for a few dollars. This is a bad Country for a <u>man</u> or <u>woman</u> to be sick in. Please <u>Air</u> my Uniform Coat the Captain's says we will all have to draw coats, after we get to Summer quarters. So get the pants and shoes if you can and lock them up until I see you. You might send me up a small <u>can</u> of Preserved Meat of some Kind. O'Connor, of our Company tells me a woman belonging to Company "F" 4th arty, was shot by a Musket going off accidentally. The ball lodged in her and it was not supposed she could live long. It took place as the Boat was starting from the Kissimmee where the woman was left. Dear Wife try not to Expose yourself and keep good health. As this is the Season people get sick. The little money you earn strive to save it as it will come good to you. Should you have any money put aside that you would not like to use let me know in the answer to this letter. So I can send you some, as I am managing with my <u>Extra pay</u> to keep 30 or 35 dolls. <u>ahead</u> for your purposes and my <u>Dear old Mother</u>. There is a rumor about that we are ordered out of <u>Florida</u> soon. If so, and you really wish to go home with your daughter and the <u>Almighty</u> spares me, I then perhaps can send you direct from New Orleans or some other Port, and comfortable at that. This letter is not very well written, as I have just been washing 7 pieces of my clothing, which will save 1 Dollar any how. I do all my own washing and I hope when you see them, you can say I am a terrible <u>washerman</u>.   *{this letter has water marks on it, probably from his wet hand.}* Poor girl how I would like to see her, now she is growing up. Kiss her for me and tell her to be a good girl and her <u>dada</u> will buy her a nice carriage like them in Newport, KY for to take home to see her <u>Aunt Lizzy</u>, (that is if we all live) I have lost much <u>flesh</u> since the 1st April.

During the months of January, February and March I made out to keep my health very well, since then I have failed greatly, well I have had a great care on my mind, the uneasiness about your being left alone and other cares, has certainly reduced to me in health and strength. Dear Wife, I hope you read that letter from <u>Kate</u>. As they all feel friendly to you– Mother says God will Bless you for your gratitude in the 1st letter and now <u>Eleanor</u> be patient and I am pretty sure we shall meet in a short time, (Say in one month) Kiss my little girl and don't neglect at night her duty to the <u>Almighty</u>. As children about <u>Camp</u> learn every thing that is mischievous. And now <u>Farewell.</u> Your Husband "Oliver"

Write Immediately, Tell me in your answer if <u>Packard</u> gave you a small parcel or not.

N.B. Your likeness looks as well as ever. Your Bible is taken care of – as for the <u>Souvenir</u> be not uneasy. J.O.B.

<u>From Eleanor to Oliver</u>

Fort Myers
may 30th 1857

Dear husband

I received your 2 letters and I was sorry to hear that you was not well and I have been very sick myself with the intemiton *{intermittent?}* fever and I had it two days and a night and never broke   I feel a little better for the fever has intinely *{instantly?}* left me and the doctor says I will soon get better   I will send you a box of things the first chance and the clothes that you want me to send you I cannot buy.   you wanted to know how much money I have   I have very little now for you must know what a large family I have to support   I do not know what patterson means he never writes to his wife   I hope dear husband that we will soon meet again   for that I am all most tired of my life   Etty is well and getting so bold that I can do nothing with her.   I have nothing more particular to say No more at present from your loveing wife E.M. Bayard

<u>From Oliver to Eleanor</u>

Fort McRae, Fla
June 1st, 1857

My <u>Dear Wife</u>,
I am improving in health, and hope you are also in Excellent health and
<u>spirits</u>. Pendergast & Kohbe has come and he rather surprised me when
he told me that you had not received my letter, but I suppose it was in the
mail that they met at **Fort Denaud**. I do not Know what to say to you to
Encourage you to <u>patience</u>, but there is no other way of getting along, but
to wait. I have suffered both <u>mentally</u> and <u>bodily</u> on account of being
apart from you, but what can I do. I hope the time will come soon, when
we shall <u>meet</u> I could send you down 40 dollars if you are in want of it,
but I am afraid it might be lost. If you can hold on awhile longer, I may
have an opportunity to send it, if it was Bills, there would be no
difficulty, but as it is in <u>gold</u> it makes too big a bulk in a package or
letter. It is the general impression that we will leave this place before
long and all hands will be rejoiced at it, as this is certainly an awful
place. Let me entreat you to have patience awhile longer and I hope all
will be well. Pendergast tells me that you look better than Ever, well
that's cheering news, "May your shadow never be less" but try to be
contented, and do not work too hard this hot weather, and compose
yourself, and He that's above will do the Rest. Pendergast tells me that
<u>Etty</u> has grown 6 inches, <u>Bless my **Cosey**</u> may she ever prosper. he also
tells me that it is supposed the Headquarters of the artilly. (4th) will be at
Fort Myers, if so we may have a chance of being stationed there,
anywhere but this place, if you and the child are present.
By the answer that I sent you, I wrote to you to send me some <u>wine</u> and
something <u>fresh</u> like oysters or Lobsters - and some <u>tea</u>, and I suppose I
will get it about the time you get this letter. I would write to my Mother
if I had a good <u>Current Bank Bill</u> however there is time Enough for that
if reports are true about leaving here, and now <u>Dearest Eleanor</u> I have
told you all I can think of at present, and hope this letter will find you
cheerfull and the young one well, <u>look to her</u> particulary, as now is the
time, if you have an opportunity to instruct her. Please not forget about
the overalls, and Boots, and a white <u>shirt </u>would not be amiss. Give my
respects to Roach and all Enquiring friends, and tell me in your answer
who writes your letters for you. From your Sincere Husband Oliver

Be not uneasy about the north, I am anxious that Etty should be schooled and she shall be if I am spared. Take Care of No. 1 and all will be right. yours. J.O.B.

From Eleanor to Oliver

Fort McRae, Fla
June 3rd 1857

My Dear Wife,
I received your letter yesterday Evening and the <u>Paymaster</u> also came up and paid the Company. I send you by the Paymaster (Lebuard) <u>one hundred dollars</u> ($100) in gold and may it arrive safely. It is directed to you in the care of Col. Waite and he will hand it to you. I was grieved to hear that you became sick so suddenly. Since Pendergast left **Fort Myers**, Fla, I have no encouraging news to give you. I believe by the last mail that we will remain here all summer and I am going to prevail on the Captain to have you sent up to me. Dear Wife it is rather hard for you to be the way you are and if I can get the Captain to consent for you to come up, the only difficulty will be in crossing the Lake. The rain has commenced and I am afraid it will be very disagreeable, however as we are situated now at present apart from each other, it is a life of anxiety and pain. I received your box, but I sold them all as I have recovered from my ill health, and when I am well, I can live on anything–
Enclosed you will find <u>5 dolls</u>, belonging to <u>Romback</u> of our Compy. He wants you to send him- wine, or something good to drink and <u>Tobacco</u> for the rest. When you send it up direct it to me. And go to the Setler *{sutler}* and see if you can get <u>10 dollar Bank</u> <u>Bill</u> on some Bank of New Orleans, or Charleston S. C. Bill. Go to Col. <u>Waite</u> and you will get the money, (100) dolls in gold. Answer this immediately, after you receive the money, and Dear Wife take good care of it. Kiss the little one for me, and tell her be a good girl. From your Husband "Oliver"

Fort Myers
June 4th 1857

Dear Husband,
I Recevied your letter yesterday morning and by it i am glad to hear you
are getting better as this leves me very wake {*weak*} at present   i still
have to ly in bed   Dear husband what made me look so well when
pendergast was here   the fever was comming on me then.   I sent up a
Boxes wich *{which}* Contains too {two} bottles of wine   too {two}
pounds of tea   one Boxes of lobsters   one boxes of roast beef   It cost me
five dollars. Mrs Moonlight is doing my worke as Mrs patterson is
Cooking for the band Master   don't say anything to patterson about it
Mereatta is well and in good helth   She is all the time asking when you
will be home   Dear husband let us Know when the company is comming
down   McSweeny and Broker come here too {two} days ago and three
more of D Compy they says **Fort McRae** is an awful place   Dear
husband you want Know who rites my letters   sometime Roche and
sometimes Mrs Mcintosh Roche sends his best respects to you. Rite to
me as soon as Possible and let me Know you are getting along   No More
at Present From your Sinceare Wife M Boizard

From Oliver to Eleanor

Fort McRae, Fla
June 1857

My Dear Wife,
I have been speaking to Captain Ireland about you coming to the
Company, and he told me that you could come up on these conditions,
that he will employ to <u>cook</u> for the officers <u>Mess</u> and Lieut. Hudson told
me also, he would like you to wash for him, as he is obliged to send his
clothes over the <u>Lake</u> to get washed, They will pay you well. It is a hard
matter to get a cook among the men that Knows how to cook well, and
<u>Economise</u>. Dear Wife I shall be so glad if your health is good Enough,
to start after you get this letter. Enclosed you will find a note to the
Quarter master, for your transportation to **Fort Center**, the Captain says
you must make your load as light as possible on account of the
transportation, be sure to bring all your cooking utensils along, as they

44

are rather scarce here, if you can purchase a <u>Gridiron</u> do so and try to bring 2 <u>Brooms</u> up with you. I think if you have good weather you can come here in 4 days, the only difficulty will be in crossing the Lake, if the weather, should be bad, It has rained for 4 or 5 days consecutively here and this the rainy month, however we will have a place fixed for you by the time, you come up. You might buy yourself and Child <u>shoes</u> and such articles as you stand most in need of – and also try get an umbrella, for yourself it will be good in crossing the Lake, on account of the sun or rain. I hope the Child will not be scared in crossing the Lake. Sergt. Hall who has charge of the Boat, will see that you are as comfortable, as possible. Try to bring my 2 pairs of <u>Cotton</u> <u>Pants</u> if you have not bought the Soldier pants, and also 1 pair Bootees, No. 8 if you can. a few Hickory shirts and Blue Flannel shirts would sell well here, and about 15 lbs of <u>Tobacco</u>. if you can get the transportation, as regards the Provisions they will be furnished out of the Commissary so you wont require much of that, however Cook yourself a <u>ham</u> before you start (you Know best) you will with my help, be able to make some money here, and then we will have the satisfaction of being together. I have been thinking of this for the last 2 weeks, and as soon as I found there were no hope of leaving here, I made the application of getting you to Cook. Should you have anything that you cant bring along, get the quartermaster, to store it for you, and be careful to get somebody to mark all your things with your name on them. I hope you have received the money I sent you by the Paymaster. Dear Eleanor, take Care of it, as we will want if some future day. I know that you are not Extravagant, but every thing is high in the Country. I collected every cent that the men owes you. I got <u>Browns</u> 4 dolls, <u>Normans</u> 75 cts and nobody owes us any thing in the Company. Now I still have a few dollars left, Try to get me a good Bank <u>Bill</u>. <u>Louisiana</u> <u>Money</u> or some good Bill, that is not <u>torn</u> so I can send it to my mother. Tell the Postmaster, to forward your letter when it comes from your <u>sister</u>. take care of the child on your <u>route</u> up here, and May the <u>Lord Bless you and Protect you.</u> I like to forgot bring 2 or 4 lbs of nails some 8 penny and 4 pennys. take things <u>Cooley</u> and all will be right, bring your tent and Poles along. As soon as you can collect what is due you from the <u>Men</u> Why then try to get along as fast as you can. Get somebody to assist you, if <u>Hahesy</u> will pay you that money, for Corpl. McCarthy well and good. Goodby Eleanor for the present your husband Oliver

Bring a fish line and a dozen large hooks. 6 Boxes of Matches <u>also</u>
Don't forget Starch & Blue   never Mind about Wash Tubs. Get me if
you can 2 sail needles, & a ball Twine You might bring some under
shirts, (good ones) Bring something food for yourself, Cordial, Wine &
c. If you have my cleaning things, bring them up, a Brick and Brush &
Blacking. I am afraid you cant think of all yours & c. J.O.B.

From Capt. John H Meland, **Fort McRae** to Capt. W. S. Hancock, Fort
Myers

Fort McRae, Fla
June 7th 1857

Captain:
The bearer of this, Mrs Boizard, a Laundress in Company "K" wishes to
join her husband at this Post. Will you please furnish her with the
opportunity to leave **Fort Myers** She wishes to leave some things
behind, and will be very glad if you let her store them with the property
of my Company.
very Respectfully
Your obdt. Servt..John H Meland
Capt. 4 Arty. For Capt. W. S. Hancock
A.Q.M. *{Army Quarter Master}***Fort Myers**, Fla

From Kate Dow to brother Oliver

Phila.
July 22 1857

Brother Oly,
I received moms letter with the check enclosed on the New Orleans Bank
24 dol 27 cents to be cashed at the broker   dear Oly Mom is well and she
very thankful for your present and she says when in danger of war the
spirit of our father is hovering around you   she hopes to live to see you a
comfort to your wife and her   and our fathers words are true as you are
now the support with Lib and me of her Old Age   Dear Olly, All we can
do for mom is not much as she did for us when we could not for our self
I am sorry to hear that Elenor is not well I am scarcely even well myself

so I can sympathize with her   I think it must be unpleasant where she is
as the weather is warm enough let alone the insects of every kind   dear
Oly if you should go to Utah I hope you will be in no danger and should
Elenor come by the way of <u>Phila</u> we shall be pleased to see her and
Marietta   I think she would be better at Pittsburgh where she is
acquainted than where she is   if you were to remain it would better for
her to stay   dear Olly we are all well at present except the great heat and
you know how that Prostrates both Cris and I   Phineas is well sends his
love to Uncle Olly   Zarty and family are well   Tourisons are as usual
Christopher saw John Dinnin Sunday he is well wish to be remembered
to you Mr Mrs Dow and girls Aunt Maggs Coss send her best respects
to you Cip Priser and family and all your friends   Dear Olly we have
lost an old acquaintance Sarah Burn Sarah Evinson was her name   I
look around and all my friends pass from this world and who will be
next   Dear Oly, we have hurd no news from Mary Jacob and Libbe
are well   Jacob look well he is never sick   has a constitution he take
from mom to think the third day of August mom will be 71   Dear Oly
Cris has gone in business for himself has invented a printing press and it
is liked by all who see it and will sell very ready after he get a full start
it is called the Star Printing press his place is on Charleston Street here
is his card and press I thought it would please you so here it is   Dear
Olly I have no news at present mom sends her love to you and never
forgets you in her prayers   Libbe sends her love to you all the family
Cris says take care of your self Old Cove   Phineas Dow is quite Large
by this time he is in North **Bonar** Grammar School.
Good By from Sister Kate.

Nebraska Territory

In the fall of 1857 Oliver's regiment was moved to Fort Leavenworth, KS to help with the Indian trouble as well as the Mormon rebellion that was taking place. It is probable that before they made the trip to Kansas, Oliver & Eleanor enjoyed a short furlough, possibly visiting Eleanor's sister in Pittsburgh, and probably visiting John & Harriet Fisher in Glen Arbor. One other thought would be that Oliver might have received a discharge at this time and then re-enlisted in 1858.

At first, Oliver's company was stationed at Fort Leavenworth, Kansas, but in August of 1858, Company K was sent to Fort Kearney in the Nebraska Territory, Eleanor traveled with Oliver to Fort Kearney. The following summer, Company K was moved to Fort Ridgely, Minnesota.[9] Eleanor remained at Fort Kearney.

Oliver received either a furlough or a discharge from the U.S. Army in the fall of 1859 and he moved for a brief time with his family to a forty-acre plot of land they had purchased in Glen Arbor, MI.

From Captain of 4 Artillery at Fort Leavenworth

Fort Leavenworth KS
May 12th 1858

I Certify that Mrs. Ellen Boizard is a Laundress of Company K 4th Artillery and is therefore Entitled to rations and Quarters. Mrs. Boizard has drawn rations to include the 20th May 1858.
{I cannot read the signature} Captain 4 Artillery
Commanding Co. K

Approved By order
Col Munroe   L. H Klouze Adj 4th Arty.

---

[9] The timeline of events for the 4th Artillery was gleaned from a website article

.

Phila
August 14

Brother Oly

I recieved your leter to Mom dated Augt 4 with a treasury note Enclosed
for $20 dollars Crisse had it cashed Mom and family are all well   I am
very glad you returned to take Elleanor and Marietta with you as it is
very lonesome I suppose where she was   I hope you are all well and
continue so I felt very sad to hear you had left for Utah   but Oly thier is
a God Every Where to protect you   look to him and he will shield you
from your foes   you know Oly thier is something in prayer to our
heavenly father   look to him and he will deliver from all that is bad   you
are the child of Mary{ I believe this is a reference to their Catholic faith
not the name of their mom}   A prayer poor mom prays three times a day
for us all but you and Mary she has spechel *{special}* prayers for you
both being absent from us   all the family Enjoy pretty good heath
{health} mom was 72 third of August she is smart of her age   her sight is
very bad and she cant walk so smart as she did   she has a good
constitution   Aunt Tourinson fails so mutch you would not know her
She wont last long we all thought she was gon *{gone}* last Thursday Mr
and Mrs Dow and famly are all well   Martha and Sarah send their
Respects to you and Eleanor   Zarty is well and Calley and children all
well   Calley a large girl and Charly he is the same very roguish   they are
very fine looking children   Phin Dow you would not know him he has
grown   he is five foot and stout in proportion   he often speaks of you
Phin has bin *{been}* drawing some fruit for Marietta   he has an idea of
drawing   the large pears are for Aunt Elenor   give my love to Elenor
and kis *{kiss}* Marietta for me   rite soon and as often as you can   by the
by I almost forgot   Brother Jacob he is well and looks well and doing as
well as can be expected for the hard times   times are hard these few days
and sister Elizabeth you would be surprised to see her   she is well but so
thin she is as thin as Calley   she has bin *{been}* very sick but is well at
present   she sends her love to you and Elenor and Except *{accept}* both a
share of mine   Oly I believe I have told you all   Mrs Copps sends her
respects to you and wife   I will leave a space for Criss I believe   good
by May the Lord Bless you all from your Sister Kate Phinehas sends his
love to you and Aunt Eleanor and kiss Marietta for him. *From Chris
Dow to Oliver written on the bottom of Kate's letter.* My Best Wishes a
plesant time to you and Family. Good Luck attend you & bring you Safe
home in good health. Your brother C. C. Dow write soon

Phila
Dec 19 1858

Dear Brother Oly
I have not yet recieved an answer to my last leter I hope you are all well
Dear Oly how did you like the papers i sent you we are all well at
present but mom Grief is the cause of her illness Dear Brother Oly we
have lost our onley Aunt she died on the second day of December my
Birthday at 6 oclok in the morning she was concious *{conscious}* of her
leaving this world of sorow and perfectly resigned to go she asked for
us all she said she would like to see you and Mary before she died it
was a sad sight around her dieing Bed she was surrounded By many
Friends for she had been a mother to Any person she knew she had a
very large Funeral it was attended with 45 carages *{carriages}* she was
taken to the church prayed for and Buried in her lott at St. Mary
Cemetery. Where Uncle Tourison and Cate Garson lays poor Mack he
will go next he is very ill I believe he has the **dropsey** on the Brain that
desease *{disease}* is seldom cuerd *{cured}* if ever Dear Oly rite as soon
as you receive this leter for we all feel ancious *{anxious}* about you I
enclose you Aunt Tourison Death in this leter the famly are all well and
send thier love to you and Wife Stephen Tourison asked partickulary
{particularly} after your health and Famly Also William and wish me to
remember them to you in my leter to you Libe *{Libby}* was up and
sends her love to you and Ellenor and Marieta Mr Lytle will not last
long he grows very feeble My dear old Friend Mrs Priser Died a
month since and I have lost severl *{several}* of my most worthy Friend
by Death this has bin *{been}* a sad year to me Dear Brother Oly we
have had no news from Mary I feel sad when I think of her she usualy
{usually} rote one a month and it has bin three long years since we have
had a word from her I hope she is living but we all doubt it but we
must not grieve as we must all pass away one by one from this Earth
Dear Oly I beleiv *{believe}* I have told you all that will interest at present
we all send our love to you and famly and mom in particular Dear old
soul Every day she grows near to us all for we don't know how soon
her time may come she take Aunt death very mutch to heart but seems
rather more reconciled Cris send his love to you and Elenor and the
little Pet Phin Dow you would not know him he grows so fast I think
he will be as tall as his uncle Oly he is five foot now that is a large boy
for 13 years is he not and as good natuerd *{natured}* as a kitten

51

Mr and Mrs Dow and famly send thier love to you all   Mrs Copps is
stoping with me a short time sends her respect to you an famly   and all
your friends   A Mrs Dean called sevel *{several}* times to hear from <u>you</u>
she dresses in Black   she say she is an interested Friend of yours   she
came from Leavenworth City send her love to you all   <u>is</u> she a Worthy
person Oly   Good by Dear Brother Oly   Absent But not forgoten
From your sister   Kate Dow

Dear Oly We all wish you a Mery Christmas and a Happy New Year and
May the Blessing from Our Heavenly Father rest upon you and family   I
forgot to say Zarty and Brother Jacob are well and Cally and Children
Dear Oly since Aunt Tourison Death I Feel rather bewildered or forgetful

<u>From Kate Dow to her brother Oliver</u>

Phila.

March 27, 1859

Brother Oly,

I recieved your letter of Feb 26th and would have answered before this
but there has been bother about the Canada papers that was in Aunt
Tourison hands for many years and being as Aunt Tourison is no more
of Course they belong to mom and mom asked for them to keep them as
long as she lived and Margareth and Elizabeth refused to give them to
mom and insist on keeping them   it has bothered mom considerable   she
is the only heir that should hold them   so we have been so full of
business that I wanted to rite but could not   they are so obstinate they
will not give them up with out going to law about them and we don't
want to do that   they want to throw of *{off ?   out ?}* mom claim   it has
annoyed us all very mutch   they think they will realize a fortune thier
family alone   I hope they will grow fat on hope for the present   Dear Oly
I am sorry to hear you are so unfortunate in money matters   Cris has lost
considerable this winter   we must take the bitter with the sweet   there are
a series of Misfortune seems to follow us all but as Chris says it is all for
the best   I think the best is now sometimes   there is no use crying after
the past we must all hope the future will be better.   Dear Oly, I have
nothing new to tell you.   Only I saw John Dinnin last week and told me
to tell you he would like to see you once more.   <u>Poor Bus</u>   All the family
are well at present and hope you and Elenor and Marietta are well   no

news from sister Mary Libb and Zarty and all the family sends their
love to you the children grow fine Cally sings like a nightingale she
takes after Aunt May Parkhurst, she looks like Charly is a singer also
they will make smart children I hope I was up at Cip Prisers they all
send their respects to you they all seem like sisters to me and use me
sutch they are all soul people they love little and love long Dow folk
are all well send their respects to you and family McNeal is the same he
suffers mutch McLytle grows very feeble he will leave us shortly for a
better world I hope Mom told me to say to you she won't give up the
ship yet at nite she grows feeble but generally healthy she keep up
through every thing considerable Cris will send you some few paper for
to read I forgot Brother Jake he is well old fashion as ever Li Dow
sends his love to you all he laughed when I told him about Etta Give
my love to Elenor and give Etta a kiss for each of us Good by rite soon
absent but not forgotten From your sister Kate Dow

From Oliver to Eleanor

Fort Ridgeley, Minnesota
July 12th 1859

My Dear Eleanor
We arrived her 2 days ago, after a march of 40 days from **Fort Kearny**.
We left Sioux City on the 20th of June and Since that time we have
Scarcely been dry 24 hours at a time, it happened to be a very rainy
Season and that accounts for So much water in the **Sloughs** and Creeks.
This Post is a very pretty location and compact. It is Situated on the St
Peters River and during this high stage of water the Steam Boats come
up here. I hope the River will Keep high until the Middle of September
and then I hope I Shall be able to get a furlough for 2 months and I also
hope you will be able to Start from **Fort Kearny** at the Same time. I
write a letter this afternoon to Mother, as Soon as I finish this, and when
we get paid off, I shall write about the Recording of the deed. My Dear
Wife you cant conceive how lonesome I am without you and Etty and
Pinky, although we have been very busy, since we came her, Cleaning
quarters & c. Company "L" of 2nd arty. Is Stationed here at present the
Battery Company and the 2 Companies of the 2nd Infy are out trying to
make some agreement with the Sioux Indians. I suppose as Soon as the

Infantry Companies come in they will march for **Fort Kearny.** There are about 15 women at the Post but most of them will go away with the 2 Compy's of the 2nd Infy. Mrs Fitzgerald and Hoffman are well and Sends their love to you, they were heartily tired of the march everybody dislikes Major Pemberton on the road, he always took us out of the way. Dear Eleanor I hope you have Kept in good health and also my little Etty, poor little thing. I never have a moment's leisure, but I think of her. She is a fine girl and I truly miss her Tell her to be a good girl and Dada will never forget her. I was just thinking whether you was in the old house yet or not, or whether they had put you in a tent. I hope the Summers heat and your washing will not effect your head, well try Dear and Keep up a good heart, and the Lord will not forsake you. By a General order all the Citizens of the Post are discharged and Soldiers are detailed to work in their places. I am at present doing duty in the Company. Well I don't care much about it for in 2 months I will try to get a furlough. The Recruits for this Post under Lt. Dana have not arrived nor any of our women yet. I believe they went up the Missouri River to **Fort Randall**, and I expect they will have to march across the Country the Same as we did – What dirty clothes I had I washed them myself, and I found them hard to get clean as they were very much stained with the Swamp mud. I have seen nobody here that I know, and in fact I don't much care about forming new acquaintences, all I think of now is getting off, and joining you and the Girl. Well my Dear Wife I have nothing more to State to you at present, but hope that you and Etty make Keep in good health and Spirits and not be too lonesome Give my best Respects to the Hospt. Steward and all the Enquiring friends, and also let me Know in your answer how the Sick man is coming on, and whether you still prepare his meals. My best wishes to Serg't Paxson and Dear Wife and Daughter receive my fervent wishes for your future welfare. Your Husband John O. Boizard Mrs. E.M.Boizard Laundress of Co. "K" 4th Arty **Fort Kearny**, NT

From Oliver to Eleanor

Fort Ridgely, Min.
July 24th 1859

My Dear Wife
Your letter dated the 7th July came to hand 3 hours since, and I hasten to answer it, as the mail leaves tomorrow morning. I received your first

letter (Murrays) and it Somewhat Surprised me to hear that he was in the vicinity of Leavenworth. Mrs Fox and Stoneham have arrived. Mrs Fox is quartered in the Capt's quarters and Mrs Stoneham in the tents. Mrs Fox's boy looks big and healthy. I have mounted 2 or 3 guards Since I came here but at present I am not quite well having been on the Sick Report for the last 4 days, with a <u>Cold</u>, however awhile I am writing this, I am much better. The Doctor has Kept me in the Hospital, in a day or two I expect to be for duty. I have written you a letter Since I arrived here about the 12th of July. Mrs Fox tells me that she did not see <u>Cleebe</u> or his Wife, but States that Mrs Dwyer has bought Cleebe out, and Mrs Dwyer States that our things are Safe. I hope such is the fact. The 2 Companies of the 2nd Infy and the Battery "E" of the 3rd Art'y. is still out. I found 2 letters Enclosed in your Envelope from Philadelphia and was quite gratified to hear that Mother received 20 Dollars I gave to Capt. Roberts. The other was from My Sister Elizabeth an answer concerning <u>Fury</u>. You Should always read the letters Coming from Philada. to me, if you have not done it. They all Send their love to you and Etty – I am Sorry my Big Dudu has had a Sore head. It is wonder it was not noticed before. I used to See her frequently rubbing her head. My Dear Eleanor you tell me that you have plenty of work. I hope you will not overdo yourself, for Health is precious. I have been in very good health Since I left you, until about 8 days ago and Since that time I have Coughed Considerable in the night but now I think in 2 or 3 days I shall be all right   Last mail I Send off the deed to Traverse Michigan for to have it recorded and to pay the first years Tax - I Suppose I will get an answer before I am ready to leave for Leavenworth. The Paymaster has been Expected to come on every Boat, if he does come Shortly, he will pay us off for May and June and then if I can collect what the men owes you, It will pay my expenses. (if the Capt. lets me go) to Leavenworth. This river Saint Peters or Minnesota is falling fast, and by the month of September, Boats will not be able to Come up to **Fort Ridgely** – Consequently, I shall have to desend a great portion of the way by Land, to Saint Paul. The women are all well and Send their respects. Mrs Fitzerald wishes to be remembered to Mrs Murphy. Dear Eleanor the time truly hangs heavily. It Sems *{seems}* like a year. Chris, tells me times are dull in Philada. And they hope to See us next November in Philada. But I think there wishes will not be gratified. My Dear Wife, I must Close as I have no more news of any importance. Give my best wishes to the Hospt. Steward and all Enquiring friends, and tell Etty She

ought to mind her book and not forget her Spelling or Reading, give her
my Embrace, and receive my blessings for your never failing Kindness –
Your Husband   Oliver

Mrs E.M. Boizard
Laundress of Compy. "K"
4th Arty Fort Kearny, NT

From US Army Paymaster to Oliver

Paymaster's Office
Detroit, Mich
November 30th 1859

John O Boizard
Late Private 4th Regt U.S. Arty
    Sir
           I enclose for your signature duplicate final statements,
upon signing and returning which to this office a draft for the below
amount will be transmitted to you. The following is a correct statement
of your acc.
Pay from June 30. '59 to Nov. 17.'59   4 mos. 16 d @ $10 per mo.
                $45.33
Ret. Do. $60.00
Due for traveling from Pittsburgh Penn__Fort Ridgely Minn. 1100 m. @
        20 m per day $20.16
Subsistence for 55 days (as above travelling acc. @ 23c per ration
                $12.65
Amt. Due you for clothing $68.30

Total – $206.44
Deduct for Asylum 59c_____ – 59
$205.85
Deduct for Ordnance Stores –_____. 40
$205.45
Yours Very Respectfully
(Signed) Sackfield Maclin
Paymaster US Army
Your furlough & discharge will be returned to you with Draft –

56

1859 plot bought by Boizards modified.jpg

S/E quarter of the N/W of Sec. 15 in township numbered 28

Research at the Traverse City office of land records revealed that John Oliver Boizard purchased a 40 acre plot of land in 1859. The plat map above is actually an 1881 plat map of Glen Arbor, but with the help of Dave Taghon at the Empire Musuem, we were able to locate the 40acre plot of land that the Boizards purchased in 1859. On this 1881 map, we see that the Fishers owned the land just north of the plot owned by the Boizards – it is probable that the Boizards were neighbors with the Fishers in 1859 as well as in 1864 when Eleanor and Marietta purchased a different 10 acre plot from him to build a cabin.

Newport Barracks, KY
1861-1863

From the time that Oliver was discharged from the army in 1859 until we read the letter that John Fisher wrote to him in December of 1861, little is known for sure about the Boizards whereabouts.

We know that they moved to Glen Arbor for at least a short amount of time, as they owned forty acres there and when John Fisher wrote to them in 1861 he told them news about their 'neighbors.' How long they stayed there, we don't know. It is possible that Oliver was not able to support his family in the still undeveloped area of Glen Arbor, thus forcing him to sell and move on. They cultivated a strong friendship with John and Harriet Fisher in the time that they did live in Glen Arbor.

Oliver apparently re-enlisted in 1860 or 1861, because we discover that Oliver and his family are stationed in **Newport Barracks**, Kentucky where Oliver is a clerk, probably in the Quartermaster Department.

Oliver & Eleanor are together from 1861-1863 and the only correspondence that we have during those years are letters to the Boizards from the Fishers in Glen Arbor, and from a military family, William and Evelena Brown. They were friends that had apparently been transferred from Newport Barracks to Fort Adams, RI.

The letters written by the Fishers to the Boizards are perhaps the most eloquent of all the letters in the collection. John Fisher was a true patriot and he was a staunch believer in the Union cause. His letters read like passionate speeches against slavery and for the preservation of this great nation.

Oliver's three-year re-enlistment was up in January or February of 1864, and at that time it appears that the Boizards moved to Chicago.

<u>From J.E. Fisher to John O. Boizard</u>

Glen Arbor
Dec 21st 1861

Friend Boziard

The last mail brought your letter, I have not received a letter in a long time which done me as much good as yours. I had often wondered where you were and what you were doing, now your letter tells me you are in the right place ready and armed to do battle for the old <u>Flag</u> and the existence of our nation. May you deal heavy blows and may the God of battles nerve your right arm; is the prayer of your Friend. History gives us no parallel to this rebellion and never did rebels deserve the halter more than the rebels of the Seceded States. I am very thankful I now know where you are as you will be kind enough to keep me posted in relation to matters and things pertaining to the war in your vicinity. Now for matters here, Mr. Goffart lives up west of Town about two miles, near Mr. McCarteys. He has **preempted** forty acres, they are well two of their children go to school. Mr & Mrs McCarty are well they with us were pleased to hear from you   they wish me to present their compliments. Mr. Dorseys, Tuckers, Rays, in fact all the old neighbors were glad to hear from you. they send their respects to you and to Mrs. Boizard. There has been some changes in affairs and business since you was here. The N T line of Propellers have called here regularly all summer, on an average of one a day for the season. it has made good times every body is busy. there has been a large immigration here this past season. Families are now living near your old place   Some are settled three or four miles back from the Lake. I am keeping the Saw Mill busy. next summer more are coming to Settle we have had a good School for the past year, and this fall a preacher moved into town and preaches to the sinners, weekly or <u>weakly.</u> So you see we are coming up. As I told you we would. I am writing this letter lying on my back afflicted as was poor Job of old; sore boils from the soles of my feet so up along. You did not mention to what Regiment you belonged, please do so in your next, also the names of your Com. Officer and Adjutant so if you move I can get a letter to you   And Dear Friend know this that the Prayers, heartfelt earnest prayers, of every lover of his country are continually offered to Heaven for your preservation and the success of your arm. Mrs. Fisher wanted to write some in this letter to Mrs. Boizard but I have filled it up. we both and our Boys send our Love and Friendship to you both   write me old Friend. Yours Truly, J. E. Fisher

I shall write again next mail.

From John E. Fisher to Oliver

Glen Arbor
Jan 2nd '62

Friend Boizard

I sent you a letter last Mail and now I am going to have Uncle Sam carry you another and by the way I love that Same old Uncle Sam. my earliest recollections of reading was how he whiped {whipped} his Dad (Old England) and told him to his face that he was of age and intended to Set up House keeping on his own account and that how he grew, prospered and multiplied till the nations of the World call him the Great Modele Republic and with our own eyes we have Seen him fostering care for and protecting his children far more than any other National Parent in the whole world – Then with what regret, grief and anger it is to us to See a portion of his Family attempt to take his life, virtually to enact the Savage custom to draw and quarter him. How often it is that the History of Families, we have often Seen the favored Son or Daughter in a family the very one that gives the Parent the most trouble So with our Nation the government has paid more of its means, given more of its appointments, more of its patronage in fact that portion of the Nation now in Rebellion has itself administered the government for four fifths of the time since we commenced our national existence. So they had but to help themselves to all they wanted and they did.

Now Friend Boizard when I think over all these things and many more connected with the history of our government my blood boils with anger while a deep, deep grief burdens my mind to think that so large a portion of our People Should be so ungrateful as to attempt to destroy tear down and annihilate so good a government. And now Friend B I have preached this little sermon it will do for this letter I shall write you next mail. you recollect our mails come and go but once in two weeks, so it will take a month maybe more to Send a letter & get an answer.

Write at your earliest opportunity – give my best regards to Mrs Boizard and your little Daughter and for your-self I feel a deep and earnest Solicitude that the God of Battles will preserve you and those with you till this Rebellion is crushed, and History Shall engrave your names on its brightest page and millions, aye, millions on millions shall point to that page, and Say, there are the names of the Preservers of the Great Republic. Yours truly J.E. Fisher

J.O. Boizard Sergt. Mj.

Glen Arbor
Jan 31st 62

Friends Mr & Mrs Boizard

This weeks mail brought us a letter from you for which accept our earnest thanks. Mr Fisher was quite sick when he answered your first letter and has been ailing, since. some of the time obliged to keep to his room. and our Lounge can testify, to his companionship. (You know what disease he suffered when you was here.) so he has appointed me his Secretary, Pro Tem. We have had beautiful weather thus far, snow now about eighteen inches in the woods, not as deep near the shore. no ice as yet on Lake Michigan. Glen Lake is covered with ice. Business is quite lively in fact the road past our House is quite a thorough fare Horse and Ox teams passing daily with cord wood & c. Mr Oliver has **Preempted** and moved on to a piece of Land near the new Dock (Mr Fisher spoke of it in a former letter) which is about four miles north of here there is quite a settlement in there. I believe they are well. Mrs Oliver had a little Daughter about a year ago. The people of your acquaintance here are well, except Mrs Dorsey and the bright eyes of her little three day old Boy will I think affect her recovery.

We had two hired men cutting and drawing saw logs the mill is not running and probably will not, untill warmer weather you have I think ere this received our second letter in which I told all the news, and as our place does not improve much in Winter I have but little to write this time. News reaches us that England is ripe for a broil with us that Canada is arming and that we are on the Eve of a terible struggle, will it be that the God of Freedom will forsake us – I think not, while her sons and Daughters, aye her Daughters too are willing to do Battle for Right. Mr Fisher had concluded our news Paper news was very imperfect, we would be very, greatfull for all information it is agreable for you to give us, in fact the neighbors as well as ourselves Hail a letter from Mr Boizard as a god send in the way of news for that we all know is reliable. The Boys attend school, they also attended a Dance last Evening, they think they are almost men, they are very anxious we should let them attend a Dancing school that is to commence next week. we have not decided yet. they send their love to Etty. Mons. Goffarts is greatfull for your kind remembrance of them. Mr & Mrs McCarty send their best regards to you both – Now Mr & Mrs Boizard at your earliest convenience we shall be most happy to receive an answer, yours with lasting Friendship J. E. & H. M. Fisher

To Oliver

To: S Burbank
Lt. Col. 13th Inft. Comm.
at **Newport Barracks** KY

Sir:
The application in the cases of, Sundry Laundresser enclosed inqs form
of Aug 20th as per statement List Subjoined, has been received. It
appears to be correct, and will be audited as soon as reached its turn, and
the result communicated to you.
Very respectfully,
Your obedient servant,
Ezra B. French, Auditor

Claim of E.M Boizard – against John Kendrick -		$3.25
Boch 8th Reg. US Infty–		
Margaret Ostermayer– Sundry Soldier same Co –		$10.10
Priscilla Michaels – — — — —		7.50
Hanny Tagier – Rudolf Howard " "		4–
Augusta Hammerle Sundry Soldier " "		17.10
Carolina Greible – " " " "		8.75
Mary Leary – " " " "		17.75
Selina W. Holt " " " "		7.25
Mary Swady Charles Butt " "		3–
Johanna Pfarromiller Sundry Soldier " "		35.20
Katharine Lang " " " "		10.50
– Buehl " " " "		21.75

Fort Adams RI
June 1st 1863

Dear Oley,
 I take the pleasure to write you a few lines to inform you that we are all
well and we hope that these few may find and your family enjoying the
same blessing. You must excuse me for not writing before but I was
waiting to hear wether we would be ordered out or not. We had orders to
leave about two weeks ago, but they was countermand we have Col.
Sheperd for our Col now   things goes on better than they did before
Col. Sanderson is order out but where to we don't know.
My wife says she is glad to hear that Mrs. Boyzard is better. She says she
expects her sickness while full in to her arms it is about time you do
something for your self we have no news but plenty of hard work   we
wash for 40 men and 3 officers   we have about 20 men on recruiting
service but no recruits coming in yet   Neley and Saly sends their Love to
Mary Etta and wishes to see her   my Wife sends her love to you all and
so do I   give our respects to all inquiring friends and we hope to hear
from you soon   no More at present. From your Effecinate Friend,
William Brown   Principal Musician 15th infy

Glen Arbor
July 6th 63

Dear Friends Mr. & Mrs. Boizard
We received your ever welcome letter a few mails since pardon us for
not sooner answering it we are very sorry to hear of Mrs Boizards ill
health I really think the climate of Glen Arbor would restore her and I
should very much like her for a neighbor again   you would be really
surprised to see how our country has improved since you left. there is no
government Land in our Town all has been taken and mostly by actual
settlers. crops are looking very well. we are living up on our farm
moved here last fall, as our sawyer lives at the mill   it makes quite a long
walk for Mr Fisher morning & evening and his health is not very good,
but our fruit trees and things were being destroyed and needed the care of
the owner so we moved on to the farm

My Brother C C McCarty is keeping a Hotell in Town, has built a little way from the Glen Lake road but a short distance from the Dock, has considerable custom there are so many Land lookers and families moving in. there were forty couples at the Fourth of July Ball held at his house. All of your acquaintances here are well and very much pleased to hear from you. we have a weekly mail. – Our peach trees are loaded with peaches we shall probably have six or Eight bushels. Mr. Barret will probably have 25 or 30 bushels of apples on his farm he has been offered 1000 dollars for his place. quite a number have enlisted from here 13, I think so you see Glen Arbor has contributed her share towards putting down this rebellion and what a terible war it is. So many lives lost I wish it would end but not untill the South are whiped. *{whipped}* I have no patience with them or those that sympathise with them it really seems to me, as though our Generals have been to afraid of hurting somebody, while the South were fighting to kill, we have been afraid of hurting our Brethren, but I think they ought to be delt *{dealt}* with like enemies for they are, and of the worst kind. I always considered family fights the very worst, and what is this, but a family fight, if I was a man I would see what I could do. I see by the papers Gen. Mead has taken Gen. Hookers place, what is the trouble with the Gen's. that they are so often changed. are they not competent, or are they considered not trusty or is it politics as some charge. I hope the right man will be found and soon to. what is your opinion about England & France taking sides against us. I think they would be glad to see us divided but I hardly think they will come out openly in favor of the South unless she frees her slaves, as both those foreign powers boast of being enemies to Slavery, but if they come we will be enough for them, crippled as we are. for if necessary a woman can carry a gun and use it too, so I think we might raise quite an army. now don't laugh at the idea for I am seriously in earnest Charly say if the war lasts untill he is old enough he shall go – July 24th You see by the first part of my letter it is sometime since I commenced it the truth is I have so little time for anything but work work I have eight & nine in my family and a girl only thirteen to help me I am from necessity compelled to work and that pretty industriously too Well Miss Etta I intended my boys should answer your nice little letter but they are both at work so I will I think you are improving nicely in writing. Charly & Franky I presume you remember, they do you, and if you was here would like to take you to the Parties with them. they both attended a dance on the fourth of July and each took a little girl. they had a nice time, Charly is nearly as tall as I am do you grow as fast as

65

that. I am sorry your ma is unwell, you must be very kind to her   when she leaves you as my mother did me this winter, we shall think of every naughty thing we ever did with sorrow   your ma may think best to come here   we should all be very glad to have you. I hope you will write agin soon. we often speak of you   do not think you are forgotten by us because we do not oftener write   I will tell you how Mr Fisher works and then you can see for yourself   to begin with his health is not very good   he gets up at four in the morning, goes down to the Mill before breakfast to oversee affairs   sometimes comes back to his breakfast but oftener I send it to him   generally is not at home untill dark   then he is very tired Sundays. I say 'now do write to Mr Boizard'   'I will'   he says 'as soon as my head feels clear, but I must lie down and rest first I am so tired and I have writing I must do'   he is the Judge of Probate for this Co. & Town Supervisor besides Justice of the Peace and School Trustee so you see his hands are full, but I am in hopes he wont take any of those offices again   then he will have more time to write to our friends.   but do write often and I will answer your letters

My father is living with us   Father & Mother came here last fall, and it pleased the ruling power to take my mother from us. she died the thirteenth of last April, after a long and painfull sickness. Father is 75 years of age and very much broken down. We are having such grand victories now we hope the war may soon close   they are trying to raise two more Regts. in the northern part of Mich. A Mr Brooks speaks in town Saturday Evening. war of course is the subject and to raise volunteers the object of the meeting. if ladies are allowed to, I shall attend. I hope you will write soon   our best love and wishes to your ma and accept the very best wishes for yourself

from your sincere Friends   J. E. & Harriet M Fisher

the boys do not go to school this summer, they will next winter, they have to work for their Father   we have so much to do   I think I will send this letter by a boat it will reach you sooner   give my very best love to your ma and accept the very best wishes for yourself from your friend Harriet M.Fisher

To Miss Etta Boizard

From John E. Fisher to Oliver Boizard

There is no date on this letter but from the events mentioned in this letter it can be assumed that this letter was written in the late summer/fall of 1863

Friend Boizard

Since I wrote you last the Union Cause has made a great progress, the taking of Vickburgh and the tightening of the **Anaconda folds** of the Union power, gives promise that treason is about soon to find that ditch of which the man Stealers and women whippers of **Secessia** have told so much. if down in the depths of the lowest hell there is still a lower hell then possibly those who have tried to destroy this only free government may there find a punishment Suitable to their crime. to think of the Hundreds of thousands of lives lost and the untold suffering endured, the Widows and orphans made – causes us to curse the instigators of this rebellion. at the same time we are thankful that their crime has developed such a noble <u>class</u> of <u>defenders</u> of <u>Freedom.</u> Freedom to <u>All</u>. ALL not a part of the people. it is a truth well known to all who have observed that where Slavery exists at all, it to a certain degree enslaves the whole, it demoralizes the whole, but thank God the people of this land are beginning to see the value of full and unrestricted freedom and though the lesson is costing dear, very dear, yet I presume we could not have learned at any other School. J.E. Fisher

Bill from the US Post Office to Sgt. Boizard

Post Office Newport KY
October 8th 1863

U.S. Barracks
To Newport Post office

For Postage during the months July, August, September '63 $8.13

Sgt. Boizard

Dear Sir– Above you will find the Barracks Postal account for the past Quarter. He cannot take the time as heretofore to copy the names of parties getting letters. They are in the office and subjection to your inspection.

Respectfully,
Mr. Andrews
P.M. *{Postmaster}* Thursday Morning Oct 8/63

Added to the bottom of this letter in J. Oliver Boizard's handwriting is the following note:

Paid $8.15 on the 9th of October '63

From Didier A Fermet to Oliver

Corinth
October 17, 1863

My dear friend Boizard,
I would tell you that a lot of things have happened since we left each other. Luck has not been on our side in our music since we left. In leaving {?} caught a rheumatism in his legs and has not been able to play since we left NewPort. Sergent Pertz is pretty sick as well. I thought we would be coming back to NewPort, going by Wisburg *{Vicksburg?}* we got the musician George of Iver in the beat. After staying a while at Wisburg {Vicksburg} we left for Memphis where we stayed 8 days and then left for Corinth but bad luck had it that we had a battle for four hours. We lost a good amount of men but were victorious. We got a musician prisoner, his name is Frederick, and the two horns captured by the enemy. We must leave tomorrow and maybe within a few days we will have a big battle. I have nothing else new to say, since you must know more than me. Sorry if I didn't write sooner because I myself was very sick but thank God I am fine now. Excuse me for writing with a pencil but it is not easy to write in the camp. I will be happy to hear your news and what is new in NewPort. I wish to return as soon as possible. I am anxious to hear your response. Write in English, I can read it perfectly. Give my compliments to the young ladies of the Barracks. I extend to you the hand of friendship and hope to see you soon.
Didier A Fermet Musician of the 13th U.S.

{This letter was written in French and translated for me by Josh Filler.}

<u>From Mrs. Brown to Eleanor & Ettie</u>

Fort Adams RI
Oct 21st 1863

Dear Friend,

I received your kind letter and was glad to hear that you and your mother and Father was well and I hope this will find you all in good health as they leaves us at present. I thought you all had forgotten us. Tell Oley if he would forget his bottle as easy as he does his old friends it would be a good thing for him. Elen says she is sorry that your doll was wounded but she has had a dozen killed since she seen you. Harry is a big boy and talk and run all over the Fort and the baby, is as fat as a pig. We have no news here only plenty of hard work. Tell Oley, that Brown is agoing to reenlist for 5 years more. Give our respects to Bridges and all inquiring friends. We May be down about Christmas. No more at present but remains your Efficinate friend till death write soon Evelena Brown

There is a lot of extra paper at the end of this letter and written on those empty lines in very 'young' writing is the following note, probably written by Marietta as she practiced her writing skills. Marietta would have been 11 years old at this time.

Dear Mother

I am writing you a note how are you I am well and I hope that you are the same I had to write a letter for school and i did so but no dictated it for me.   To E.M Boizard   Newport KY

<u>From John E. Fisher to Oliver</u>

Glen Arbor
Nov 5th /63

Dear Friend Boisard

you are thinking I am not useing you well in not ans'g your letters but if I do not write it is not because I do not think of you, no, we often think of you and your Family and wish it was in our power to See and have one good familiar chat with you all. I have to work as hard as my poor Strength will bear. when I come into the House I am so tired I have not

69

the energy to write. my health is improving I am better this fall than I have been for the past two years, and am quite free from pain.

I was talking with Mr Goffart about your wanting a few acres and he said he would Spare you ten or twelve acres, at gov't price. He owns and lives about two & a half miles west of town and is doing well. his land is good, it is the nearest place that I could find where you could buy a piece of good land cheap, if you should like to have Mrs. Boizard come here I will See that She has some place to go into. there is also about 44 of government land adjoining the piece you can get of Goffart but it is marsh and is only good for grass, yet I would advise you to buy it if you buy of Goffart. if you Should not want the whole of the 44 acres I would be glad to join you and buy half of it. the country has filled up verry fast the past Season. it is verry different from what it was when you was here it is much more like an old country. Mr Dorseys - MrCartys, Rays, and all of your acquaintance here are well. Mrs Fisher and the Boys join me in Sending our best respects to yourself Mrs Boizard and Etta and believe us always your friends and well wishers.

  J.E. Fisher

The Chicago & Glen Arbor Years
1864-1870

Oliver's term of service was up with the U.S. Army in January or February of 1864. After his discharge he moved to Chicago, Illinois and was able to find employment as a clerk with the US Mustering and Disbursing Office. I believe that Oliver was a civilian employee at this job, because Oliver refers to it as 'employment' and he always seems to wonder how long he will be able to keep his job. Oliver was also responsible to provide his own living quarters while in the employment of Colonel Pomeroy.

In May of 1864, Eleanor & Marietta take a boat from Chicago and move to Glen Arbor. Eleanor had recurring headaches and bouts with a poor heart and these health conditions may have been the motivation behind their leaving Oliver in Chicago to move to Glen Arbor.

From 1864 until 1870 when Oliver dies, the Boizards communicated mostly by letters. There were occasional visits to Glen Arbor by Oliver, and during the winter of 1867-68, Eleanor & Marietta moved to Chicago to be with Oliver.

William and Eliza Bridges and their daughter Emma, are introduced to us during the time period of 1864 -1870. These close family friends had also been stationed at **Newport Barracks** in Kentucky and after the Boizards' move, their friendship continues through correspondence. Marietta Boizard and Emma Bridges developed a special childhood friendship that endured for many years.

There are photographs of Emma and her husband Edwin in a family photo album and a handwritten note on the photograph indicates that there was a family relationship between Emma & Edwin Brown & Eleanor. So far, a family relationship has not been discovered in any research.

During these later years we also meet a single man named Austin Newman. Austin served in the Civil war and it appears like the acquaintance was made when he too was stationed at **Newport Barracks**. He visited the Boizard family and seemed to have an interest in Marietta; he was sixteen years older than her.

In 1867, Marietta Boizard and Charlie Fisher began to take special interest in each other. They wrote often during the winter that Marietta and her mother spent in Chicago. They were married on January 19, 1870. Marietta was 17 and Charlie was 21.

All correspondence ends between Eleanor and Oliver in November 1870. It is believed that Oliver died in Chicago in November 1870.

From William Brown to Oliver

Fort Adams RI
Jany 17th 64

Dear Oly

I now take the pleasuer to write you a few lines to informe you that we
are all well and I hope that this few lines will find you and your family
enjoying the same   I wrote to you the 20th Dec to let you know that we
could not come to see you by Chrismas on acount of the weather being
so cold but you may look for us when the weather gets warm   tell
MarryEtta that we wont forget her shells   please tell Mrs Smith that we
have wrote two letters to her and has received no answer to ether *{either}*
of them   I hope you had a merry chrismas at Newport   we had a big
diner *{dinner}* hour and plenty of Egg Nog and Lauger *{Lager}* Beer
tell Marry Etta that we named the baby Malisa it was a favarit name of
the grandmothers   she is four months old and she weighs 16 lbs and can
sit alone   tell Marry Etta that when my Wife can go to town She may
look for her chrismas gift   Nely and Saly sends their Love to you all and
Shoney is the bigest rowdy in the crowd   Dear Oly please to do me the
favor to ask Col. Sanderson if he knows any thing about the wash Bills
that was against Elev of the 2nd Bat. they was put in hands to Colect and
{he} Colected the Sutters *{sutlers}* Bills and let the wash Bill lay   I
understand that they are laying at the auditor office and I think that it is
his place to see to it   that is about all I have to say   give our respects to
all enquiring friends and the same for yourself   Write Soon   I remain
yours for ever Wm Brown
Pr Musian 15th Infy.

From Wm Brown & Evelena Brown to Eleanor & Marietta

Fort Adams RI
Jan 22nd 1864

Dear Friends

We received your kind and welcom letter and we was glad to hear that
you was all in good health as this leaves us at present only my Wife has a
felon on her hand and she aint able to do mutch Dear Friends I am very

sorry you was so lonesom on Christmas   but I hope you had a happy
New Year   my Wife would like very well to be with you

when you write again please let us know what kind of place it is for a
Baker or any sort of work and if there is a place near yours   we will buy
it so we can be nabors *{neighbors}*   Santa Claus com to see the children
Christmas and New Years both Neley and Saley wants to see MarryEtta
the next time I write I will send you our potagraphs. *{photographs}* when
you write to your Father Please send him our best respects and the same
to you all we have no news worth writing I hope to hear from you soon
we remains yours forever. Wm Brown Evelena Brown

From Didier A Fermet to Oliver

Huntsville, AL
February 28, 1864

My dear friend,

Excuse me if I am slow to write but I am so greatly busy that I could not
answer your letter. I am in good health and desire that this letter find you
the same way.   I cannot tell you anything about the war but you can
rather hear about me. We cannot see anything from where we are, the
town is very pretty but there is no pleasure. The women behave
extravagantly and don't like soldiers as us but this is not worth NewPort.
I have heard that we are returning to NewPort and if we return I will tell
you what intentions are. At this moment I am working so that when I get
to NewPort I will choose myself a little wife and get married, make a
home for myself and a family and make some money. I think it is the
best way to secure a job for myself. Please inform me if I really have to
do five years of military service or only three. You know I enlisted for
five years and some of the officers are saying that an order of congress in
Washington announced that those enlisted for 5 years only have to do 3.
Please inform yourself because I would wish to be able to cut two years
off but I need to at least be sure. Mr. Clark compliments you and your
family. All our musicians are well and compliment you as well. Our
sargent William Besse passes his complements as well as his wife's.
Give a friend's handshake to the young ladies that I know and tell them I
wait impatiently to get back to NewPort and choose which one I want to
marry. If you can embrace them for me. I have nothing else to say.
I shake your hand friendly, Didier A Fermet Musician of the 15th

Excuse my writing but I am tired and I have a heavy hand.

{This letter was written in French and was translated for me by Josh Filler.}

From E.J. Bridges to Eleanor, second part of letter is from Emma Bridges to Marietta

Newport KY
March 11, 1864

Dear friends,
we received your letter today we were all glad to hear from you that you arrived safe there   we are all well at the present   we got your photograph and i give them Mrs. Johnson and Mrs. Jones. there has been some changes here   a order came to send some men away   in the order they named the men, oscar, harry, with several others too numerous to mention   we were very sorry to hear that you had a cold and hope that you will get over it soon   poor picket is gone at last he died last night at 1 o clock Mrs Alberty moved into your house without ever cleaning she just swept out and put down her carpet.   you did not tell us where to write so i did not no {*know*} what to do about senden you your money   it has been payday here and all the men that owed you paid my father, but one   and he was not paid off   Jack doran and Mcloney were transferred to their old regiment the fourth artilery. sergent devere took them there Mr Johnson took the others   Emma is sleeping with Mrs. Johnson every night   it was reported around that Mr. Boizard was in newport. hanigar said he seen him up at rits and spoke to him   no more at present but rite soon, yours truly, E. J. Bridges

Dear Etta,
lets have a little chat   sarah Maryan Jiny tomy is all well but we missed you from amonst us   we were all lonesome   on sunday i went to church with Sarah   mother went to sleep on the chair Mrs devere came up in the afternoon a little while   oscar newman give me something for you   i would not send it this time for fear you would not be there to get it   he went down to the boat and got yours and paid a quarter for it and got 6 of

his own   he gave me one and gave me one for you the day he was a
going away   he had great times running in and out giving us all little
things   he gave jiny, a bucet *{bucket or bouquet}* and a box of butons
{buttons} and a botel *{bottle}*   he gave Maryan a box of butons *{buttons}*
he gave me a pertfoalia *{portfolio}* full of writing paper   tomy said for
me to write about him a running a way and cetching *{catching}* whiping
{whipping} poor oscar   tommy is teling me what to say in my leter   i
must stop now as it is time for me to quit   it is 9 oclock and i must go
down to Mrs. Johnsons   no more at present   answer my leter as soon as
you get this   yours forever
E. Bridges

From Wm. Bridges to Oliver

Newport, KY
March 24th 1864

Dear Friend
I lift my pen to drop you a few lines. hoping and trusting thay may find
your self and famley enjoying the verry best of health by the blessing of
god our heavenley father--
Bus -- I had a verry hard spell of it. for about ten days -- all hopes of
men were given up and dispared of -- I trust to god it may never be my
lot to pass through such an ordeal again. I supose you guess what was
the matter   I have onley bin *{been}* out ove *{of}* the Hosptel 3 days and
am not well yet -- I succeeded in collecting $2.75 cts of your bill which
you will pleas find enclosed   one man received no pay -- now for sum
{some} nuse *{news}*   the Depo *{depot}* is broken up & the P.P. & Band
ordered to **Governors Island** we leave on Sunday week the 3rd of April.
Eliza goes a long sum *{some}* two or three other famleys   Gallagher was
discharged & enlisted again   farewell to Newport Ky. and old senss
{sins} -- My cousen tens *{?}* due sume *{some or soon?}* to come forth
and pay up   Wm Bridges

Etties Letter of the 20th was received   Eliza happy to hear that Mrs
Boizard had recovered from her cold   the hole *{whole}* famley was hapy
to hear that you were all well as this leaves them that these few lines may
find you in the continuation of the same favored blessing   glad to hear

that you had gained employment we have bin *{been}* successful in
selling off our furnature   Tommy is a bad boy he wont keep still while I
write but sends his love to Ettie & Mrs Ard-- I dont know ov *{of}* any
thing more to say at this time   more next time   we all join send our love
and best wishes to you all   wish you were her *{here}* to go a long
answer this soon in order that we may hear from you before we leave   I
remain yours for ever   Wm Bridges

From Emma Bridges to Marietta

March 1864

dear Eta,

i take the pleasure to write you a few lines to let you know that i am well
and hope that you are the same   when oscar newman went away he left
his photograph for me to send to you   you will find it enclosed in here
and he bought one of yours and paid a quarter for it   he said for you to
write to him   i cannot give you that until he writes   sarah does not
know that we heard from you this time   for we had to get supper and we
sat down to answer   i am sory that you are not here to go with us   my
cousin is spending the night with us   Jiny was up there two nights   i
was not up there yet   we are a going take diner with my aunt on sunday
and then we are all a going down to Mrs. Johnson on friday evening and
stay till sunday evening and then we will start for the depot   this is all at
present   write before we leave. yours forever   emma bridges.

From Eleanor and Marietta to Oliver
(Marietta is writing the letters for her mom now)

Glen Arbor, Michigan
Tuesday May the 10th 1864

Dear Papa

I take the pleasure to let you know that we are well and hope that you are
the same   we did not get here until Saturday morning we laid at
milwakee all day   the boat run about two hours and then laid up the rest
of the night at a wood yard.   we were very sea sick. we ate breakfast
and dinner at Dorseys and then we went to Fishers and staid there until
Monday morning   we live in the house at the mill.   we don't know
wether it will be two or three dollars a month for rent   it cost us three

77

dollars for to get our things into the house. we have been hard at work cleaning house. they was glad to see us. potatoes is a dollar a bushel. when you get my shoes made   get them with pegs in because the sand cuts the sewed ones. we think that the place has improved much since we was here before   we don't see anybody here but has strange faces we have not seen of the old neighbors yet. will you send us the ledger the last number was eleven and the next one is twelve you might send us the daily paper as the war news is acceptable Fisher got the paper you sent him no more at present as it just now struck 10 oclock and we are sleepy and tired We Remain Yours Truly   Eleanor M Boizard Marietta Boizard

From Oliver to Eleanor

Chicago
May 18th, 1864

My Dear Wife,
Your welcomed letter came to hand this morning with the Detroit Post Mark on it. It has been 7 days on the road. I felt somewhat uneasy about you, I though you might be sick. I send this by the Propeller "**City of New York**" and also Etty's shoes. They cost $2.75. I send you also a music box, which I received from the Post Office. No letter came with it. I suppose it came from Austin Newman. I bought at Auction 2 packages of Soap, I send you one, with the shoes. I am very busy in making out Muster Rolls, the Capt. Has employed one more clerk. (5 in all). I am boarding at Pfeiffer's. I sleep by myself, there are 2 others sleeps in the same room. About the beginning of next month I will try to send you some Mackrel.   There has been terrible Fightings between the Two Armies, and I suppose they will fight terribly at the taking of the Rebel Capitol (Richmond)   You state that Potatoes are $1.00 per bushel, I hope you will content yourself and keep your health. After you get fixed let me know how you get along and the price of articles such as you use about the house. Also let me know how you can secure yourself a homestead. Tell Fisher I will send him the news of the Big fights. I suppose by this time you have seen many of the neighbors and you might answer this letter on the first propeller. Well Ellen, I will close for it is time to go to work. Give my best respects to Mrs. Fisher, Dorsey and all enquiring friends, not forgetting Mr Goffart & family. Truly yours, your husband, "Oliver"

Tell me how the house looks after its fixed and about the stove. JO

Kiss Moll the Madd" for me, She is 12 years old today
I found your pictures in my stockings, best I have seen.
(Note) Write soon. How is Dick   J.O.B

From Eleanor & Marietta to Oliver

Glen Arbor, Michigan
Saturday 21, 1864

Dear Papa,
We received your letter and was glad to hear that you was well as this
leaves us the same. I got my shoes and they was most to small me but I
can just wear them we got the papers and was glad to get the ledger as
we have nothing much to read here   you wished to know how the house
looked   it looks very well but it looks empty   momma says you had
better send her a table and an oil cloth instead of fish   a good one for the
things that we got from that man is a coming apart   momma wants you
to send in some barley and wheat as a substitute of coffee and some teller
stamps   also a small jar of lard   we was up to Goffarts and he has a fine
place he has about six acres cleared   Alix is here and is married to that
Irish woman the one he used to go and see and he has two children and
he also has a place on the homestead bill   but mama spoke to Mr. Fisher
and he said that you would have to come and see about it yourself   you
would have to go the land office yourself and that you would have to pay
about 14 or 15 Dollars and it would be about 5 or 6 miles away   mama
thinks that we had better buy a few acres of land   be as saving as you
can because if mama has the money to pay for it right down she thinks
that she might get it cheaper   we had not much time to look about yet
you wished to know how much the things are here   flour is nine dollars a
barrel and tea is $2.00 and $2.50 a pound and it is not as good as that we
brought   and for the worst brown sugar they ask twenty two cents a
pound   eggs is twenty five cents a dozen   pork is 15 cents a pound
there is no school here there is no teacher here   they are looking for one
there is not hardly a boat but that they bring more settlers   Mr. Fisher
says that when you have any papers   for you not to tear them up for to
send them by the boat   Mama says for you to send them to us   Goffart's
sends their love to you   we can get fresh white fish here for 10 cents a

79

piece when you write send the things in care of Mr Dorsey for he is always there   the stove is as big as ever only it wants a length and an elbow   we can do without it until you come up   no more at present but remaining yours   truly yours forever   Oh we forgot Dickey he sings as loud as ever   he was on a visit for a week to Mrs. Fishers.

Mrs. Eleanor M Boizard (mama says do not laugh at her name)
Miss Etty Boizard.

{Eleanor had signed her own name in a very childish script.}

There were three columns of figures on the back side of the letter.

Table 8.00	15.75 old w	74.25
Glue 0.25	2.50 coat	37.25
Lard 2.00	2.00 (?)	37.00
Box 0.25	14.00 board	
Pomatum 1.00	2.00 washing	
Wheat 0.50	36.25	
Oil cloth 1.50	1.00 stamps	
Freight 2.00	37.25	
15.75		

From Eleanor Boizard to the Land Office

Glen Arbor Michigan
Monday 23rd 1864

Dear Sir

I take the pleasure to ask you to let me have the southeastern part of north east quarter from sexion 30 township 29 arrange 14 does it belong to the government yet   can I have it on a homestead bill   my husband is not *{here}* for he is a clerk in Captain Pomeroys office in Chicago   be so kind as to tell me by letter   Eleanor M Boizard

{Written on the bottom of the letter}
A married woman cannot enter land under the Homestead Act.
Yours, Morgan Bates   Register

Glen Arbor, Michigan
Tuesday, May the 24th 1864

Dear Papa
We are well and hope that you are the same   mama was speaking to Mr.
Fisher and he can spare 10 acres of land and there is two acres almost
cleared   mama was to look at it this morning   there is water about thirty
rods from where the house would be built and he would ask one hundred
dollars   it is east of Mr. Fisher's farm house about one half mile and
there is a wagon road cut through to the clearing. if you can send forty
dollars to mama then she can have it to pay right down for it them.
mama can have 10 dollars for to pay the rent and other expenses   you
need not send the table this time as we would rather do without it just
now and pay for the land now   I will tell you about what Mr. Goffart
says   I don't think that is worth while but I will tell you what he has to
say as Mons. Goffart can't sell before the terms of four years   he has a
log house just the frame of logs   he will let us lease it for twelve dollars
and he will rent us 10 acres of land for 4 years   he will ask one dollar
and a half when we would clear it per acre and at the end of 4 years he
will sell it to us for 8 dollars an acre   now you see that Mr. Fishers offer
is the best one   Monsieur Goffart wants you to send him some things to
make medicine for a sick woman   one quarter of a pound **camphor germ**
one pint of the **spirits of hartshorn**   quarter of a pound of **bitter aloes**
one pint of alcohol when you get them send a receipt of how much they
are and then he will pay me   did you ever answer Bridges & Joneses
letters   no more at present But remaining yours true
Mrs. Eleanor M Boizard
Miss E.E. Boizard

Dicky is well and he sings like he was a going to deafen a body
signed by Richard the 1st
*Eleanor signed her name in a childish script. There is a picture drawn
of the bird Dicky*

*There are some figures written on the page, probably from Oliver as he
calculated the cost of the provisions they requested. Other figures seem
to be his budget.*

81

1/4 camphor gum	$0.60	Pffeifer	$15.00
Pints Spts Hart	0.40	Tailor	2.50
½ lbs Aloes	0.20	Purdee	2.00
Alcohol	0.50	Capt.	5.00
	$ 2.70	Mach st	0.50
		Mitchell	0.25
		Table	8.00
		Lard	2.00
		Lamp	1.50
		Wheat	0.50
		Sundries	1.00
		Pomatum	1.50
			$ 37.50
		Goffart	1.75
			$ 39.50
		Washing	1.00
			40.50 74.25

40.50
33.75

74.25
39.50
34.75

<u>From Oliver to Eleanor & Marietta</u>

Chicago, Illinois
June 3, 1864

Dear Wife,
I send you by the "**Propeller Granite State**" your table and oilcloth.
Cost $8.50. also a jar of lard, a bag of wheat and $30.00 enclosed in the
letter. You Speak of buying 10 acres of land from Fisher, well it is a
good idea, but you should not pay for it at once, Say you might pay
$60.00 down and let him wait for the balance 40 doll., which I will pay
in 4 months, 10 dollars per month, because if you pay all the money you
have, in case I Should get out of employment you have nothing to subsist
on. Keep the $30.00 which I Send you until you can get another
remittance. You will require Some provisions Shortly, and I Suppose it
will take $100 to put a house on the 10 acres, and at the present prices it

82

will take at least 100 dolls. for your winter stores. Things are still getting higher, my expenses have been high this month, I paid for my board and have to pay $1 per dozen for washing and I bought 2 linen coats, I got them cheap. I paid $2.50 for fixing my overcoat, and a number of other little expenses. I also Send you Goffarts medicine which amount he must pay you when he gets them. You will please find the bill with them. I hope that you will remain contented in good health, also my big Dudu. I am busy now in making out muster rolls for the 100 days now. After that is done, there will be a Slack of business. I would try to do more for you, but is it rather hard to be without money all the month. Next month I Suppose you will require some provisions, you will tell me what you want and I will Send them to you. Try to keep Etty in her Studies, don't neglect her. Tell me in your next letter whether Fisher has any lumber to build a house for you and tell me if the land is good. I suppose the timber is not very good. Act for yourself for the best and I hope all will be well. I still board at Pfeiffer's. He talks about raising the price of board. How did your pickled Beef turn out, and tell me how your coffee and Sugar holds out. If I can keep employment this Summer, well enough, if not I must go elsewhere. I will try to come up and see you about October, if nothing happens. How do you spend your time, do you not get lonesome. I wrote to Bridges but have got no answer. I felt no desire to write to Jones, well I will close this letter hoping you will receive the articles safe and the money. Give my complement to Mr. Fisher and Lady and all enquiring friends. Kiss Etty for Me. Tell her to take more care in her writing. Truly yours
Your Husband "Oliver"
Patrick send his compliments to you. J.O.B.

From Eleanor and Marietta to Oliver

Glen Arbor
Michigan
9th 1864

Dear Papa
I take pleasure to let you know that we received your welcome letter and was glad to hear that you was well   we got the table and the oilcloth and the jar of lard   there was no wheat put ashore   did you mark the wheat as they wont be accountable for things that is not marked   mama is sorry

about it for she wanted it as a substitute of coffee we got the money and Goffarts medicines and we got the Hair oil and it is very nice our meat kept very well you asked about coffee and sugar we dont use much of it but as to the coffee it goes the fastest mama paid Mr Fisher for two months rent 4 dollars for May and June you wished to know about the 10 acres of land the timber is good it is principley beech and maple mama thinks we could not do better there is two acres of it cleared you wished to know whether Mr. Fisher had any lumber yes he has plenty of it mama thinks that it would be cheaper to put a log shanty on it she was speaking to Mr. Fisher about one and he will see what it will cost to put one on it and we will tell you some other time and we will have to get on it by fall for Mr. Fisher might get another miller and he might want the house mama feels better than she has been these two summers you wished to know if we was lonesome we are some times I wish that you would send us the ledger every week as we have nothing at all to read the last number was 12 there is 4 back number you will find money inclosed in it for it and some books and the name of them on a slip of paper I go to school and I think that the teacher is a good and educated one she explains things to us children when you write tell us what str. your office is on and what number of the haus {*house*} and where you board as we forgot the number Mr. McCarty went to chicago and we could not tell him where to find you and maybe Mr. Fisher will be out this summer tell us what butter is per pound we will tell you in the next letter whether we want any provisions mama could have got some boarders but the provisions will cost more than it would come to as they don't pay much for board here if there is any money left get a copy book No. seven there will be fifty cents for the ledger and two dollars for books no more at present but remaining yours. yours Forever Signed by Eleanor M. Boizard
Signed by Marietta Boizard
Postscript Don't be downhearted it is nine o'clock.

Chicago
June 13th '64

My Dear Wife
I have received no acknowledgment I Sent you $30 by the Cap't of the
"**Granite State**" along with the Table, 1 Jar of Lard, also a Bottle of
Pomatum among the articles for Goffart, if you have not Send me a
letter Stating that you received the money you should immediately
apprise me of it, for Such things Should be promptly to. I Saw Mr.
McCarty and was highly gratified to think I was so lucky to meet him, he
gave me pleasant news of you, you will answer this direct on the 1st
propeller and let me Know what articles of Provisions, you are in want of
I will also send you Some money about the 1st of July for your 4th of July
Anniversary. I Send you 2 papers and also 2 for Mr Fisher   I am well
and hope that you and Etty are well. I was dreaming rather an unpleasant
one about you. I suppose you will require some Tea   I forgot your
Wheat but I think the Best Coffee is the original. Tell Mr Fisher I went
twice to hear **Leo Miller** lecture on Truth & Philosophy. I like him well.
I Send him a copy of one of the papers of that denomination Give my
best wishes to all Enquiring friends and let me know whether you
received the money or not and how you liked your Table and oilcloth, the
Pomatum I suppose has been applied to your head allready. Let me
Know how Goffart likes his medicines for "Sick Women" a hard dose I
should think and whether he paid you for it. I have no more to Say,
Yours truly Your Husband "Oliver"

Mr. MrCarty told me he saw the Table & carried it to the Store but did
not Know whether your received the letter or not.

From Oliver to Eleanor & Marietta

Chicago Ill
June 15th 1864

My Dear Wife
Your letter dated the 9th just came to hand this Morning, and I hasten to
answer it. I Send a letter by the Prop. **Cleaveland** Scolding to you for
not acknowledging that letter with the money & c. However I went to
the post office and found the letter. I Send you with this letter Ettys

Books and 4 Copies of the Ledger, which will Keep you in reading Some time. Mr.Dakin has gone East to get married and Capt. & his Wife are going East also for a Short time. we have been very busy, we have 5 Clerks in the office now - besides the Captain. I will Send you $30 dolls. at the End of this month, also what provisions, you may need. I Suppose you might buy the Land from Mr. Fisher I Suppose he will take $60 down and rest in 3 or 4 months, try to get a good house if you can on it for the Winter, it will require a tight house on account of the cold. There is news that Gen. Sturgess of our party has been defeated in Mississippi. I am sorry for it. No More at Present Do you think the Table is worth $6.00 and the Oil Cloth $2.50   The Lard cost 3.20 Yours & c. Oliver

From Eleanor and Marietta to Oliver

Glen Arbor Mich.
June 17, 1864

Dear Father,

We received your kind letter and also the papers and was glad to hear that you are well and we was sorry that you didn't get our letter as we wrote right away   we put it in the post office and we told them to put it on the boat and Mr. Ray might not have done it he might have sent it by mail we got the money $30 the table and the rest of the things   we put $2.50 in the other letter for the papers and some books **McNallys Geography** and **Sanders new series spelling book Clarks Grammar** and a number 7 copy book and the numbers of the ledgers is 13.14.15.17 and so on until you send them, because we got the 16 no. please send them as it is lonesome here and we have nothing to read   Mr. Fisher is having the logs cut for our shanty as he might sell the mill and they might want this house Mr. Fisher might come to Chicago the latter part of July you might send us some tea and butter as butter is 40 cents a pound here we aint quite out as we might have a bee and then we will need them things and also a smoked shoulder or ham and when you send the things you might send some rhubarb always for Mrs. Dorsey to eat as she has the sore mouth and she can't get it here   we have some lectures here twice a week   Mr. Gofferts son lives on the corner of Huron and Pattin, northeast side or southwest it is in the same place that they used to

live in no more at present.
But remaining yours truly yours
Mrs. Eleanor M. Boizard
Marietta Boizard

P.S. We have not seen Mr. McCarty since he came in.

From Eleanor and Marietta to Oliver

Glen Arbor
June 26th Michigan

Dear Papa,
We received your letter and was glad to hear that you was well   we are
well but mamma has the headache today   it is the first time she has had
it since she came in. we got the books and would like to know the price
of them as the teacher wants to know the price. they have commenced of
our house   mamma was up there and she says that they have to get the
log together and then we will have to have a **bee**   Mr. Fisher wrote on a
piece of paper what things that we need and you will find it in the letter
you said that you would send us $30 at the end of the month   get the
things and send us what you can   we got the ledgers and the last number
is 16 no more at present. But remaining yours, Yours truly
Eleanor M. Boizard
Miss Marietta Boizard.

*A small piece of paper was found with the following supplies written on
it:*   get Sash for five Windows, 12 lights in each. also one Box glass
8 by 10. See that the glass to sash correspond as to size. get lock &
cheap trimmings for door. and 40 lbs 10 penny Nails

From Oliver to Eleanor

Chicago Illinois
July 3, 1864.

My Dear Wife,
I send you by the Propeller **"Cleveland"** 20 lbs. Butter, 2 lbs Tea, Sash
for 5 Windows, putty, also 3 hams, and 40 lbs nails & lock & c. I find the
things are So very high, that I cannot Send you any money (of any

amount) this time. Consequently I will defer it for this month (June). Hams are 18 cts. Butter 35 cts. Flour $11. by the Hundred Barrels, Tea $2 per lbs (good). I hope you will Still retain your health, and Keep up Cheerfully. I will try to reach you about October next. You Stated that Mr. Fisher proposed coming down about the end of July, tell him to come to no. 70 Washington St. near Washington St. Etty wants to know the price of the Books, as far as I recollect the Geography was $1.25, the Grammar 90 cts, and the spelling Book 50 cts. You did not inform me whether you purchased the land or not, but I suppose you have. Let me know how you Stand in circumstances and also the progressing of your 'Shanty'. Will you Shingle it or not. Etty Says in her letter about your headache and that can't be helped. I hope that you will keep your health. Tomorrow being the (4th) we will not work. We are very busy at Present, there are now 6 Clerks in the office, and I presume that there will be Employment for the Summer. It is astonishing how every thing is raised. I think hereafter it would be better to Send you Monthly a Barrel of Flour, for it is hard to tell what prices May come to. I presume your coffee is going fast, also your Sugar. Let me prevail on you to take Care of Etty. See that She attends to her **cyphering** and let her take more pains in her writing. Let me Know as Soon as you have your "**bee**" but don't Entertain <u>Boarders</u> you will find that you will be loser at the present prices. Try to get along, if you find that you are pressed for Money, let me Know I can get it from the Captain. On the receipt of this please acknowledge it on the first Propeller, No more at Present, your husband "Oliver" Kiss Etty for me. N.B. My Compliments to Mrs. Dorsey & Husband and Fisher & Lady J.O.B.

<u>From Eleanor & Marietta To Oliver</u>

Glen Arbor, Michigan
July 6th, 1864

Dear Father

We are well and I hope that you are the same We received the things the window sash and 2 lbs of Tea and a jar of butter and 3 hams   a box of glass and a box of nails and no letter no papers. the last was number 16   mama thinks that we can afford 6 cents a week for her a paper   no more at present   but we will tell you more in another letter as we wrote a few lines to let you know that we did not get any letter. We remain Yours Truly yours Marietta Boizard

From Oliver To Eleanor& Marietta

Chicago, IL
July 14, '64

Dear Ellen,

Mr. Goffart just came in this morning and he told me he had put a letter in the office for me. I went up and took it out. I was quite surprised to hear that you got not letter with the articles I sent you. Those articles should have been shipped on the **"Cleveland"** I went there saw them weighed, marked myself and paid $1.50 for the Freight. The boat Started in the night and next-morning I went down to See if she had gone, and there I found the agent had neglected Sending them he had got asleep, however it caused Some delay. The hams cost 20 cts per lb. $7.00, the tea $4, the butter and jar $7.00. The sash cost $5. The glass $5.25. The nails 4.00. The Lock & c. 1.25, the putty 80 cts. ($34.30) in all. He told me the logs were put up and boards were being hauled down I am quite glad to hear that they are getting along So well, You have not told Me whether you have bought the land or not, Mr. Goffart Said he thought you had. Let me know all about it how you Stand, and whether you owe much or not and what it will Cost. I send you 5 Copies embracing no's. 17 & 21 of the ledger. You must not think hard because I did not Send you the Ledgers, I also forgot the rhubarb for Mrs. Dorsey. I have So much on my mind, I can attend to all the small matters, I look principally to the high price of Provisions, at Present Flour $12 a barrell, pork $45 barrell and in fact a pair of Common Shoes Cost $4.00. Pfeiffer has raised his board to $4.50 cts. Washing $ 1. per dozen. I hope Etty is well and attends to her Schooling, don't neglect her in regard to her religious duties -- Does She grow much. I have a Small locket for her in my chest and when Mr. Fisher comes down, I will Send it to her. Tell me whether you will Shingle the house or not. I suppose they can't make it a tight room without them Mr. Goffarts Son looks Bad he has had the **Typhoid fever**, I don't mean Felix, he looks Strong. Mr. Goffart told me he had no meat for 2 weeks. Is that So. Please answer this at your earliest opportunity no more at present Truly yours your Husband, "Oliver"

*The date on this letter is actually **June** 14 '64. However in the sequence of the letters, I believe that Oliver mis-wrote the month, I believe it should have been July and I have amended the date and placed the letter here where it seems to place chronologically.*

Glen Arbor
Michigan
July 18th, 1864

Dear Papa,

We received your welcome letter and papers also and we was glad to
hear that you was well we was glad to get a letter as it is almost a month
since we got a letter   you wished to know whether we got the land
Mama thought that she told you   now we will tell you all about it
Mama has paid Mr. Fisher $80 on it and she owes 20 on it yet   She
would like you to send her $25 next month if you can so that she could
pay Mr. Fisher and get the deed and then she can have $5 left Now I will
tell you about the house it is 12 by 24 and Mr. Fisher says that it will cost
$75   Mr Fisher pays the men and we are pay him   It would have been
done but Mr. Fisher cant get men to get to work on it when he comes
down you and him can arrange it about the house as mama is anxious to
get the land paid for now   i will tell you what we want   some flour we
are not out yet but we wont have enough to last the month out and next
we want some shugar *{sugar}* and also some wheat or barley as Mama
does not want to buy any Coffee until we get out of debt   that is all until
you come in yourself   you say you have a locket for me and I thank you
for it Mama says that I am getting big and I am getting fat   I go to
school everyday and the teacher says i am learning fast   Mama is
knitting you a pair of socks.   you spoke about Goffart not having meat
for two weeks   Mama says that she cant see how that can be he has had
since we come in two barrels of flour and some meat besides and she got
some flour down town the day that he went away   there is plenty of flour
down town but Mr. McCarty had none as his dock is not done   it was
last week $14 downtown and Mr. Dorsey says that it has come down
since then   Mr. Fisher has sold his mill   he is about closeing the bargin
{bargain} and we dont know what moment might they may want the
house as they are talking about keeping **bachelors hall** until fall you will
find the monthly report of school. no more at preasent But remaining
truly yours forever, Mrs. Eleanor M. Boizard Miss Marietta Boizard

Post Script Come Home as soon as you can. Dickey is well and sings as
loud as ever. Signed by King Richard the Third.

You ought to know Mr. Goffart better than that, because you know he is always growling

<u>From Oliver to Eleanor & Marietta</u>

Chicago Ills
Augt 2nd 1864

My Dear Wife
Enclosed you will find $25- I also Send you 1 Bll. Flour $13 and 10 pounds of Sugar at 25 c'ts per lb. The Flour cost $13 and Some Wheat. I could not think of Sending you 1 Bll. Of Corn Meal you would soon get tired of it having no Flour. I also Send you by the Propeller "**Young America**" 4 pieces of Pipe (new) and elbow which costs 3 Dollars. You Say Mr Fisher will be down tell him to come No. 70 Washington St. near Dearborn Street he cant miss the office. I almost had made my mind up to come and See you for 10 days, but as Mr Harris is going East to See his mother, it would not do for both to go at one time and so I did not ask the Captain. Try to Keep cheerfull I am very lonely and I must come up next month to See you. In fact my clothes wants overhauling "Button Come off" and I want some rest. the weather has been intensely hot and these **Dutch Stews**, and **Slush** takes away appetite. I dont feel none of the Best. Tell Fisher the Rebels are making another raid into Pennsylvania. I have nothing more to add of any interest   Has Goffart got home   he returned from the country without finding any work but left his son there, he came to the office and complained of being Sick and wished me to let him have money to go home on. I told {*him*} it was pretty hard for me to loan money as it took every cent I could earn to get along. however I had made up my mind to let him have $5 Dolls. but the Capt. went East that Same day and I did not get it for him, however he did not Come back to the office, and I did not Know whether he was taken worse or not or whether he went to Glen Arbor or to his son's house. Tell Etty to be a good girl, and let her not forget her <u>Maker</u>   you will find her <u>great monthly Report</u> with the money. No. of Days without whispering "15" rather extraordinary feat - an awful task for her.--
And now **de olddest of de wimmins** Good Bye.
 Your Husband Oliver

Answer this at your first chance Gen'l Grant has mined & Blown up a Rebel Fort at Petersburg, VA   Loss Great N.B. Kiss Etty for me, and tell her to take Care of Dick Please send my Black Thin Coat down by Mr Fisher J.O.B.

I Send you 2 Ledgers No. 22 & 23

From Eleanor & Marietta to Oliver

Glen Arbor Mich
August 2nd 1864

Dear Father
we are all well and i hope that you are the same   Mr Fisher will go out on the Maine and we will send this by him   they are working at the house and as soon as they are done we are a going to move in it. dont wait untill Mr Fisher comes back but send the provisions before because we will be out of flour   mama told you what to send in former letters dont forget wheat and you may get dicky some seed ask for seed mixt for a canary.   dont forget mamas papers the last number was 21 no more at preasent but write soon   remaining yours   truly yours
Mrs Eleanor M Boizard
Miss Marietta Boizard

From Eleanor & Marietta to Oliver

Glen Arbor Mich
August 7 1864

Dear Papa
We received your welcome letter and was sorry to hear that you are not very well   we got $25 in the letter   Mr Fisher started the same night   the same night that we got the letter he went on the **maine** and so we could not send your coat to you   perhaps you can come in with Mr Fisher   we got a barrel of flour   a sack of meal and package wheat and some sugar and the stove pipe and the papers and was glad to get them   when you come in you can have as many fresh fish as you can eat at 10ts a peice mama hops *{hopes}* that we will be in our house before you come we are on our second ham and it is not very good it is very strong   we use more butter than meat   that butter was very good   mama is very glad that you

did not give Goffart any money   them shoes that you sent in mama had
to get them mended and pay a dollar and i will have to have a pair before
winter   no 2 and high in the in step and high around the ankle   them
others would have been to small for to wear with woolen stockings
mama had to pay $1.80 for 3 pairs of misses hose or stockings   when
you come in dont forget dicks seed   he sings as loud as ever and eats as
much   here is my 2nd monthly report   mama has two hens now F
{Fisher?} gave them to her and I have kitten so you see we have a large
family   now if we had a little piggy   we will have one when we get in
our own house   no more at present   but remaining yours
Mrs Eleanor M Boizard
Miss Marietta Boizard

From J.E. Fisher to Oliver

Denney PO Ill
Aug. 12th /64

Friend Bozard
I became so overpowered by the heat in the city that I was compelled to
leave, though I should have been glad to have stayed longer.   I left on the
Evening train on the Burlington & Quincy Road on the evening of the
10th I went to your office to tell you but you had gone   I am now safe
and sound at with my friends all right.   Enclosed I send a letter I wish
you would forward to Glen Arbor by the first Boat   if I send it by mail it
will not get there in time   Your Friend   J.E. Fisher

From Marietta to Teacher

Glen Arbor Mich
August 23 1864

Dear Teacher
I take the pleasure to let you know that I am well and I hope that you are
the same.   We are moved in to our new house and we like to live here.
The water is so nice and cool it is just like ice water.   I expect my father
home the first of the month I will be glad to see him   he said that he
would bring me a present when he came in.   We were thinking of going a
black berrying this week if it dont rain I went to get my tooth pulled but
Mr Walters had taken his instruments home and I will have to put it off

untill I come to school next week. I wish that you would come back next summer and teach school for I like you better than any teacher I ever went to   I dont expect that I will go to school much this winter because the snow will be to deep but I will try to go if I can. Excuse my short letter as my hand trembles. But I remain yours truly yours
Miss Marietta Boizard

Throughout this letter, there are pencil corrections that have been made over lower case letters that should have been capitalized.

From Oliver to Eleanor & Marietta

Chicago Ill's
Sept. 13th 1864

My Dear Wife,
I send you by the **"Young America"**, 1 Shoulder, 3 lbs. Cheese, 3 lbs Candles, 4 packages of "Extract" and a Jar of Butter. I also Send to Mrs. Tucker 10 yds Plaid and Braid & 2 Dolls. Worth of Green Tea with the Bills attached to her Packages   I felt Sorry that I could not See you but it was Lucky Enough to get off so soon. I went to work on Monday and to day I made out a large Muster Rolls Satisfactory to the Captain -- Excuse this writing as I am writing it on the Head of a Barrel, on the Wharf -- I had to hurry up as I just quit work, and the Boat being ready, to start Mr Fishers files are aboard with the Cap't. I have a Slight pain in my Side I presume it is cold, from the Lakes as it was pretty rough, give my regards to all Enquiring friends. I hope that dress wont get greased. Kiss Etty for me and receive my Blessing Your Husband Oliver

Note: Write Soon J.O.B.
Butter 48 cts a pound

From Oliver to Eleanor

Chicago Ill
Oct 3rd 1864

My Dear Wife,
I just received your letter, and I had made all my purchases, and it took all the money I had Except the $5 Doll's enclosed. I am Sorry that I

cannot Send Mr Tucker his oil, but if he can make out till next month, I will Send it to Him. I send you by the Steamer "**Maine**" the following Articles of Provisions & c. 2 Bll's Flour. 15 lbs. Dried apples, 3 lbs. Tea, 5 lbs. Coffee, 10 lbs. Sugar. 12 lbs. Parched Rye, 5 lbs. Prunes, and Cod Fish 1 Platter, 40 lbs Bacon, 2 Prs' Shoes (which I hope will be big enough) 1 Iron Tea Kettle & c. And Some Reading Matter, and Ettys **"Day School Bell"** which I hope She will improve in it. Your letter must have been overlooked at the post Office, for I went every day. Still no letter, and then I thought of McCarty's Dock, and then I saw the Captain of the Young America and he told me he delivered every thing right. Had I not got your letter this morning you would have had to do without money until the End of this month, however 5 Dolls may suffice until the month of November, and then if nothing happens I can send you some money My pay has been raised to 100 Dolls. per month Commcg. The 1ˢᵗ October, 2 ½ Dolls. for Tax, leaves me $97.50 and that is good enough for an old Soldier The articles are well packed in 2 Boxes, and the Shoes, Papers & Ettys Books and the letter in the hands of the Captain of the Boat. Kiss Etty for Me and Receive my blessing.
Your Husband Oliver

From Oliver to Eleanor

Chicago Illinois
Nov. 4ᵗʰ, 1864

My Dear Wife,
I Send you by the Propeller Empire the following articles of Provisions & c. Butter, in a jar 20 lbs, 20 lbs Lard, 3 lbs Candles, 1 lb Yarn, 1 Shovel, 1 Rake, 2 yds Flannel, 2 Cakes Chocolate, 1 Dos. Extract Coffee, Sena, Oil 1 can 3 galls. *{gallons}* 1 Bll. Flour 1 Bll Corn Meal. 1 Day School Bell, 1 Steel Thimble, 1 broom, 100 lbs Pig Feed, 1 Hind Quarter Fresh Beef. I should like to have Sent those things on the **Maine** but as the month was not out, and the Captain having been gone to Cincinnati, I could not do it. I suppose you will have them to haul up from McCarty's pier, as I understand the Boats all wood there. You will please find Enclosed the Sum of $10 Doll's, which will probably do for November, the Boats are not insured for running later than November 15ᵗʰ. I hope Mr. Fisher has surveyed your Land, and gave you the Deed for it, if not you must demand it of him, as you have no voucher for it at all, don't neglect it, and as I pay the installment on the house take the necessary

receipts for it. I am not able to purchase that Sheeting for Mrs. Tucker as I have purchased Some articles for myself and the expenses which takes all my funds at present, the price of Sheeting per yard from .30 to 80 cts. Enclosed you will find a list of Prices paid for the different Articles. I am glad you are comfortable for the winter and also that the Shoes am sure that they are not the first rate Article but I guess they will do. Tell me how you like your Shoulders & side meat and cod fish, do you think that you will have Tea, Coffee, Sugar, enough if not I must try to send you more before the boats stop Running. Try to be careful of your provision., for there is not doubt you will have visitors this winter. You say you want **Sena** has Etty <u>worms</u>. Kiss Etty for me and tell her to try improve herself in writing this winter. Tell her to take her time and write plain. Give my best wishes to all Enquiring Friends and please accept my blessing. Your Husband "Oliver"

N.B. Etty will find enclosed a little ornament for her hat, which I found in the Street. J.O.B.

From Eleanor and Marietta to Oliver

Glen Arbor, Mich
Nov 11th 1864

Dear Papa
We are well and I hope that you are the same the things came in at McCartys but we have not got them home yet owing to bad weather it is a snowing   If you can send anything more in Please don't forget Mrs Tuckers muslin don't pay more than 40 or 50 cents a yard. we got 10 bushels of potatoes at $1 doll per bushel from Mr. Tucker and he worked 6 days on the house plastering at a $1.25 per day. you may send us eight yards of dark calico for aprons as we are entirely and you may send dicky some more seed   one night the mice broke dickys leg and mama splintered it up and it got well and so you see that she is quite a surgeon you asked if we would have tea enough I don't think we shall as I had to part with a pound of it for to get corn for the piggy   you may send me some sugar   get it cheaper don't get it so white. we liked the cod fish shoulder and side meat very well   we are sorry that you didn't get it all side meat as the side meat was the best   you might Send us a barrel of apples if you can   coffee we have plenty of it and some matches Ettie

would like to have a Bottle of **Dr Hooflands German bitters** and send me 1 lbs of salts and some Ind corn or wild turnip and some bitter aloes not the powder that what looks like {?} when you break it as the people all around has the fever either the **Typhoid** or **Billious** and we want to have some medicine in case we get it   Mr. Tucker has had it going on three weeks don't be frightened as we are all well Ettie is as fat as a little piggy. And I am not far behind mamas shoes is to large for her she thought they would fit her but as she came to try them on she found out that they was to large Mrs. Fisher thinks that she will take them if mama can get another pair because they just fit her   they are no. six mama wears wide fives but don't get them so broad across the toes   mama says don't be frightened because we send for so much as we cant get any thing more untill the first of May   now for the village news they have been drafting Dorsey is drafted and Parker and I don't know how many more they have to go Traverse the 16th. send me a box of pens **Gellots 303** Mrs E M Boizard   Miss Ettie Boizard

Written on the back of this letter was the following:

Nov 12 1864

Dear Dada

I am going to finish my letter   we got our things home today and they was all right and we got the letter and the money   we did not find the thimble   the beef was very nice   Ettie likes her flannel   that yarn is very coarse and I don't think that it is very good   Mrs Fisher got some just like it and she says that it is a mixture of that stuff that they call shoddy. Mama says that she expects that she will have to pay $2.00 for getting the things hauled down from McCartys I saw Mrs Fisher and she said that Mr Fisher would come and survey the land tomorrow if the day was fit   No more at present

write every two weeks and we will do the same

From Oliver to Eleanor

My Dear Wife
You will please find Enclosed $15, it was my intention to Send you
more, but I found the expenditures So much, I could not do it. I bought a
new hat and a pair Shoes for myself. I See the last Boat Started
yesterday "**City of New York**" I Send you Apples and a Box of Sundries
on the "**Empire**" with a letter with Ettys thimble Enclosed. I hope you
will have provisions Enough for the Winter, the weather is very mild. I
Should have liked for you to have More, but everything is So high that
the months pay Soon goes, but now the Boats stop I will not be able to
Send you any more provisions, except your Monthly Amount of money.
We must try to pay Mr. Fisher from this month out, December, I find you
will have to be quite Economical with your Winter Stores, as the Meat
part of them may not hold out. However I think if you occasionally buy
Some fish, you can do well Enough– I would like to Know how you
managed your Quarter of Beef – it Cost $10 - I should like to Know how
you stand with Mr Tucker I Send him 1 Bll. Flour, 1 Can of oil and 15
yds sheeting at 50 cts per yard. You Say you got 10 bus. Potatoes,
$10.00. 6 days work at 1.25 per day 7.50 in all $17.50. The Flour I
think cost 11.50. The Sheeting 7.50, The oil & can $4.00 and 45 cts for
Braid, making in all $23.45 cents His Bill against you would be – deduct
17.50 due EMB 5.95 Besides what the Freight cost.
I Sincerely hope I Shall be able to Keep my place as there is 7 Clerks and
I don't Know whether the Capt. Will Keep us all or not. Patrick told me
that he had a talk with the Captain about me and the Captain Said I was
all right for the winter as long as I choose to stay with him. Let me
Know whether the Snow beat in the house or not, and how the Pig stands
the cold weather, and also the Chickens. Tell Mr. Fisher that I will
Commence paying him Sums Every Month hereafter. I forgot Etty's
pens, I am Sorry, the <u>vagabond</u> will think I neglect her but Kiss her for
me and that I know will pay her for the neglect. I Saw the Steamer
Allegheny coming down with Some Blue Jackets aboard her, She
touched at Traverse City – and I thought of Mr. Dorsey and Parker. I
suppose they were among them. Dear Ellen I had a Strong notion of
Coming to See you, on the Empire, but I Know it would not do if the
Capt. had give me leave. However you must keep up a good heart this
winter, you must not be lonely. I hope you will have Enough to Eat and
you have Enough to Keep you warm. Answer this letter as Soon as you

can, as it takes fully 2 weeks to come & go. I hope you will put Dick where the mice wont Kill him. Give my best respects to all Enquiring friends   And receive my blessing. Your Husband "Oliver"

Pffifer has raised the Board to $5 per week.
Kiss Etty for me and tell her she must not forget her schooling

From Eleanor & Marietta to Oliver

Glen Arbor Mich
Dec 14th 1864

Dear Papa
We received your letter & was glad to hear that you was well   we got the money   there is about 1 foot snow   you asked if the snow blew in the house   it dont and the house is quite comfortable considering as there is no carpet on the floor   you said that you wanted to know how the pig got along   she gets along very well   when you write tell us how much the first shoes cost that you sent in as we didnt know whether they cost $3.00 or not as they were different from the others Mr Tucker cuts our wood and we dont burn any small quantity either   Mama says that when you write dont send so much paper when you write   one of them big **fools cap** sheets of paper weighs a good deal and we have to pay <u>more postage</u> Sarah Tucker is very sick they dont expect her to live   Mama set up night before last and I expect that she will have to set up to night again Dorsey & Parker ate supper at the **soldiers rest** and then they took the cars and went to **Jackson**   you spoke of paying Fisher all along untill we get the house paid for I will be better satisfied as we want a kitchen built   Mama wants to know what you sent that thin stuff in for aprons   it is not fit to make up   again it is washed there wont be nothing of it but a rag   that she would rather had two yds of good calico   when you come in will you fetch me a christmas gift   no more at present   But remaining yours Truly Yours Mrs Eleanor M. Boizard   Miss Marietta Boizard

PS dont get mad at us about the calico

<u>From Oliver to Eleanor & Marietta</u>

Chicago, Ill's
Dec. 16th 1864

My Dear Ellen

Your letter came to hand this morning it has been 12 days on the road, it was post marked December 3rd. I was getting uneasy, I went to the Post Office everyday, and this morning I got it. the Snow must be very deep on the roads in Michigan, hence the delay. I am glad you are well and also Etty. I am also pleased to hear that Mrs. Tucker has partially recovered. I am sorry that the House leaks. I expected it would. I Send you a letter, on the 30th of November with 15 dollars Enclosed. I Suppose you have received it before this. After the 1st January I will Send you money, and then you must pay Mr. Fisher 25 Doll's. for the 1st Installment, you did not Say, whether he had laid out your 10 acres or not or whether you had got the deed or not. I am in moderate health at present. the weather has been intensely cold, but it has moderated Since. I Bought me a new Hat and a pair of Shoes everything is very high (provisions particulary) It will be good Enough to be frugal with your winter Stores, as you wont have much to Spare I am glad that you got So many Candles off the Beef, and I hope the Beef was nourishing to you. As Regards taking that Boy I hardly know what to Say about it You will be obliged to Clothe him & c. and you Know we have our house to pay for, and a number of other Expenses, however do as you like about it. You must tell me in your next letter whether the house is cold or not you must try to Keep the Snow off the Roof. have you bought any fish yet, or do you think that you can fish during the winter when you want them and now Ellen I must close this letter hoping that you will Keep well, also Etty, tell me how She liked her Thimble I forgot her pens. I am sorry Give my best wishes to Mr Fisher and Wife Mrs Tucker and Wife and all Enquiring friends Truly yours your husband
   "Oliver"

N.B. Enclosed you will find a few lines from Emma Bridges with no date or place, the Envelope was Post Marked Nov. 11th New York it was directed to me J.O.B.

100

From Emma Bridges to Marietta

Dear Eta
it is with pleasure i take my pen in hand to set you a few lines to let you
know that we received your leter and was glad to hear you were all well
as this leaves us all at present   for chrismas stuf your fat turkey make
your good diner *{dinner}* for we are all a comeing   the wether is very
moderate now but i guess we will have very cold now for it snowing hard
we keep a litle *{little}* store   I go to the city every morning with 30
dolers *{dollars}* to buy apeels *{apples}* belove *{?}* cheese. and you used
to be afrad *{afraid}* a dolers {dollars} for fear she would lose it.   Ma
and me have made a hundred and 20 dolers *{dollars}* since we comenced
{commenced}. mrs donelson is at the same   buy *{by}* a fortune she is
goin away soon- for he had an ordnace *{ordnance}* apoinment
{appointment} sergant galuger was sent away recruiting but him and
vater was sent in the other day and put in the recruits and sent to the field
they don't know what for   and my father is at the same truble *{trouble}*
geting drunk every day. He reenlisted and got 7 hundred dolers *{dollars}*
and i want you to tell us how land is for we are comeing there to buy
you must have the house to buy and ma say she wishe your mother was
here to go to the thater *{theater}* and mr boizard in front with the
umbrela under his arm and my fater *{father}* behind bringing up the rear
jiney and tomy goes to school and tomy got on his first hats and thinks
himself quite a man and i think its is time to quit as i have to go down to
the dock to get the pies   my mother gives her love to you and your
mother and farthe *{father}* the same yours truly Emma Bridges

From Oliver to Eleanor

I wrote this letter on the 30th Dec. but dated it on Jany 1. '65
                    U.S. Mustering and Disbursing Office
                                                     Chicago, IL
                                             January 1st 1865
My Dear Wife
Your letter came to hand, on the 29th Dec '64 and I was glad to hear that
you and Etty was well, but was sorry to hear of the Illness of Mrs
Tucker's daughter, but it is to be hoped that ere this she is well.

Enclosed you will please find ($35 doll's) which amount you will please pay Mr Fisher the Sum of 25 Dollars, as the 1st Installment on the House and take his receipt for it. You did not State in your letters, whether he had Surveyed your land, or gave you the deed, these things should be attended to, and if you have done so why not let me Know. It being New Years, I have the not the pleasure of Knowing how you May Spend yours. I don't think I will spend mine with much Satisfaction. I went to St Charles, Ills for 3 days, the Capt. Send me up there to take the Estimate of Public Property & c. as the Barracks are about to be Sold – I found it cost me $10. to live notwithstanding the Government paid the transportation on the Cars and Back – the answer of letters come Slowly from Glen Arbor, are there no Speedier way of getting letters from there. One of your letters I see was dated the 30th of Nov. and the Post Mark was Dec. 3rd. It appears letters are irregular in that Post Office Dept. As regards to the price of them Shoes, the 1st pair was $2.75 and the other was $2.75. I never enumerated freight for articles I Send up, you did not tell me whether the apples were as <u>miserable</u> as the apron stuff. I hope they were Satisfactory as for the Calico I thought that Lake Street <u>Gentleman</u> was not honest as poorer folks are. Well now I suppose I have Said more than I Ought to (with propriety) but hope you and Etty may keep your health and it would be good Enough not to lose your rest <u>to much</u> as you are Subject to <u>Coughs</u> in that climate particularly – Give my best respects to all Enquiring friends, and Kiss Etty for Me and tell \

her, (If I live) I Shall buy her Something for a New Years <u>present</u>.
Your Husband "Oliver"

answer as soon as possible

From Eleanor & Marietta to Oliver

Glen Arbor Mich
Jan 6th 1865

Dear Father
We received your letter and was sorry to hear that you are not very well but this leaves us well as the pantry shows   Mama says for you to get one or two blankets for to keep you warm at night and keep yourself clothed warm   It is not very cold here and the snow in not any deeper than it was   you wished to know if we bought any fish   no they dont

catch any now but I got some pork and had to pay 25 cts per pound. you wanted to know if Mr Fisher surveyed the land yet as he is not at home he is at **North Port** he is a Judge or some thing but he will when he comes back you wanted to know whether the house is cold or not no but it is as comfortable as can be expected as it is we was to a party Monday afer *{after}* New Years. it is right lonesome here I liked the thimble very well. Dickey is well and sings very loud no more at present but remaining yours Truly Yours
Mrs Eleanor M. Boizard
Miss Marietta Boizard

From Eleanor and Marietta to Oliver

Glen Arbor, Michigan
Jan 20th 1865

Dear Papa
We received your letter by the last mail and the money also 35 dollars. Mama says that she will give Mr. Fisher $30 so that we can get out of debt as soon as we can for then I can get the shingles made for the house. Mr Fisher has not surveyed the land yet as the snow is so deep that I don't think that he can as it is two feet deep but it is not very cold. It takes Mr Tucker one day in the week to cut us wood. we received a letter from Emma Bridges last mail and it had neither date or anything and I made out that they was all well and Mr. Bridges has reinlisted for seven hundred dollars **bounty.** the mail only goes once every week we write every other mail. those last shoes that you sent Etty the uppers are all ripped to pieces and she only wore them a week and I will have to go and pay $3.00 for her a pair for it will cost more than they are worth to get them mended for they ask $1.00 for putting just a couple of little soles on. Mama says for to tell you that she is a baking bread and pies our coal oil is all most gone we will have enough to last untill we get another letter from you. Mama has not had a bit of cough since she came in. when Mr Tucker or any man comes in dicky will commence singing just as he used to when you were home. no more at present.
But remaining yours Truly yours
Mrs. Eleanor M Boziard
Miss M E. Boizard

Post Script We are well and I hope that you are the same.

103

<u>From Oliver to Eleanor</u>

U.S. Mustering and Disbursing Office
Chicago, IL
Jany 21 1865

My Dear Wife
Your letter dated Dec'r 26th came to hand about 14 days after it was
written, and I received the other one dated 6th Jan'y. I am glad you are
well. I am not So well, as I might be. I Send you a letter dated Jan'y 1st
with $35 dollars enclosed, in order to pay Mr. Fisher $25 for the 1st
Installment on the house. the weather is very mild, at present I expect we
will have rain. I will Send Ettys Almanck in February, after I get paid
off – I expect nothing else, but Some of us will be discharged the end of
this month, as our work is pretty well Squared up, Should I be discharged
I shall try to Come up and See you I Shall have to foot it up there. I
hope the Captain will Keep me until we get out of Debt. You Spoke of
being at a party. I hope you enjoyed yourself. I spend my Christmas &
New Years like all other days, except we had Some little extras for
dinner. I read Bill Browns letter, but did not answer it, as I get tired of
writing. I hope You have received that Money, $35– You Say you paid
25 cts for Pork per pound, I hope your bacon is not used up – I have
nothing more to add, Give my respects to all Enquiring friends and
please receive my blessing, Your Husband (Oliver)

Kiss Etty for me
and take Care of Dickey
Tell me if you think your provisions will hold out

<u>From Eleanor & Marietta to Oliver</u>

Glen Arbor
Feb 2nd 1865

My Dear Father
We are well and I hope that you are the same   we received two daily
papers   Mama gave Mr Fisher the Money and took a recipt. you must be
right saveing this winter as we must have a new set of chairs in the
spring as these are comming all to pieces   they cannot be touched but
they come to pieces. Mr Tucker has been sick but he is better. I go to
school and the weather is very mild   Mr & Mrs Goffart was down to day

and they sent their best respects we are making soap and the cat is in the box asleap and the pig a squealing and the rooster is a crowing and dicky is a calling for more seed our house is very cold no more at present but your must try to come home in the spring. We remain yours Truly yours Write soon as you get this PS You spoke of my New Years Gift Get me something Nice
Mrs Eleanor M Boizard
Miss M.E. Boizard

<u>From Oliver to Eleanor</u>

Chicago, IL
Feby 3rd 1865

My Dear Ellen,
I received your letter dated, Jany. 20th acknowledging the receipt of the 35 Doll's. I became quite uneasy, as I had written the letter Jany 1st. However I Suppose the delay, is on account of the roads. You will please find Enclosed $30 – as Soon as you received it answer immediately. I don't Know of any thing that hurt my feelings So much as the Death of that Girl of Mr. Tuckers. She was an affable and Kind girl and then so much Company for Etty, truly I can not help thinking about her. You Spoke about Etty's Shoes and the Coal oil – try to make out the best you can until the Month of May. I am glad to hear that you are So well also my <u>Big Dudu</u>. You think of having the Shingles made, well act as you think proper, and probably we will get along By and By – I bought Myself New Books, and Some Clothes, which Cost Considerable, at the present prices, for Board, Washing & c. a person Cannot Save much, however after the property is paid for, it will be ours, and a home for you and Etty – You Spoke about getting a letter, from Bridges, there are Big bounties on hand at present, however that don't Effect me. We are busy now, as there are new Reg'ts raising. There are negotiations now for peace, and it is to be hoped that it will be Satisfactory. Gen. Sherman is moving on to Charleston S.C. and likely there will be heavy fight in course of 2 weeks. Gen. Lee is still about Richmond, and Grant is watching him. However we will change the Subject. I am glad to hear that your Daughter & Self is well. May you Keep So. Tell Mr. Tucker and Lady that I feel quite hurt about the loss of the Girl. However it cant be helped. "<u>All must die, who live, passing from nature into Eternity.</u>" Give my best respects to Mr. Fisher & Lady Mrs Dorsey and all Enquiring friends.

No more at present Your Husband "Oliver"

N.B. Kiss Etty for me Twice
I Send you Some papers

To Marietta from Emma Bridges

Fort Columbus New york harbor
Feb 4 1865

dear Eta

your leter came to hand this day in wich we were glad to hear that your
were all well and in good sprits {spirits} as you say you goin to the
party i am happy to inform you we were all wel and i trust the pen line
may find you enjoying the same to   i dont have to go to the city so often
now as they have stoped the people from selling now for the sutter
{sutler}. Dear Eta we hope that as soon as the weather gets a litle
{little} beeter {better} that you wil come to see us. and take giney home
with you.   it is not very cold here no more. i supose things is very high
every were {where} we pay {?} cents for calico & 50 a barel of potatos
Eta sarah is not here but her fathe {father} is phildelphia recruiting i
hope your {?} may come the for i want you to come as soon as the
weather is fine and so does Austin Newman. try and come. i send you
by this male {male - Austin Newman or mail} a rich valentine wich you
will pleas acept. tommy says he will writ to Eta   I guess i will have to
stop to start the fire   you must write the minute you get this. my father
and mother send their love to your mother and father and my father to
write to him now for he has got nothing to do and he can write   giny and
tommy send their love. no more at present   do try and come. Yours truly
Emma Bridges

From Eleanor and Marietta to Oliver

Glen Arbor, Michigan
Feb 10th

Dear Papa

 We received your letter and was sorry to hear that you are not very well
but I hope that you may be well by the time this reaches you. you spoke
of coming home if you are discharged I hope that you will not be

discharged untill we get Mr. Fisher paid   if you should come get a large pair of boots so you could put on two pair of stockings and dress yourself warm   you wished to know about our provisions   our butter meat and lard will be out first   we have over a barrel of flour and a good deal of cornmeal   we will have to feed it to the pig. we guess that we will have enough of other things to last us   Ettie is growing so that I have to put a piece to all of her dresses you must save all of your old clothes and bring them home   we can allways get wood cut or something done   no more at present   But remaining yours   Truly yours   Mrs. Eleanor M. Boizard Miss Marietta Boizard

This is Dickys picture but the artist didnt draw it very well
There is a hand drawn picture of Dicky with a text bubble that says "more seed"

From Oliver to Eleanor

Chicago, IL
Saturday Feby. 18.'65

My Dear Wife,
Your letter dated Feby 2nd Came to hand yesterday, and I am glad to hear that you & Etty are well.   I am in moderate health at present, now and then my Side hurts me, and then again it feels well enough. Business is very brisk in regard of Recruiting, at present we are busy in the office, we worked all day Sunday last, and I suppose we will have to work Tomorrow. You spoke of being Saving in order to get ½ doz chairs, I will try to purchase ½ doz chairs, in order to Send or bring them to you, in May. I bought me a coat & pants, as my old pants were getting Shabby. I will have to pay for the Coat at the End of this month. The next installment I Send up, let me know, how much more we will have to pay for the house. I think another payment of $30 ought to close the Bill. I suppose I will have to bring up Some Provisions with me when I come to See you. Let me know what you have left in the provision and whether that pig is worth anything. I Send you $30 Doll and a number of Papers. I suppose you have received them. I must order 2 pair Shoes for you & Etty, (Calf Skin) before May. I have still the old ones for measure. Everything is very high. I have to pay $5 a week for Board, and $1 for washing a dozen pieces. I bought me Boots, cost $9.00. The coat will cost $20.00 Pants $4. And then with other Expenses I cant save much. However after the House is paid for that much will be Saved

107

during this year. Etty is quite amusing, in her letter, I showed her letter to the Clerks, and they Spoke highly of her, the cat asleep, the Pig Squealing, the Rooster crowing and you making Soap, it was quite a Programme. Kiss her for me and receive my best wishes.
Your Husband "Oliver"

From Eleanor & Marietta to Oliver

Glen Arbor
Feb 26th 1865

Dear Papa
We received your welcome letter and the money $30 and was glad to hear that you are well we gave Mr F $20 we needed the other 10 dollars mama says that she would like for you to send her $50 the next time and then we can pay Mr Fisher all and have done with it   Mr T is working at the shingles and then we will have him to pay after.   we had to kill our little pig as we could not get feed for it and we wanted the meat anyhow Mama's shoes is not worth anything she has paid $1.00 for getting them mended   the leather is rotten for are all going into holes. I want stout gingham domestic for dress   get one green and white and the other brown and white narrow bars   9 yds   you can get them in the spring as I am all in rags   mama is not very well that whatever it is a bout her heart trouble her dreadfully   I go to school and the teacher's name is Miss Cooke   Mrs Tators Sister   Mama thinks that the rye coffee hurts her and our other coffee is all most out   we received the papers   save all the books and papers that you can for they come good here   save me all the cards and gift paper that you can find   No more at present But remaining yours Truly Yours Miss Marietta Boizard   Mrs Eleanor M Boizard

From Oliver to Eleanor & Marietta

Chicago
March 3rd 1865

Dear Ellen,
I am well, and hope <u>the tall girl</u> and yourself are well. You will find Enclosed <u>Thirty five</u> (35) We are very busy. We have Sent off <u>two</u> Regiments {the letter has a hole in it, causing words to be missing on

108

both sides of the paper} and a large portion of another Regiment *{missing word}* organizing. I received a letter from Mr <u>Dorsey</u> and I Enclosed it to his <u>Lady</u>. Please ascertain how you Stand with Mr. Fisher and let me Know the particulars. I have been Somewhat uneasy about you, I dreamed that we met, and also Etty and you told me that you had to go home, as you feared the water was coming into the upper room-- I hope you are well and also "<u>Dudu</u>" try to get the shingles, made if Mr Tucker is well. I hope Mr. Fisher is well, as I understood in the <u>Dream</u> that he was not well. Try to take everything particularly and I have no doubt, but we will get along in another Year. The weather is very mild, at present, and I hope the navigation will be opened early, however you cant get passage much before the month of May. I know it requires a great Economy to make your provisions hold out, I hope *{missing words}* not want. By the By, how does your Pig, will *{missing words}* a barrell of meat, in time, Beef is *{missing words}* per Hundred on the <u>Hoof</u>. Pork is cheaper than beef -- Coffee is about the Same, Sugar Some few cents lower I must try to get your <u>Chairs</u>, I would like to get a number of things for you if nothing happens. I have not received an answer from the last letter, but I Suppose it will arrive tomorrow, the Post Office is Closed to day, on account of the Inauguration of <u>Old</u> <u>Abe</u> an <u>Honest Heart</u> The Rebels are getting <u>down</u> in <u>the mouth</u>. Wilmington N.C. and Charleston S.C. being lost, and nothing remains much Except Mobile, and Galveston, on the Texas Coast and it is to be hoped, <u>Everything is gone up.</u> I shall close this letter, hoping you are in excellent health and also my Big Dudu. Give my best Respects to all enquiring friends and receive my fervent wishes. Your Husband "<u>Oliver</u>"

<u>From Oliver to Eleanor</u>

Chicago, IL
(Sunday) March 12th 1865

My Dear Wife,
Your letter dated 25th Feby. 1865 came to hand on the 9th of March and I have felt quite uneasy about you Since. I hope you are better, by this time. I cannot rest easy, when I know that you are Sick. and Etty tells me that She is all in rags I thought that She had Clothes enough to last her till Spring, as for Shoes wearing out that cant be helped, as the Shoes that you buy already made are not worth much. Although you pay a big price, for them. Etty tells me that you had to Kill the pig. I find it takes

a quantity of provisions to last all winter,. I cant brag much about my health at present. I feel no appetite and my Stomach hurts me frequently it is something like "<u>indigestion</u>" I Set So much we are So busy that we are obliged to work till 6 O'Clock in the Evening, we have been at work including this day, four consecutive Sundays. Two of the Clerks are Sick, and the work comes heavier on the remaining Six. The Captain works very Steady himself. We will get off another Regiment in 3 days. And there is nearly another full regiment not yet organized. I Send you on the 5th March $35 I hope you have received it. Keep up Courage and all may go well. Kiss Etty for me and tell her I will bring her some gingham for dresses. Maybe in the month of May or June. Give my best respects to all friends, and receive my best wishes. Your Husband "<u>Oliver</u>"

<u>From Eleanor & Marietta to Oliver</u>

Glen Arbor
March 24th 1865

Dear Papa
We received your letter the 20th and we received the money and was glad to hear that you are well as this leaves us at present. all but mama she has the headache. Mrs Dorsey received the letter and they are all well we got a copy of the times from Emma Bridges. Ettie was at a childrens party at Mrs Fisher's last week. I got eight pounds of meat for $2.00 as our butter and Lard is out they dont catch fish yet but as soon as they do we will buy some. We will pay Mr. Fisher $25 dollar's. we will have to get some sugar. We have payed Mr Fisher $75 out of $98, we will have to keep $10 to pay the school bill and other expenditures I hope we will be able to pay Mr Fisher all in another month Fisher's folkes is well. but Mr. Tucker is not very well. When you come in fetch in a mate for Dickie and bring it in a square cage as he is calling for young birds all day when you write next time tell me what flour costs outside we have bread stuff enough untill you come in in May. Come in as soon as you can if they have any paper boxes at the office bring in some as we have use for them. Bob Oliver is married he is married to a Miss Smith that came in last fall and Mary is married to that Miss Smith's brother. and Sallie was married to James Kilderhouse, when you get lard get it in a pail that has not painted in the inside. no more at present but remaining yours truly yours. Miss Marietta Boizard & Mrs Eleanor M. Boizard

Both of Glen Arbor Mich

How is Heopshies or Whatever them German folks names was that used to live in the same house with us that live on pope st

From Oliver to Eleanor

Chicago, IL
March 31st 1865

My Dear Wife
Your letter dated the 18th March, Came to hand this morning, but it appears that Etty did not State whether you received the $35 or not. I see by your letter that you have to pay Mr. Fisher 48 Dolls. Enclose you will find $35- (Dolls) and when the <u>Maine</u> Starts from here, which will be about the 20th or 25th April, I will Send you Some Coffee, Sugar, and Meat. I may not be able to See you until the 1st June as we are very busy, and I think there will be a change before the month of June, but I would like to come up about June, if nothing happens. I feel moderately well at present, but for 2 days last week, I was quite unwell about the middle of this month, my nose took to bleeding, and I bled the part of one day about 5 times, and once in the night, but it Stopped by itself. Mr Pfeiffer Boy "Emil" 10 years old got his leg fast in a wagon and made a hole in his Knee, that took place today at dinner time, and his father is gone to the Country till Tomorrow. I hope you will keep your health, as I can't brag much about Mine. Give my best respects to all Enquiring friends. Kiss Etty for me, and receive my best wishes.
Your Husband "Oliver"

From Oliver to Eleanor & Marietta

Chicago Ill
April 16th 1865

My Dear Wife
I Send by the propeller **Maine** 1. Bll. Flour, and a Box of Groceries, which I had put up in good order. I also Send you a copy of the News, which you will find deplorable news, as regards the murder of the President. The whole Country is placed in Solemnity. All Buildings in the City of Chicago are decorated with crepe. Old men weep in the

Streets, men appear to be infuriated at the dastardly act. **J. Wilkes Booth** the actor is Supposed to be the murderer -- **Sect'y Seward** was also stabbed in Bed, but his death requires Confirmation his Son was also wounded badly by the Murderer   I will write again the 1st of May   I Shall not be able to See you before the 4th or 5th of June -- I hope you are well and also My Big <u>Dudu</u>   Kiss her for me, and receive my Blessings. Your Husband "Oliver"

<u>From Eleanor & Marietta to Oliver</u>

Glen Arbor
April 24, 1865

Dear Father

We received your letter and the money but was sorry to hear that you was not very well but this leaves us very well at present   I have paid Monsieur Fisher the last $20 on the house   I have got 1,800 feet more lumber from him.   we paid $5 for drawing lumber & logs we can pay him   I have paid over $3.21 school money for Ettie   there were three or fore *{four}* Propellers in yesterday up at Macks dock and we dont know whether there was anything on them or not for us. and they brought the news of the assination *{assassination}* of P Lincoln. now for domestic affairs   we are very glad that the Lake is open so that the boats can run as we have to pay $2.00 for 8 pounds of meat and that wont go very far where there is not butter or lard. our tea is allmost out as I let Mrs. Tucker have a pound of it in the winter. Please send Ettie in a pair of shoes as hers is so much worn out that she gets her feet wet every time she goes or comes through the swamp. if you can send them in by the next boat. I have made about 10 or 12 lbs of maple sugar   we have pretty near two barrels of potatoes. if you can I would like for you to send me in some dryed beef   we will have to have some kind of a fence around the clearing before we plant. no more at present but remaining yours truly yours. Mrs. E.M. Boizard

<u>From Eleanor and Marietta to Oliver</u>

Glen Arbor, Michigan
April 25 1865

Written at the very top of the letter.
Mr. Fisher is not very well he is troubled with **boils**. When you send
things in send them in at Todd dock as it costs so much to send up to
Macks dock as it takes a man and a team a whole day we guess the
buffalo boats will stop here at todds dock but we don't know yet for
certain

Dear Papa *{crossed out}* Oliver
We are well and I hope that you are the same. We received the things a
box and a barrel of flour we was very much pleased to get the butter and
Lard as we had got tired of fat meat we was very glad to get the tea as we
were just out I guess that we will let Mr. Tucker have the flour as we will
have enough to last us untill you can send us in some more as he is out.
When you write tell us the price including the freight   there is a letter
and a paper over at Mr. Fishers but we have not got there yet please
excuse the blots   you may get this letter before you do the other and I
will tell you about my shoes. please send me a pair of shoes as soon as
you can   you may get it quicker as we are going to send it by a boat if
we can   by the teacher as far as Milwaukee any how on the boat they are
expecting a boat any minute   Please send me in some writing paper and
a box of pens. paper is so dear   6 sheets for ten cents. I just finished
you a shirt. Mr. Tucker will finish the shingles in a couple of days and
then he will put them on the roof. no more at present but I remain your
affectionate wife. Mrs. Eleanor M Boizard

<u>From Eleanor & Marietta to Oliver</u>

*The top of this letter is missing, so we cannot see the date or the
salutation. Based on the contents of the letter, I believe that it fits in here
chronologically.*

We are well and I hope that you are the same. the kichen is up and part
of the roof is on. they are working at it now   it takes six thousand
shingles. we got the sash down at the store enough for three windows
and six pounds of meat & the sash & meat cost 5 dollars. we had the

113

ham but it would not go far where there is work men. please send us 4 or 5 pounds of putty as Mr. Tucker says it will take that much. Mrs Tucker wants 4 pound of tea. send Ettie 9 yds of pink calico you will find a sample in the letter & send Charity Brotherton 10 yds of the same piece that you get Ettie but have them measured seperate and two yds of plain **jackonet** you will find a sample of it also and one yd of white **drilling** as mr. Brotherton is working here helping Mr. Tucker please send an ink powder   Mr Fisher has been very sick he has had a **carbuncle** on the back of part of his neck   I don't know what to do about planting as I cannot do it   yesterday I set out a few currant bushes and to day my heart pains me dreadfully   but I will have to try to put in a few garden seeds if I can get them   no more at present   But yours with respect
Mrs Eleanor M Boizard
Miss Marietta Boizard

Please come home as soon as you can. this is the last sheet of paper and there is not more at the store

From Oliver to Eleanor & Marietta

Chicago Ills
May 3rd 1865

My Dear Wife,
I send you by the Propeller **Granite State** a small package containing Some Garden Seeds, Etty's Shoes, and Gingham for a Dress, also a Spade, you Stated in your letter which I received this morning "post marked" Milwaukee, that I should Sent things to Todds dock. I Sent them by the Maine supposing they would land there, it appears there is antipathy arising about the Quality of the wood and the Boats wont stop there. Consequently, you are obliged to pay high to get them from the other Dock. **Booth** the Murderer has been Killed by a Sergeant of New York Cavalry. They fired the barn, arrested his accomplice, and exterminated the Murderer. President Lincolns remains will reach here Sometime on Monday and all business will cease, in regard of public offices. Capt Pomeroy leaves here on Sunday night, he goes South to transact business for the Government, he will be gone about 3 months. We have got the hurry of business over and 3 Clerks will be transferred from this office. Which leave 5 in number left. Government has issued a General order to reduce the force of Employees, also Stopping

Recruiting for Volunteers   Many officers will be dropped, as the war is coming down to a point. Gen'l Johnson has Surrendered all the forces of Georgia & North Carolina, and there is another army (Rebel) west of the Mississippi, which will have to give up. I paid for Flour $7.50 and $1 for Freight 50ct's for the Box of Groceries. I am glad to hear you are well, also Etty. Mr. Fisher I hope will get clear of his Biles *{boils}* Soon. I know what they are. Ettys shoes cost $2.50 and hope they will answer her, as it is the most difficult thing to get good Shoes. I could have ordered them made, then I dont Know whether they would fit her or not, they are number "3's" they are large Enough, that's a sure thing, I think if her foot has grown much. I Suppose her foot is like the **Oldest of the Wimmens.** I enclose you $10 Dolls. My Expenses has been large this month. I paid 35 doll's for Provision, and $1.50. Freight.
I Shall try to Start from here about the 1st June, and then I will try to bring you 6 chairs. I am Glad Mr Tucker has the Shingles ready, and hope he will be able to Shingle the house as soon as possible. I met the young Goffart, moving up to Glen Arbor on the **Young America**, and now I will Close for awhile. Kiss Etty for me, and receive my blessing.
Your Husband Oliver
John O Boizard

From Eleanor & Marietta to Oliver

Glen Arbor
May 12th 1865

Dear Oliver
We received the letter and a package also the money $10. I hope that you will come home soon. We are out of flour and have baked the last baking   We received the shoes and the dress Ettie foot has not grown much and so her shoes are full to large No 2's are pretty large for her. the roof is on the house Mr Fisher is better. We hope you will stay more than a day or two this time. Etty says you promised to bring her a present and she says She would like to know what it is going to be   there is no school yet and we guess it wont commence untill the 1st of June we expect the teacher that taught last summer will teach, Mrs Tator. we got one hen setting. Ettie has found three or four nests this spring today she found a nest with 8 eggs in it. Mr. Goffarts folks Says that you and me and Ettie has to go up there to their house when you come in.

You did not send me in any onion sets no more at present   But I remain
your ever affectionate wife Mrs Eleanor M. Boizard

Write soon or come in soon I dont care much which you do but I would
rather you would come in.

<u>From Oliver to Eleanor & Marietta</u>

Chicago, Ills

June 22nd 1865

Dear Ellen,
I arrived here this morning at 7. all Safe. I went immediately to the
office, to report and found Capt. Hill, all right, go to work tomorrow,
plenty work, office full. I Send you by the boat, **"Empire"** 1 box
containing clothes & c. which I presume will Suit. The Calico prints I
could not well find, and I thought I would Suit my own taste and I hope
it will Suit the rest. I paid 26 dolls. for two coats $6- for pants, 4 dolls
for vest and $1.75 for Hat. (20 yds of Calico $6.00) in all $43.75 without
the price of the freight, for Mr Brotherton's family. they owe you 75cts -
- it amounts to $43.75. I send you 8 spools of white cotton, also **skeleton
hoops** for Etty, cost $2.50 the salesman told me a Lady shed tears,
because she could not find any of the same kind. at that time he had
none on hand. I think he lies-- I do not Know how Miss Charity and
Etty will like their dress patterns & c. But I did the best I could -- I could
not get Mrs. Brotherton's pattern of calico, and I chose that quality.
After the 1st month if nothing happens, I will Send your little necessaries.
I left Mrs Akeu about to look for her Sister. Give my regards to all
your Husband "Oliver"

<u>From Eleanor and Marietta to Oliver</u>

Glen Arbor, Michigan

July 1st 1865

Dear Father
We received your letter and the things and all the things were right but
the stuff for the white waist it was **paper cambric** instead of **Jaconet** it
was stuff for linings. it has rained more or less since you went away and
I guess you took all the mosquitoes away with you. the old hen has all of

116

her little children. Jenny has little birds and they are just like a nest full of worms as the man says but his was a mouth full. I go to school and I wish you would send me the **History of the United States** as the Teacher says I must study it. Mrs Tucker says if you cannot get photographs to get them on plates and get them varnished but not in cases as she wants to send them away in letters to her people. perhaps we will send this out on the boat Dorsey has not come home yet his regiment was sent back to Louisville KY and he says there is no knowing when he will come home. Mr Tucker planted the rest of the potatoes. Harrison Brotherton finished the fence. I like the ribbon very much I guess this is enough for tonight so no more at present but write soon. Yours forever Mrs. Eleanor M Boizard   Miss Ettie Boizard

there is a drawing of a bird with a text bubble that says "more seed more seed"

From Oliver to Eleanor & Marietta

Chicago Ills
July 3rd 1865

Dear Ellen,
I Send you by the "**Young America**" a Box containing Groceries, Hardware, and also your Dress, Shoes for you & Etty, which I hope will Suit, also a Small pocketbook, containing $15 Doll's. (all I could Spare). I hope you are well also Etty, and will Spend your 4th July, agreeable, without any disaster. The Captain has not returned yet. Expect him daily, dont know how things may turn out after his return. I hope I shall be Employed, this Summer, try to get along as Economical as possible, as we dont Know what May turn up. I will Send Mrs. Tucker's pictures during the month July -- I have nothing of importance to relate. Give my regards to all Enquiring friends. I Sent Mr. Lindsleys papers down for Signature. I expect to hear from Mr. Dorsey shortly from Louisville, Ky. I Send a letter from him to Mrs. Dorsey -- Truly yours Your Husband "Oliver"

By the By how is Miss Charity's dress write in answer also Ettys

NB How did the clothes answer of Brothertons

<u>From Eleanor and Marietta to Oliver</u>

Glen Arbor, Michigan
July 9th /65

written at the very top of the letter:
We owe Brotherton's 5.25 and they want you to send them 1 pound of
tea the same kind we have and the rest in unbleached sheeting the same
you sent Mrs. Tucker not to coarse don't pay more than 41 cts

Dear Papa
We received the things and the letter and the pocket book with $15 in it.
I like the pocket very well. Ettie's shoes does but mine is very large but
I guess I can change them. I liked my dress very much. I got the flour at
Mr Field's. The next things you send try and send them in at Todd's
dock. I paid Harrison $4 for making the fence and cutting some wood.
When you write next time write and tell me whether I can get my winter
wood cut. Please send me two yards of white **drilling** lining and send
Ettie two round combs. two doz of glass with colored buttons with eyes
in as large as a cherry. Mrs Tucker wants you to send in Willies pants
one pair any how as that pair that Mr Tucker bought that day is allmost
wore out. The young birds are all dead   I guess the old bird did not feed
them as she ought to. The day that we went to see about the things the
fox came and took the old hen that Ettie had   the little chickens and the
little chickies go all around crying after her. the potatoes are growing
nicely and what cucumber we had left   we enjoyed the fourth very
much. what few there was down at glen arbor dock they went a boat
riding on the Caldwell. over to the south Island and they paid $50 for the
trip but we didn't go   we went up to Mr Macks as there was a team down
and we had a very nice time as every thing went off quietly Don't forget
my **History of the U.S.** Mr Lloyd was here to clear up the log's off of
the lot but I would not set him to work on it untill I know what you was
going to do whether you was going to stay with the Captain or not   Send
me in a Flour Sieve our butter and Lard will be out by the 1st of August
send me a jar about 4 or 5 gallons with a lid and put either the butter or
Lard in it as it will do me as a churn   have the lid so it will fit down in
the inside no more at present   But I remain yours truly yours
Mrs. Eleanor M Boizard

Chicago, IL
July 14 1865

My Dear Wife,
Your letters dated respectively the 1st and 9th July, are now before me,
and in reply, I have to State, that I am glad to hear that you and Etty, are
well and passed your 4th July, happily without any disaster. I am sorry
that your shoes, did not fit you, for I took the precaution to have them
made for you, thinking they would give Satisfaction. I paid $3.75 for
your Shoes and $2.25 for Etty's. You spoke of getting your winter wood
cut, you might Employ Lloyd to clear your logs from the clearing and
make Fire wood of them for 1 week and I will pay him at the End of the
month. The Captain has Come home and we are busy, but I do not
Know whether he will remain here during this Summer or not. However
I will let you Know if any Change takes place. Employ Lloyd for one
week if you can get him and I will pay him in August. It wont cost more
than $10.00. I will try to Send all the articles required for yourself and
Mrs Tucker Mr Brotherton at the End of this month. I heard
McWickham had a fight with Bailey the 4th July – So the fox got the old
Hen at last. I am Sorry, I would soon have lost 5 Dolls- than that old hen
– Tell Mrs. Tucker I will Manage her Pictures this month, I have not
been to See Mrs Kuntz yet with the Bag for Goffart, I forgot I happen to
See the Bag under my Bed – Kiss Etty for me and tell her to be a good
girl. I sent a letter to Mrs Dorsey from her Husband. I will close this
letter as I am down hearted– Good Bye "Oliver"

From Eleanor and Marietta to Oliver

Glen Arbor, Michigan
July 18th/65

Dear Papa,
We received your welcome letter and the papers and we was very glad to
get them as reading matter is very scarce. You spoke of getting Mr.
Lloyd to cut wood and clearing up the lot if we was to get him now he
could not clear it up untill fall   the hemlock logs that are on the lot we
could not burn as it will our stove out in- no- time.   Mamma has spoke
to one of the Brothertons boys for to cut it by the cord and we can get
(Lloyd) to clear the place up this fall. Tucker's want 1 lb Tea   I got 14
lights of glass at 15 cts a light. I changed my shoes and I had to pay 50

119

cts for getting them changed they was (no) 6 but 4 will fit me if they are high enough in the instep and they are wide enough. We have eight more little chickens. The Old Waddler is their mother we have the other eight and some of them crows and they go in with the other chickens Harvey says the young chickens that is a week old lays eggs every day. Papa will you get me a strand of Amber beads don't get them if cannot get amber as they say that amber will keep my neck from getting any larger as I am getting a large neck like Mrs. Tucker's no more at present but remaining yours Truly Yours Mrs E. M Boizard &
Ettie Boizard

Write Soon   PS send me three or four spools of colored cotton 2sps 40 & 36

From Eleanor & Marietta to Oliver

Glen Arbor
July 28th/65

Dear Father
We are well and I hope you are the same   Mr Lindsley got the money and handed us the letter but he never said as much as thank you or anything   but you could not expect anything better from them the low lived set that they are   I will give you a specimen of Mrs Parker (our news carrier) You know when you were in here I had the prickly heat very bad and she was here and she saw it on my neck and she asked Mama what it was and mama told her what it was and she went around and told that I had the itch   I am not the only one that catches her tongue as you will see in the end of this letter but everybody.   Mr Tucker is working at the house and he wants you to send in a trowel   we are out of cornmeal and we would be glad if you would send us in some for the little chickies   if you can please send in some rice as our potatoes are out and we have nothing to put on the table but bread and butter and fat meat our butter is out also the lard   the little chickens crows no more at present but remaining yours Truly Yours Mrs. Eleanor M. Boizard
Miss Ettie Boizard

{There is a picture drawn of a lady with a text bubble-- with the following words:}

120

John Dorsey has deserted and he got as far as chicago with a cow and he was caught and taken back.   this is another one of her lies. Mrs Parker our news carrier

P.S. Dont show this to anyone

From Oliver to Eleanor

Chicago, IL
August 5th 1865

My Dear Wife
Your letter came to hand, dated the 28th July, and I find that Mr Lindsley received his money. I am Sorry to hear that he did not Even thank any body for the Kindness bestowed. However let it now. I would have Sent your little Stores before now, but as the Boats (Northern Transport) do not land at Todds wharf, I Send a Box containing sundries, also a Can of Kereosene, and a jar of Butter. I found the jar you required, but the weather being so hot, I though I would not Send the Lard this month, as it would be all Solution. The corn meal I will try to Send up during the month of August. I tried to find Amber Beads for Etty, But I could not find them. The original Amber Beads are costly. And the idea of her wearing about her neck for Cure that's all Bosh. Apply friction of Iodine or Liniments if you have them, and if not, I will send them at the Earliest opportunity – You will please find $10 Enclosed. I could not Send you any more but will try to make it up next month. I bought a pair of pants & c. You will find (I hope) the articles well packed. Groceries are Somewhat higher, Tea is about the Same $1.80, Sugars higher, I also Send you 2 cans peaches which I suppose you will relish –   The Photographs are pretty well taken and hope will answer. Give my regards to all Enquiring friends Your Husband Oliver

Kiss Etty for me and tell her to Keep her temper

Glen Arbor
August 13th/65

Dear Father

We received the things   butter and money and also the photograph and
they were well pleased with them.   Mr Tucker has worked Eighteen days
on the House and he is not near done yet   I guess you forgot the Trowl
as you did not send it in.   We had to get 5 bushels of Lime and five lbs
more nails.   Mrs Dorsey has got the **Typhoid Fever** and she is at
Tuckers.   Mr Collins oldest Daughter has it also and they dont expect
her to live as the Dr. has given up all hopes of her recovery   We was not
out of tea and Mr Tucker took both pounds of teas as they owed a half
pound.   but we had enough to last untill the last of the month.   Mr
Tucker wants you to send in a iron tea kettle like ours   but get it no. 9 or
10   and send Mrs T a **skelaton hoop** skirt the same as Etties but get it
larger around the top if you can and send us in a barrel of flour as ours is
allmost gone and it is not fit to pay Tuckers with   we have to feed the
chickens with it (as we have twenty four young chickens) and Mr T is
boarding here and it takes a great deal where there is no vegetables and
we have no cornmeal to feed the chickens with   we like the cans of
peaches very much but I would rather have had pickels.   we have picked
20 quarts of whockle {huckle or whortle} berries and I am drying them
most of them for winter.   I got four pairs of colored hose and I had to pay
60 cts a pair   two pair for me and two pair for Ettie.   Mr Tucker would
like for you to Send him a barrel of flour as he is almost out   you could
send the things in at todd's dock for it costs as much to get them down
from McCarty's as it does from chicago.   We got the wood cut and we
will have to pay for it at the end of the month   we got nine cords cut
will you please get me one of Sarah's photographs if the artist has the
negative as I would like to have one   no more at present But we remain
yours truly.   Mrs Eleanor M. Boizard

Glen Arbor, Michigan
August 20th

Dear Father

We are well and I hope you are the same.   Mrs Dorsey is no better and
she took a whim that she must go down home and Fisher took her home

122

in his wagon. we have one of the children up here. Collinses daughter is no better she may linger along for two or three months but the Dr. says she cannot get well as she had the hemorage of the bowels and stomach. Harrison says he wants you to send him in $7 worth of blue **drilling** and Hickory blue and white 9 yards blue drilling and the rest in Hickory don't pay more than 40 or 50 cts a yd as it is towards cutting the wood don't forget the flour as both families are out as it takes so much to feed the chickens that we have to bake every day as we have nothing to feed them   our potatoes is not large enough to dig and there is so few in a hill as the ground is so hard   it not being worked any   we have to buy them from the neighbors   potatoes is going to be very plentiful this year. when you get these things send the bill as people asks us what the price is we cant tell them they asked us the price of willies pants and we could not tell them papa I would like you to send in my chain and pin as you might lose it. If you can please send us in some casteel **{castile}** **soap** no more at present. But we remain yours truly yours
Mrs. Eleanor M Boizard
Miss Ettie Boizard
Glen Arbor

From Oliver to Eleanor

Chicago, IL
October 12th 1865

My Dear Wife,
I arrived here this afternoon. We had a very Stormy time this morning about 5 O'Clock it lasted about 3 hours, just when we left Milwaukee, I thought it would become Serious, however it got Calm. I gave Mr. Sheridan $5 dollars he went off the Boat at Milwaukee and was going in the Country about 12 miles– and he told me he was a going to buy Some Butter and I gave him the Bucket, and he told me he would do the Best he could   he thinks he can buy Butter for 30 cents in the Country. I went to my grocer and he told me he was retailing Butter at 45 cents a pound. I will be obliged to get my Shoes mended it will cost me 75 cts and I think I will look around for one day and if I don't find anything to do I will be obliged to go to Springfield. I hope you and Etty are well. Keep up a good heart and don't be uneasy. If I go to Springfield I will write to you as Soon as I get there. If I can't get nothing to do there, I will try to go to St. Louis, if my money holds out. I paid 5 dolls, on the Boat and 5

dolls for the Butter and my shoes may cost me $1 and then it will cost me something for Board and I wont have much left Mrs. Tator got off at Milwaukee. I expect Mr. Sheridan will go down on the same Boat, if So you will get your Butter Sooner. I Send this letter by the **City of Boston.** No More at present But remain yours with respect – your husband "Oliver"
Kiss Etty for me.

From Oliver to Eleanor & Marietta

U.S. Mustering and Disbursing Office
Springfield, Illinois
Saturday October 14th 1865

My Dear Wife,
I arrived here this morning, from Chicago Ill's, and I immediately went to the Captains Office, he had Sent for Mr. Truesdell and me to Chicago, but being in Michigan, he could not find me it was the Same day I left McCarty's Dock. I found Mr. Truesdell at work, and another new Clerk consequently, he filled the vacancy. however the Capt'. has given me a Situation in the State Armory, he has charge of the Ordnance but it does not pay so well, it will pay $2 per day (Except Sundays) but he told me that he would do better for me, as Soon as the opportunity offers. Enclosed you will please find Three Dollars. all that I could possibly spare, until the 1st of next month, and then it will take till the 16th Nov. before you get it, leaving out Sundays it will be about $50 per month, however I am glad I got this job, as the winter is coming on. the Capt. used me very well. It happened that a young Soldier want to quit work this day, and that just left a vacancy for me, for the Capt Said he was glad I come. There is a man & wife by the name of Hartmann here, they Stopped at Pfeiffers Some 4 months ago, he had just left the Army, at that time, and I became Somewhat acquainted with them, and I am not Staying with them at present. She owns the Brick House, She lives in, and he is a machinist and I may probably board with them, but I am afraid it is rather too far from my work -- I Suppose the Board will be $5 per week, I have not asked them yet. I go to work on Monday. Dear Ellen have patience, I will not be able to Send you any provision, but I will try to Send you money monthly. Mrs Pfeifer and Lizzy is on a visit to this family, and will go back on Monday next. I will write again on the 13th of the month (November) if I live. Kiss Etty for me, and give my

Compliments to all Enquiring friends, and receive my blessing. I hope
you got your Butter.
Your Husband Oliver

Direct your answer to John O. Boizard
PO Box 107. Springfield. Ill's –

From Eleanor & Marietta to Oliver

Glen Arbor
October 17th /65

Dear Papa
We are well and I hope that you are the same   we have not had any snow
yet only once and then it was only a little spit and now it just like Indian
summer. I have 14 quarts of **beechnuts** gathered for winter. our house
is plastered upon the outside and it is very comfortable. our flour is out
and we will have to eat cornbread untill we can get the means to get
some   it will cost us almost as much again to get our things in here this
winter as every thing is so high but we will have to do the best we can.
Mr Lloyd has cut our wood so far. I got half lb of tea since you went
away and had to pay $1 and it is not very good at that   I would not know
what to do if it was not for my chickens as we dont have any meat no
more at present But remaining yours Truly Yours
Mrs. Eleanor M. Boizard
Miss Ettie Boizard

P.S. write soon

October 18th

This letter was written last night and this morning we received the letter
and the money which will go towards getting a barrel of flour. we have
not got the potatoes from Mr. Miller yet as he is waiting for snow to
come so he can get them here with the sleigh and ponies. we was glad to
hear that you was well. we got the book and two papers and was glad to
get them as we haven't any reading matter   we dont know whether we
can get the stove as Dorsey has not moved yet and cant untill the man
gets out of their house but we can get one from Tucker if we could get
pipe any where

From Oliver to Eleanor & Marietta

Springfield, Ills

Oct 31st 1865

My Dear Wife,

Enclosed you will please find $12. I Signed the vouchers for $28, but I could not wait till they were Sent to Saint Louis and back, as the amount is paid by the Chief of Ordnance, and So I borrowed it from the Clerk, for a few days until the money comes. I have to pay 12 dolls. for my Board & 1 Dollar for Washing for part of the month of October. which will leave me $3. for expenses during the month of Nov. I hope you will be contented and also hope that your provision will hold out till you can get this money. There being no vacancy for a Clerk in this Dept. I am reported as Laborer, but I dont do any thing but write. Capt Pomeroy is not a Major by **Brevet**, and I expect he will be the Principal Must'g officer and then I may get $3 per day for he told me that he would give me the first chance I am at Present in his Employ, only I am at the Arsenal which belongs to the State of Illinois only that there is Government property on hand, which the Captain is accountable for as he is the ordnance Officer -- I wrote you a letter from Chicago Ill also one letter from Springfield enclosing $3. which I hope you have received. It takes so long before a letter reaches here, it would be much better for you to Send your answers on the Propellers while they are running as it Saves about 10 days -- I hope that you will Keep your health also Etty. Tell me in your answer about Mr. Lindsley whether you got any more Potatoes or not and whether Mr. Miller paid you in Potatoes or not -- Tell me whether you have had any cold weather and what chance there is for Mr. Dorsey's Stove I will close for awhile Give my regards to all Enquiring frinds, and Kiss Etty for me. Please write Soon So you can put the answer aboard the Boat before the Navigation Closes I am yours, till death closes the Scene Your Husband "Oliver"

From Eleanor & Marietta to Oliver

Glen Arbor

Nov 1st 1865

Dear Papa

We received your welcome letter and was glad you had employment at Springfield Ill. it is not very cold here yet as we hadnt any frost untill the 27th of October everything was as green and as nice as it was when you

left. I am digging my large crop of potatoes   I have about a barrel.
Flour is $14 a barrel down at Todds & meat is 28cts per lb   we got the
butter 12 lbs. -- Mr Lloyd is got so that he can be around. I have been up
to goffarts   we had our first chicken today and we wished you were here
to have a piece of it   they are in good order   I traded a quilt for potatoes
and corn as I was out and Miller did not bring them   they owe us them.
we got only a bushel of potatoes and a bushel and a half of corn that
made about $1 from Lindsley. I hope that you will get a good boarding
house and a good wash woman. I sent to Traverse for $1 worth of tea by
Mons. Brotherton   no more at present   But remaining yours truly
Mrs. Eleanor M Boizard
Miss Marietta Boizard

P.S. We are well.

From Oliver to Eleanor & Marietta

Springfield, Ill's
Nov 8th 1865

My Dear Wife
Your letter Came to hand this morning and I am glad to hear that you and
Etty are well. I am Sorry that you were obliged to part with your Quilt. I
hope you will not be obliged to Sell any more -- Enclosed you will
please find $4. and I hope that you have received ere this the 12 Dollars
which I enclosed to you in a letter dated the 31st October. You Spoke of
the weather being good, the weather has been very favorably here   we
have had no Snow yet. Last Sunday I went to Oak Ridge about 2 miles
from town, and I Saw the Vault of Mr. Lincoln he lies there in view, with
his Son Willie aside of him. he is Enclosed in a Metallic Coffin, and
there is also a Square Walnut Box outside, also the Son   the doors are
Stone and Iron grating inside. 4 persons are allowed at a time to look at
the Boxes, through the iron Grating. The Place is the most Beautiful I
See   there are a Squad of Soldiers Stationed there the Sentinel walks in
front of the Vault. they are about commencing the monument, and then
they will remove him, only a few rods, where they now lie. I am in
hopes you will be able to weather the winter, by Sending you Small
Sums of money every two weeks -- Boarding cost me 22 1/2 dolls. per
month my wash Bill amounts to 1.50 and I dont have much left at the
End of the month   I shall have to get Boots for the Winter, Clothing is
higher here than any part of the Country I have See yet. An overcoat is

worth from 40 to 80 Dolls. pants 15 dolls, prices are awful. Have you received your <u>Deed</u> from Mr. Fisher yet. By the time you get this Navigation will be closed, and then I will have to wait a good while for an answer. I shall be quite lucky if I can retain my Situation this winter Kiss Etty twice for Me, and receive my blessing Give my best respects to all the neighborhood-- (I send you some reading matter) Your Husband "Oliver"

From Eleanor and Marietta to Oliver

Glen Arbor, Michigan
November 24 1865

Dear Father,
We received your welcome letter dated the 8th of the month and the money also. We are well and I hope you are the same. I got the barrel of flour and it cost $12 and when it is made up it looks as though it had molasses in it, it is so dark. the weather is very mild and we have not had any snow it has hardly froze yet some of our hens lays and one of this years pullets lays she is only 6 months old and she lays the cunningest little egg we have killed 5 chickens and we will have some more to kill when they are large enough my Tommy cries after me every place I go as soon as he finds out that I am going he begins to cry. dicky sings as loud as ever and Jenny she prates for some one to talk to her mama is knitting and she says she don't know what she will do for yarn school has commenced and I don't know as I shall go or not but I would like to go this fine weather no more at present But remaining yours truly yours Mrs. EM Boizard   Miss Ettie Boizard

From Oliver to Eleanor & Marietta

U.S. Mustering and Disbursing Office
Springfield, IL
December 1st, 1865

Mr Dear Ellen and Big <u>Dudu</u>
I received your letter this morning and was rejoiced to hear, that you were both well. The answer was two weeks a coming, I am glad you got the $12 about the 4th or 5th of December, as Soon as I can get Some

money, you may expect it about the 20th of this month, as it takes 15 day to reach you. Try to hold out and I will try to Spare you all the money possible I have had a rather bad cold, and have not get rid of it yet. I am glad your house is plastered, and you are comfortable I wish you had Some Pipe for the Stove. I Send you Some reading matter, be patient I think I will get more pay in January 1866 if nothing happens. Give my best regards to all Enquiring friends and receive my best wishes (Kiss Etty for me) Your Husband "Oliver"

From Oliver to Eleanor

Springfield, IL
Dec 8th 1865

My Dear Wife,
Please find Enclosed $20. We did not receive our money until this morning, as Lt. Col. Pomeroy was away in Chicago, and yesterday being "Thanksgiving" there was nothing done. My pay will be raised this month, and if nothing happens, I will be able to Send you $40 in January. I hope you have been able to hold out, it takes so long for letters to reach each other. the weather has been Cold for 2 days past but today it is quite pleasant. I hope you have had no very Severe weather. It will be not So hard for you to get along after this month, December. I have had a bad cold for about 10 days, but it got better without any treatment. In order to raise my pay 25 Dolls, the Capt gave me and the other man the job of watching the Arsenal, we have to Keep awake half the night and I suppose that gave me the Cough but now it is better. I Send you a letter a few days ago with Some reading matter. I Suppose I Shall receive an answer from a letter written a month ago containing $4. I Send with this letter a Magazine directed to Etty. I hope you are well I have Changed Boarding house, on account of the distance. I Sleep at the Arsenal when I am not on Watch, Answer this as Soon as possible, Kiss Etty for me and give me all the particulars, and receive my best wishes.
Your Husband "Oliver"

Springfield, IL
Dec 20th 1865

My Dear <u>Ellen</u>
Enclosed you will find Five Dollars. I am well and hope you and Etty
are also well. I Suppose you received $20, which I enclosed on the 8th
December. Before you receive this letter, Christmas will be over, and
another year will Commence. Still nearer the <u>End</u>. I am Sometime quite
uneasy about your welfare, this Winter. The weather has been moderate
So far, until this day, Snowing has Commenced, which reminds me of
your Situation this winter, in that Solitary Abode, however I hope you
will get through without much Suffering. I frequently Send you reading
matter. I had Some notion of Subscribing for **Peterson's Lady**
Magazine it is $2. Payable in advance for <u>one year.</u> I Suppose you will
have to pay 3 prices for your provisions this Winter. If I can remain in
Employment I will try to remit you money to carry you Safe through. I
am afraid you will get Sick from the Cold. Especially if you have no
heating Stove. In your answer tell me what you have to Eat, and tell me
whether your Chickens will hold out. I will close this letter and receive
my best wishes. Kiss Etty for me, and try to Keep her warm and
Comfortable. Give my best respects to all Enquiring friends.
Your Husband "Oliver"

N.B. Direct your answer as usual Box 107 No. of Bill No. 549175
My pay has been increased I watch the half of Every night beside my
daily labor J.O.B.

Glen Arbor
December 22nd 1865

Dear Father
We received your letter dated the first of this month but we did not get it
untill the 19th I am sorry that you have a bad cold but you must keep
yourself dressed warm. we have had very cold weather for about two
weeks and the snow is about 6 inches deep. we have got the stove from
Dorseys and the pipe from Burdicks Charity and George and I go to
school down town to Mr. Smith I hope that we will get the letter with
some money in it as everybody is thinking of christmas but us and we

have not anything to think about   but we will have our Christmas when you come home   Mr. Fisher has not gone to northport yet but when he goes he will see about our deed as he has got several deeds to see about send us two almanacs for 1866   no more at present But remaining yours Truly yours
Mrs Eleanor M. Boizard
Miss Ettie Boizard both of Glen Arbor

From Eleanor & Marietta to Oliver

Glen Arbor
Dec 29th 1865

Dear Father
We are well and I hope that you are the same   we never spent such a poor christmas as this christmas was   we did not know it was christmas be we thought it was sunday and we went down to Mrs Dorsey's to spend the day. every thing is very high   tea is eighteen shillings per pound and butter 50 cts when we can get it to buy and everything accordingly   it takes one man a day every week to cut us wood enough and that costs $1 1/2 but that is nothing to what it would be if we had to buy it at $12 or 15 per cord I made a pair of pants for one of the Millers and I got $1 for it and a vest also and I guess that will be 75 cts I will have to get Ettie a pair of shoes made as it is better to get them made and then they will be worth something they will cost $2 as she is almost barefooted. try and have a christmas Gift for us   I would like to have a set of new knives and forks for my christmas fit small ones   Ettie says she would like a pair of black bead bracelets   you can get them for about $1. We got the money and the letter and reading matter also. no more at present But remaining yours Truly yours
Miss Ettie Boizard
Mrs Eleanor M. Boizard
{There is a drawing of a bird with the words 'Dick or Jenny', *also a picture of a person on a pig.}*

131

Springfield, IL
Jan 12th 1866

My Dear Ellen,
You will please find Enclosed Thirty Five (35) Dollars. Which will
Enable you to pay a portion of your debts. I enclosed you on the 8th
December 1865 Twenty (20) Dollars which letter I have received no
answer. I also Send you about the 20th of December the Sum of 5
dollars, however it is hardly time for that letter to be answered, but the
letter which I wrote on the 8th Dec I am Somewhat uneasy about it,
however I may get it Tomorrow, or next day. I hope it has not been
Stolen, for to lose 20 dollars, would be too hard for us. I Send Etty some
papers & Books, with the two fifty cents currency in them. I hope She
will get them. I had Some clothes made for Myself. The Stuff I bought
at Auction. I also bought Myself a Hat & Boots, I Send you with this
money, Some Reading Matter, I Suppose the Roads are Blocked with
Snow, which detains the Mail. However the letter which you Sent, dated
the 22nd Dec. Came to hand in 14 days. I was in hopes that the letter
dated the 8th Dec would reach you about Christmas. So to Consider it a
Kind of Christmas Gift. Tell me your answer, how you get along
whether you Suffer for any thing, or not. Also tell me how often the
Mail leaves Glen Arbor. Tell me all the particulars about your Potatoes,
Provisions & c. If you receive this Sum of Money, in good Season it will
help you along, the Col. (Pomeroy) has just returned from Cincinnati
where he took his Wife (who was Somewhat rounder than usual) and he
returned this morning So we did not get our Money untill to day. My
Shirts, are getting Much worn, and I am getting myself 2 pairs of drawers
made. And now my Dear Wife I will Close this letter hoping that you
and Etty may Keep your health, and tell Etty Mr Smith must learn her
how to **Cypher.** Kiss Etty for me and tell her not forget her Dada.
Give my best Respects to all the neighbors and receive my blessing.
Your Husband "Oliver"

N.B. If our work holds out to the month of April, I will consider it lucky.
J.O.B.

From Eleanor and Marietta to Oliver

Glen Arbor, Michigan
Jan 26th 1866

Dear Father

We are well and I hope that you are the same. the weather is very cold
the snow is so deep that it covers a barrel when it stands on the end so
that you can use it. it keeps me making fires. it is very lonesome here I
have not been out since New Years and I hardly ever see any one this
winter. Ettie goes to school when ever there is a road broke. I got her a
pair of shoes made and I had to pay $4.00. we burn half a cord of wood
per week and so you see that there is no danger of us freezing this winter.
our kerosene is out and we will have to get some   we had not any
candles and so Ettie went to the store and paid 30 cts a pound and they
are made out of this stinking lard and one of them would not burn an
hour.   coffee is 50cts per lb   I am making a new dress for Mrs Tucker to
pay for some butter   if ever you get a chance I wish you would get some
yarn. but don't get that nasty shoddy stuff   you can keep it in your chest
or trunk   we have to pay $3 a pound in here and then it is not very good
at that   get it a dark blue gray   if you get it get a lot of it as we all will
need stockings. Robinson and Hatch have not been heard of yet. I
received some reading matter and the book you sent is continued and I
wish you would send me the continuation of it which is entitled. Clara
St. Johns or the mystery solved. We had not had any letter since new
years day and I think it is about time to have one. no more at present.
 But remaining yours Truly yours, Mrs Eleanor M. Boizard
 Ettie Boizard

Dicky and Jennie are both well and prating away like every thing

From Eleanor and Marietta to Oliver

Glen Arbor, Michigan
February 2nd 1866

Dear Father,

We received your welcome letter and the money also. we were glad to
get the letter and the money also. I paid Mr. Tucker $15 which makes
$20 in all that I have paid him. I have a barrel of flour to get and some
other little things in the house and I have to finish paying for Etties
shoes. We have got the deed it is recorded. you wanted to know how

often the mail went from here it goes out but once per week   we got the Almanac's and the reading matter also. You spoke of your clothes being wore out. I am sorry to say that ours is wore out to   we must have some coarse unbleached sheeting and you must have some fine unbleached for shirts. but however we must try and get out of debt for we owe Brotherton's some for the little things that we got from them also for the wood they cut for us last summer. you wanted to know how our potatoes hold out we have enough to last until spring but we will have to get some seed potatoes in the spring. The weather has been beautiful and mild for the past week we have not had any snow. The crust will bear us we can walk all around on it.   our hens has commenced to lay this fine weather I am very sorry that I haven't the stuff to make your shirts now so I could have them ready when you come in the spring no more at present but remaining yours truly yours. Mrs. Eleanor M Boziard   Ettie Boizard

From Eleanor and Marietta to Oliver

Glen Arbor, Michigan
Feb 9th 1866

Dear Father
We received your welcome letter dated the 29 of Jany. and the papers also. I have not received the bracelets yet. I did not want you to get me a pair of costly ones I only wanted you to get me a pair of black bead bracelets and they would only cost about $50 cts or 75 cts at the farthest. I wanted a pair as all the rest of the girls had some. I got a barrel of flour I was not quite out but I would not had enough to last untill I got some more money. it cost me $12 I got half a gallon of kerosene at $1.25 cts per gallon and I got half a pound of tea at 18 shillings and it was not very good at that and a few lbs of meat. I signed for the **rural new yorker** at $2.50 I had to get some more yarn to knit Ettie some stockings as she is almost barefooted and I paid Mr. Tucker $15 (after I finished paying for Etties shoes) now I have told you all my purchases and I have the large sum of 20 cts left out of $20   no more at present. But remaining yours truly yours. Mrs Eleanor M. Boziard   Miss Ettie Boizard

From Oliver to Eleanor & Marietta

Springfield Ills
Valentine's day
Feby 14th 1866

My Dear Wife

I Send you by mail a Small Box containing a Bracelet, which I hope will please you as every body expects Something in Shape of a New Years Gift. I hope this will Suffice -- Your letter dated the 26th Jany 1866 came to hand. I thought it might be an answer to the letter containing 35 dolls. We have not been paid off, for January yet, as I expect, they have run out of funds. So Soon as we get our Money, I will Send you $50 which will Enable you to get out of debt and then you will be able to Save Some money, that is, if my Employment, Keeps until May. There are but 7 Illinois Regt's. to be mustered out, and when they turn in their arms, I think the work about the arsenal will close. I also Send you 2 Papers, 1 with the picture of Gen. Grant which will do to nail against the wall of your Log Cabin. I hope the Snow will Soon disappear about your neighborhood. this day it is blowing and the Snow drifts very much. Kiss Etty for me, and give my best respects to all Enquiring friends, and receive my Blessing -- Your Husband "Oliver"

N.B. answer this immediately

From Oliver to Eleanor

Springfield, IL
Feby 20th 1866

My Dear Wife,

You will please find Enclosed a <u>Fifty Dollar Treasury note</u> which money I hope will Enable you to pay Some of your debts. you might pay Mr. Fisher a portion and also Mr. Tucker, but be Sure not to let yourself out. I have not received any answer from the letter dated Jany 12th which contained 35 dolls. I answered your letter dated 26th Jany and Enclosed you a <u>Bracelet</u> also Send you Some reading Matter. We had no mail from Chicago, for 5 days. The Snow blocked up the Railway, but now it is open. I Suppose by the time you receive this letter, the Snow will be mostly gone. I Suppose the Snow must be very deep, between Grand Haven and Traverse. I am in moderate health, and I hope you and Etty are in the same state of health. Although I have been uneasy, as you told

135

me in your last letter, that you were lonesome, and you had not Seen any body Since New Year I wondered how you could get any thing for to Eat, Such Weather --

I hope our business will last till May and then if the Capt or Col. is not ordered away, I think he will let me go for 20 days. My Shirts are nearly gone. I will have to get two made up. Give my best respects to all Enquiring friends Your Husband "Oliver"

P.S. I looked for that <u>Clara St Ive</u> but could not find it. Kiss dudu for me. J.O.B.

From Eleanor & Marietta to Oliver

Glen Arbor
March 2nd 1866

Dear Father

We are well and I hope that you are the same We have not had any letters from you for almost a month   any how we have not had a letter since January the 19th 1866 and we are beginning to feel anxious about them. Dicky and Jenny are both dead   they both died the same time I broke a basin full of oil and the scent went all through the house and I expect that was what killed them. It is dreadfull lonesome   if it was not for a party occasionally we would not know what to do.   there was one the 23rd of February there was one the 21st & 22nd but we did not go to them   one of them was at Mr Todd at the hall and two at Mr King   the 23rd there were 26 couples at Mr. King's and we went. I wish that you would get 2 lbs of yarn you will find a sample in the letter dont get it any coarser than the sample and get it as near the color as possible   you can get it cheaper out side then you can in town   they charge $3 a pound in here and you can get it outside for $2. I am quilting Ettie a skirt   she does not go to school as her eyes began to hurt her and so I thought I would not let her go any longer.   she got her bracelets and she says she would rather waited a while longer and got another pair   she say that they are not worth the wait and she says that she can never have anything like any person   I am in hopes that by this month and another one we will be out of debt   it cost so much to live and it seems that we dont have much to eat   the meat that we got down at the store is not fit to eat and they charge 25cts per lbs we get an egg occasionally   the weather is very fine but the snow is very deep   where there has not been any path broken

the snow is 4 feet deep   Charity B has had that fever but she is getting
well now   no more at present but remaining yours truly
Mrs. Eleanor M. Boizard
Miss Ettie Boizard

From Oliver to Eleanor & Marietta

U.S. Mustering and Disbursing Office
Springfield, Illinois
March 7th 1866

My Dear Wife
You will please find enclosed $40 (Two 20s) Feb'y being a short month
my pay was considerably less. I Send you 1 Bill of $50. on the 20th
Feby, but have received no answer So far, also Bracelets for Etty and one
nice one for you. This money will Enable you to pay Mr. Fisher, and all
your debts, I hope, for we must try to Save Something for next winter,
for fear I should run out of work for I think our job will close about May,
if So I Shall be obliged to Come and See you, and then I will require
money to take me out again. I Know you are Saving, Still it requires to
be careful, for I dont want you to be so pinched as you were this Winter
for provisions & c. I bought myself a hat, and 2 new Shrits as my old
one's are worn out. I have bought you a dress and Some yarn, and I
purpose buying Ettie one also, and Keep them in my trunk. I want Some
clothing but I will try to get a Suit about the month of May or June. I
hope you will receive the Money Safe. let me Know whether you Suffer
for anything or not. Tell me all the news and give my best respects to all
Enquiring friends -- Your Husband "Oliver"
Direct your letters as usual Box 107

From Eleanor & Marietta to Oliver

Glen Arbor
March 9th 1866

Dear Father
We received your welcome letters one dated the 14th and the other the
20th of Feb. one contained $50 and I was very glad to get it as I could
pay some of my debts   we did not get them untill the last mail I got the
bracelet and the papers also   I was very much pleased with it and the
picture of Gen Grant   if only had a Frame for it I would be glad. I am in

137

hopes that the next remittance will put us out of debt and then we have to get the lot cleaned up. You spoke of coming home in May I hope you will   and you say that your shirt being worn out you must save money enough and when you send us some more money   get a bolt of muslin get it fine unbleached shirting and get it over a yard wide. and get two or three yards of fine Irish linen for the bosom. get a couple doz of pearl buttons for the bosoms and some Coats & Cotton No. 30 & 50   there is not any muslin in here and when there is it is three prices and it is all gone as soon as there is any brought in from outside   by the time you get this I expect we will have another remittance and that will be enough to get us out of debt and after that you need not send us so much   send us about 10 or 15 dollars monthly. for I am tired of buying things in here, save as much as you can to bring in provisions and things with you. the weather is very fine and the people are commencing to make sugar. I will not try to make any as I do not feel strong enough and if I did I have not got any kettle to boil it in. it would cost me as much to get the wood chopped as it would to buy the sugar   let lone all the trouble to get the trees tapped and carry the sap and everything   we would give anything for a piece of beef. I have not got any lard and I dont think it pays to pay 50 cts for butter to shorten pie crust or anything else and I will have to have some lard. I have got fifteen dollars worth of butter this winter from Mrs Brotherton at 50 cts per pound and we did not eat much meat as it so rancid that we cannot eat it. I have paid Mr. Fisher $15. and I want to pay Brothertons what I owe them. the remainder I will need about the house as I need several small articles about the house   no more at present but remaining yours Truly yours
Mrs. Eleanor Boizard
Miss Ettie Boizard

From Eleanor and Marietta to Oliver

Glen Arbor, Michigan
April 6th 1866

Dear Father
We are well and I hope that you are the same. The weather is very stormy at present it storms every other day   but the last two days have been very warm   we have not had any sugar making yet as the weather has been so stormy. The snow is going off very fast   our hens lay every day we get 3 eggs sometimes it is very hard to get any butter you have to

all most beg for it and pay very dear for it 50 cts per lb is about what we have to pay. I will be glad when you can come to bring in some provisions if you can I wish you would bring in a large handled scrubbing brush like they used in the army because we cannot mop the kitchen with the mop the other scrubbing brush is wore out bring Ettie in three yards of pink ribbon a little wider then the sample you will find in the letter don't get the kind they call {? } ribbon get it the same kind as the sample but get pink. no more at present. but remaining yours truly yours. Mrs Eleanor M. Boizard Miss Ettie Boizard

From Oliver to Eleanor & Marietta

Springfield, IL
April 7th, 1866

My Dear Wife,
I hope you will find every thing I send you Satisfactory, about Ettie's dress, I looked as Some Lawn but it looked So flimsy, that I thought I would not buy it, but you will find I have bought her a good gingham dress, which cost 55c. yd. I think it is very genteel and more durable, it is very much worn here by women. the other two dresses, I do not Know how you will like them, they cost 35 cts. yd. the bolt of muslin cost 29c. by the Bolt. I think it is very Strong for Shirts, the linen cost $1.00 yd. I Suppose it will answer, there are 3 yds. I bought you Some fine and Coarse Yarn 2 dolls. there are Some other little traps, Etties' pennies and c. I Suppose they will Send you the Groceries. I Send the Grocery men $35. and that will pay for Freight. I cannot Send you any money, as it nearly cleaned me out. We are working hard Shipping all the Stores to St. Louis Arsenal. I cant tell you exactly when we will be done but as Soon as we get through, there will be no further use for us here, and then I Suppose we will be discharged. I expressed the little trunk to the Grocers. I have got me a new chest made, and have had it Stained and varnished it looks like walnut. I hope you and Etty are in good health. Give my regards to all Enquiring Friends Your Husband "Oliver"

N.B. After you receive your things try to get the answer on a Boat JOB

139

<u>From Oliver to Eleanor</u>

Springfield, IL
April 11 1866

My Dear Wife
Your letter dated the 23rd March, came to hand on the 6th of April, and I
would have answered it before but I was awaiting for Col. Pomeroy, to
return from Cincinnati Ohio. I find he will not return until the 17th the
consequence is that we will get no money until he returns. I must get me
a Common Suit of Clothes, as my clothes are getting quite shabby. I am
glad that we are out of debt. I been looking for that announcement for a
great while. Try to get along until I shall be able to remit you Some
money. I have spoken for 2 dolls. worth of good Seed, of different
Kinds, from a Dutch woman who tells me they are all good and fresh
Seed. I rather think our Arsenal will Close on the Govert. Account about
the latter of May, and then I don't know what will turn up. I have been
writing at Cols Pomeroy's office this last month (March) and Still kept
watch at the Arsenal at night. I am well and I have gone to my old
Boarding house, where I still get my washing done. I Suppose by the
time you get this letter the Snow in your neighborhood will have all
melted away. I hope so for you must be tired of So much Snow. Tell
Etty I will try to get her **Lawn** dress when I go to buy Some clothes for
myself. I have two **Merrimack** prints in my trunk. I propose getting
Some <u>domestics</u> and provisions about the last month, as this job may run
out in 2 months – I would like you to try to get the lot cleared up – in
order that you may plant – well I have nothing Strange to tell you of any
interest, this day the Election takes place for Mayor and City officers &
c. Give my best respects to all Enquiring friends, and receive my best
wishes– Kiss Ettie for me. Your Husband "Oliver"

<u>To Oliver from Higley & Huntley</u>

Chicago
April 17/66

Mr. Boizard
Dear Sir Yours of the 16th is just rec'd in reply I would say that we are
still located as when you were in C- {*Chicago*} and were much pleased
to hear from you and to know that you were enjoying health and
happiness. Enclosed I send you the list as you request and should you
order goods of us and the market have declined you can depend upon the

market price. Hoping to hear from you soon. Feeling confident that we will give you satisfaction. We are truly yours   Higley & Huntley

codfish 10cts
Best Sugar cured hams 22 cts choice
Best Sugar Cured Shoulders 17 cts
Flour winter white $11 $12 $12.50 (choice)
Flour Spring 6.50 com 7.50 fair   8.00 good 8.50 choice
Butter today is worth 35 cts
teas Japan $1.00 to 1.50 good
green teas 1.40 1.60 1.80 good 2.00 choice
good Rio cof 30 cts
Kerosene oil 60 cts
sugars
brown 12 ½ - 14 & 15
yellows 15 & white 16 cts
Hard Sugars 18cts.

From Eleanor and Marietta to Oliver

Glen Arbor, Michigan
April 18th 1866

Dear Father
We received your welcome letter dated March 23rd we were glad to hear that you were well but we were sorry to hear that you cant come home in May. I will be glad when you do come to bring some provisions in with you. I will have to get another barrel of flour before you come in. I am not feeling well this spring my heart troubles me a great deal. You spoke of having the lot cleared up. The snow is not all gone yet   there is over a foot of snow on the ground and there has not been very much sugar made yet. Ettie was at a little sugar party last evening which the young folks had at Mr. Wells Miller.   We are out of debt now I guess. Ettie will soon be 14 years old and it seems but yesterday that she was a little baby. She is almost as tall as I am. Mr. Fisher was up at the marsh after hay and he cut his foot   it rains more or less every day and the snow is going off fast. I would like to have a beefsteak for dinner as I have got tired of eating pork such as it is.   I don't know whether there will be any school this summer or not. I have just got some more pickles from Miller   I

should get potatoes from Tuckers for seed. no more at present. Truly
yours Mrs. Eleanor M. Boizard Miss Ettie Boizard
1866 Please write soon

From Oliver to Eleanor

Springfield, IL
April 20, 1866

My Dear Wife,
You will please find Enclosed $20 doll's. The Col. Has just arrived from
Cincinnati with his wife. I have written to the Grocers in Chicago and
they had Sent me a list of prices of provisions & c. and I expect that the
Boats will commence running Soon, however if nothing happens you
may Expect to get Some provisions about the 10th May, 1866. I think our
work will Soon be over, as there are only 3 Regt's of Vol's in the field
yet, and when they turn in their arms I suppose the Arsenal will close
then. I am about to purchase Some Summer cloth, and get a Suit of
Clothes made. The articles that I have now in my trunk and what I will
buy next month, I will Express them to my Grocer, and he will Ship them
with the Groceries to you, I am well, hoping that you and Ettie are also
well. Give my best Respects to all Enquiring friends, and receive my
best love and wishes. Your Husband "Oliver"

P.S. Write soon   should a boat stop try to get a letter aboard. J.O.B.
I have purchased a stuffed squirrel, for Ettie it is in a case.

Written on the back of the letter: Since Writing the within I received your
letter dated 6th April '66. I will get Etty's ribbon also Brush J.O.B.

From Eleanor and Marietta to Oliver

Glen Arbor, Michigan
April 27th 1866

Dear Father
We received your welcome letter dated April 11th and we were very glad
to hear that you were well as this leaves us at present. We are very sorry
that you cannot be at home for Ettie's Birthday as we expected you
would as it is the 15th of May. That little boy has gone back to the shanty

that we had all winter   I thought I could not keep him any longer as the snow has all gone off. I spoke to Mr. Brothertons about clearing up the lot. I will have to get the land plowed as I will not be able to dig it. There were some passengers come in last Sunday on the boat for this place. I do not know what to do as I shall be out of flour before you come in and I don't care about getting another barrel in here as I have not had any good bread this winter out of the flour they bought in the fall. Try if can to send in some lard with you. Ettie was over the lake she went Friday and came home Monday. Charlie & Frank Fisher went over Sunday and they had a nice time as there were two girls over there. Mr. Freeman and Mr. Baldwin's daughters. Ettie is going up to Goffarts tomorrow as she has not been up there this winter. Mr Fishers foot is better. You spoke of having a couple calico dresses I am very glad of it as all my calico dresses are almost all worn out   all my dark ones. be sure and get Ettie the kind she wants, either one with white ground and purple or pink figures   very small figures. you must come home as soon as you can. if it were not for our hens I don't know what we would do we have eggs every day. No more at present but remaining yours Truly yours. Mrs Eleanor Boizard Miss Ettie Boizard

From Oliver to Eleanor

Springfield, IL
April 30th 1866

My Dear Ellen,
Your letter dated 18th April is now before me, and in reply I have to State to you, that I am quite troubled about your illness, about the Heart, but I hope Ere this letter reaches you, you Shall have got over it. This coming Month (May), I am Sorry to Say, will be my last Month for Employment here. We have received an Order to Ship all the Government Ordnance and Stores to St. Louis MO, I Suppose it will take the whole of May, then good bye John   I watch the **Chicago Marine List** and I can See when the Boats arrive from your country. I See the "Cleveland" has left for Ogdensburg, some time ago, She wintered in Chicago. Ere you have received this, you shall have received your provisions, as I intend as Soon as we get our pay, to Send 40 dolls. to the Grocer and he will attend to it. You Say Ettie has grown So big. I am very anxious to See you both, I hope She is a good Girl, and has not forgotten her precepts of

morality and Goodness. I Expect to Start home in June. Give my best
Respects to all, and Kiss Ettie for me. your husband "Oliver"

N.B. I am Sorry Mr. Fisher has cut his foot My best regards to Mr. &
Mrs. Tucker (J.O.B)

I send you some reading matter J.O.B.

*This previous letter actually has the date of April 30, 1865 but it is a
response to a letter written in 1866 and it fits chronologically here in the
story. He is about to be let go from his job. He is also writing from
Springfield, IL. I feel like he just made a mistake in his date when he
wrote this letter. So I have opted to amend the date and place it here
where I believe it actually belongs.*

From Higley & Higley to Oliver

Chicago
May 10, 1866

Mr J.O.B.
Dear Sir We shipped your goods today on board the propeller **Brooklyn**
which left this am at 7 oclock   Enclose find your bill and bal. 90c your
due Many goods have {?} much since your letter enquiring price was
recd. Hoping all will be satisfactory and that the goods may reach Glen
Arbor in safety we remain as ever thanking you for your patronage
truly yours H & H

From Eleanor and Marietta to Oliver

Glen Arbor, Michigan
May 11th 1866

Dear Father
We are well and I hope you are the same. We received your welcome
letter dated April 20 1866 and the money also. Mama has gone up to the
other dock and I am staying at Mrs Fishers this week I expect mama
back Sunday. the boats stop here almost every day. The **Brooklyn**
stopped her last Tuesday She is the new boat that was launched last
February. The mosquitoes are so bad that I can hardly write they bother

me so   you must excuse this short letter or note. no more at present but
remaining yours truly yours. Miss Ettie Boizard

<u>From Eleanor & Marietta to Oliver</u>

Glen Arbor
May 18th 1866

Dear Husband
We are we well and I hope you are the same   We received the trunk and
box and one barrel of Flour. I found your likeness and I think it looks
like you   There were three dresses. I would rather had a dark calico
instead of the blue {?}   I shall have to take the Gingham one but is
almost to good to wear every day. Ettie wanted a light dress the kind
she sent for as all her dresses are dark. The muslin is entirely to heavy
for shirts. There would not any person wash it as it will full up so. You
sent sheeting instead of shirting. But I can make use of it. You will find
a sample enclosed. There is not any shirting in here   when there is you
have to pay two prices 40 & 45 cts a yard. You ought to try and bring in
some stuff for shirts   bring me in a large kerosene lamp with a marble
bottom as those that have a glass bottom tip so easy. You will get a nice
big one for about two dollars   I borrowed one from Mrs. Dorsey and it
has a glass bottom   I am afraid to move it for fear it will tip over.   What
provisions we got we could not get for $50 in here   we had to pay 50cts
for butter I just paid $5 for some that I had got. The things that we got
from Chicago as near as we can guess Tea 4 lbs sugar 5 lbs   coffee 5
also Butter & {?} pail about three parts full   Lard a 3 gal crock full
Smoked meat 20 or 25 lbs we are guessing on the amount but we don't
know for certain. I had to get Ettie a pair of shoes and I paid $3 for them
if you get my muslin get it as wide as you can don't get it less than a
yard wide I got Ettie a {?} for $1   I got some tea   I was out and I had to
get some and some other {edibles} I have not got the lot cleared up yet
as it is so hard to get any person as they are all so busy. Today is Ettie's
birthday she is Fourteen. No more at present   But remaining yours
Truly Yours Miss Eleanor M. Boizard   Miss Marietta Boizard

From Oliver to Eleanor

Springfield, IL
June 7th 1866

My Dear <u>Wife</u>
Enclosed you will please find ($40) Forty Dolls I presume we will be
discharged this month, I do not Know, whether we will be kept all the
month or not, the stores are nearly all Shipped to **St. Louis Arsenal**, I
have worked harder Since the 1st May, than I Ever did, there was such
heavy lifting all Lead, Balls & c. Try to Save one half of this money as I
will be out of Employment, I will Start for home, as Soon as I can,
probably about the beginning of July (if nothing happens) I may bring in
some more provisions. I would like to work out this month, but thing's
look like a close. Col. Pomeroy is getting ready packing up & c.
expecting some orders. I have not been as well as usual, these last two
weeks, but I still worked, I took medicine, am better, Give my best
respects to all Enquiring friends, and Kiss Ettie for me. I will try to bring
her <u>Squirrel</u>, <u>Safe</u>, also my dog "<u>Charlie</u>" No more at Present
Your Husband "Oliver"

N.B. Answer this by a boat if you can. J.O.B.

From Eleanor and Marietta to Oliver

Milwaukee
Sept 8th 1866

Dear Father
We are well and I hope that you are the same, I am in Milwaukee as
you see by the heading of this. Mrs. Grandz wanted me to go out and
help her take care of her two children, she pays my passage and so you
see that it will not cost me any thing I shall stay about a week Mama
gets Charity or some of the children to stay with her at night I shall not
be able to write any more excuse this poor writing as I am in a hurry
no more at present I remain yours Truly your Daughter Ettie Boizard

From Eleanor & Marietta to Oliver

Glen Arbor
Sept 15th 1866

Dear Father

It is with much pleasure that we received your welcome letter, we were
glad to hear that you were well as this leaves us at present you need not
worry about us because we don't stand in need of anything our potatoes
are yielding very well we got fourteen out of one hill, and they were
about as long as your little finger Ettie has been out to Milwaukee, but
she has got back, she went out to help Mrs Grandz take cares of the
children and they paid her passage there and back and it did not cost Ettie
any thing we got all the potatoes out of one hill of those that were
planted last I guess that I will not be able to write any more as they
expect the **Brooklyn** in and I shall have to take the letter down to send it
out by her give our love to Mrs Pfeiffer and the children and a part your
self no more but write soon Mrs. E.M. Boizard

From Eleanor & Marietta to Oliver

Glen Arbor
Oct 29th 1866

Dear Father

We received your letter and the butter which we were glad to get as we
had not any butter in the house and hardly any meat. I am just going to
bake my last baking of bread there is pipe for the stove but we shall
have to get elbows we shall have to get two you will find a measure in
the letter for the elbows as quick as you can get it you must send a barrel
of flour and after you get the flour you will have to get some more butter
and lard groceries also as soon as you can, because we cannot get
butter in here and that butter wont last us all winter I am just done
digging our potatoes and I am very tired I have six bushels we have
got the corn from Dorsey you must send us a dog chain because we
cannot have that dog following us every where that we go we have not
got the potatoes from Dorsey yet and we wont need them as we have
plenty of our own and what we had are splendid and I wish that you
were here to help eat them. the school commenced today but I shall not

go I shall have to learn at home, please excuse this short letter as I am in a hurry no more at present but write soon Yours truly
Mrs Eleanor M Boizard
Marietta Boizard

send us two elbows 5 inches round
Mrs Fisher let us have one elbow and you need not send but one

From Eleanor and Marietta to Oliver

Glen Arbor, Michigan
Nov 6 1866

Dear Father
We received your welcome letter dated the first which we were glad to get. We were glad to hear that you had found employ for we were all most out of every thing to eat but we have plenty of potatoes and squash. Mr Tucker wants you to send him in a 7 inch elbow. The weather has been quite cold for about two weeks and its rained all most all the time but has moderated some, and we are having fine weather now. I am taking music lessons at Mrs. Fishers on the **melodeon**. I help Mrs Fisher when she wash and irons and I don't have to pay anything for learning. I am making a pair of pants for Silas Miller. Our chickens don't do us any good this fall, because when you were at home you fed them so well that you stunted them and they have died and the hawks have carried them off.   Lloyd has cut all the wood. The dog all that he is good for is to bark and eat. he wont eat anything but bread and meal and it costs more to keep him than it would a pig. I don't know what I shall do for soap grease I have just 5cts left. don't forget a chain for the dog. No more at present but write soon. We remain yours Truly Mrs Eleanor Boizard
Miss Ettie Boizard

From Eleanor & Marietta to Oliver

Glen Arbor
November 16th 1866

Dear Father
We have got the flour home from the store house, and it is splendid   it is the same that they charge $14 and $15 for in here   the sugar and all the rest were good   we have got the stove up it burns the wood out very

much because we have not got any elbows for it   if you can you may
send us in two 5 inch elbows you need not send in any for Mrs Tucker
we had one that we got from Fisher but it was to small   we will have to
get Lloyd to cut some more wood and pay him when I can   if you can
you might send Ettie in a pair of calfskin shoes number three and have
them come up high on the ankle   those that I just riped {ripped} on the
back   The soles are good yet of both pairs but the rip on the side and on
the back and there is not any person in here to mend shoes. I will try and
send this by boat so that you can send my shoes by the **Brooklyn** if you
can send them in   no more at present but write soon.
Yours Truly Mrs. E.M. Boziard Marietta Boizard

PS. We have got the potatoes from Dorseys MB

From Eleanor & Marietta to Oliver

Glen Arbor
Nov 28th 1866

Dear Father
We received your letter and the provisions which we were glad to get I
have not been very well for a week past but I feel much better now
Ettie is as tough as ever. the weather is very fine now but for a week past
we have had very disagreeable weather. the clock wont go and we are so
lonesome that we dont know what to do   I guess that when the cat
knocked it down off of the shelf that it injured it some how   I guess that
as soon as I get a pair of shoes that I shall go to school I guess that it will
be very lonesome here this winter   We will have enough to last us 4
months if we had some kerosene for lights   Mr Tucker has not plastered
up the kitchen yet but I expect that he will come this week. McCarty has
failed   all the girls have gone out to go to school but two or three   I have
been troubled with job's plague I had some of his boils   one of the
Brothertons boys has got the fever   no more at present but write soon.
Yours & c. Mrs. E Boizard

I got the shoes and they were quite large, but they will have to do. I will
write you a longer letter when I get some paper This is the last piece of
paper that I have Mamas hair is all coming out every time that she
combs her hair she combs out great hands full. We are well and hope

149

you are the same Ettie can play three pieces on the **melodeon**   no more at present but write soon.

From Oliver to Eleanor & Marietta
Dealers in Paints, Oils, Varnishes Glass & c.

Office of
Heath & Milligan
167 Randolph Street
Chicago, Ills. Dec. 16 1866

My Dear Wife,

Enclosed please find Two Doll's I received Etty's Letter dated Glen Arbor, Nov 28 and <u>Post</u> <u>Marked</u> <u>Milwaukee</u>, Dec. 14. I did not understand how it was, as the Boats are not running. Etty acknowledges the receipt of her shoes, but Says they are large, they are number Three. Etty states that you have been unwell but getting better. I hope you may Keep well this winter. I have a rather tight time to get along, my pay is so small, that I dont know what I shall do for clothes. My clothes are getting shabby, and my Stocking's are getting very much worn. You must try to get along with the small sum of Money I Send you, better Small Sums than none. You must Keep up a good heart, and try not to Worry. I hope your chickens will do you some good. Give my regards to all the neighbors and receive my Blessings. Yours "Oliver"

<u>This is the 3rd remittance</u>   <u>How about the Dog</u>

From Eleanor and Marietta to Oliver

Glen Arbor, Michigan
Dec 18th 1866

Dear Father

We received your welcome letter dated the third of this month we received $1 also which we were glad to get. we are all well with the exception of colds which every person has. The flour is just the same as the first barrel. Charlie Fisher is clerking in the store for Mr McCarty. The snow is about a food deep and it is real lonesome. They are finishing the Hotel that they commenced in July. Since I commenced my letter Austin came and he says that he is going to stay until after

Christmas. I wish that you were here to spend Christmas and New Years with us. I do not think, that I shall go to school this winter as they say the school teacher is crazy. My mother is getting dinner. Mr Fisher hauled up our wood for winter We have not had a letter from Mr. Bridges yet. Have you heard from Browns lately. I guess that I shall close as it is getting late and I have some work to do. Write as often as you can and we will do the same. no more at present but write soon. Yours truly   Mrs Eleanor M. Boziard   Marietta Boizard

Written on the bottom of the letter:
Ettie & her mother said that I might write a few words so I will wish you a happy New Years hoping that next winter you will be some where nearer home enjoying yourself. You and Charley had quite a time together so he said. Good bye till we meet. Austin Newman

From Marietta to Charlie

Glen Arbor
Dec 22 1866

Dear Charlie
I will keep my promise to you about going to the Party as Mrs Tucker told me that you left word for me about the party. Mr. Newman is here and I guess that he will stay untill after Christmas but he is going to take my ma. If you and Frank can I would like for you both to come over Friday and spend the day or evening as I would like to see you. You may consider it all right about the party. I am going to your house to spend the evening and wish you was there. I remain yours untill death.
 May Bee

From Eleanor & Marietta to Oliver

Glen Arbor
January 4th 1867

Dear Father
We received your welcome letter which we were glad to get and we received two $1 bills also. we got a letter Christmas with two dolls in it also. We are well with the exception of colds. It was quite lonesome Christmas & New Years   Austin stayed untill after Christmas   and New Years morning mama and myself went down and spent the day at

151

Mr. Dorseys The snow is only shoe top deep we have got both the corn and the potatoes from Dorsey We get along very well. The stove that we have in the room takes a great deal of wood as we have not any elbow for it you must get yourself some clothes and keep yourself dressed comfortably. I have two pairs of stockings here that I wished you had I wish I had plenty more yarn so I could knit you some more socks and plenty muslin so I could make you some shirts. Mr. Lloyd has gone to live on his homestead and I have to get Mr. Tucker to chop my wood for me. I have one hen that lays. The dog is here, he lays around the stove and barks when he hears any person at the door, stamping the snow off of their feet he flies at them as though he would tear them to pieces and barks we have not heard from Bridges yet. I don't know what Ettie shall do for her schooling as the snow is too deep in winter and the heat is so great in the summer that it makes her sick she ought to be at school she is growing up without any learning Goffarts were here today and he sends his regards to you. There was a Tug here last saturday with a crew of sailors from off some vessel that was {?} on the coast some were {where} below here I am knitting Ettie a pair of stockings out of that fine blue yarn that you sent in May There is a stage that comes through from Traverse, every week it brings the mail in every week. We wish that we had some apples They have them down at the store for $6 per barrel if you can get any book save them and bring them home and save all your old clothes and I can take them for carpet rags my kitten has grown so large that you would hardly know it if you was to see it. The dog and kitten sleep together and they play like two cats I cannot write any more at present as I have to go and get supper and wish you were here to drink a cup of tea with us no more at present but write soon
Yours Truly
Mrs. E.M. Boizard
Miss M. E. Boizard

The previous letter had the date of January 4, 1866 written on it, but taking the letter in context, it follows chronologically to actually be January 4, 1867.

From Eleanor and Marietta to Oliver

Glen Arbor, Michigan
Jan 25

Dear Father
We received your welcome letter dated the 5th and two dolls also which
we were glad to get. We are well but mama has two boils on her foot
and she cannot wear her shoe   her blood is very much out of ordinary.
The snow is very deep it is very lonesome in here this winter. You must
keep up courage as there are several Fisher kin a great deal worse off
then we are. Mr. Lloyd he is worse off then we are, he had but one small
quilt to put over him and two children untill Mrs. Dorsey and mama went
around amongst the neighbors and got things enough for him a quilt.
save all of your old clothing and they will do for his little boy as he is
almost naked. Mrs. Dorsey & mama made the quilt on mama's birthday.
Mr Fisher is not very well. What is the name of the person in that picture
that you sent to me in the last letter we know her name is Bertha but we
don't know her other name. Mrs Aikens has had the Ergsiplos
{Erysipelas} but she is better now   it is hard to get anything to write as
we answer every letter that we get   if you can get any papers send them
in as we don't have very much to read. no more at present. But write
soon. Yours truly   Mrs. E.M. Boizard   Miss Ettie Boizard

From Eleanor and Marietta to Oliver

Glen Arbor, Michigan
Feb 15th/67

Dear Father
We received your letter dated the 16th and two Dolls which we were glad
to get. Mama has not got any better of her cold. I was coming down
stairs and had my hands full and one of my ankles turned and I fell and
hurt one of eyes it is black and blue. the snow was so deep that we could
not get any mail for two weeks from Traverse City. there is something
killing all our chickens and we will have to get another chicken house
built. You say provisions are getting cheaper I wish they were in here.
Meat is 25 cts sugar 20, muslin is 45 & 50 cts per yd   as quick as you
can you must put some money away to get some muslin for your shirts.
It has rained for about twenty four hours. Mama has not been out of the
house since New Years only to a funeral. you must send the muslin as
soon as you can after the boats run. I will take this two Dolls that you

153

sent and get yarn for to knit you some stockings. I am sorry that you fell and hurt yourself you must be careful, we would like to be out there be we could not live and pay rent and buy wood. We will soon have to have some dark calico dresses as we are almost naked we have plenty of others though. The tea at 20 shillings in here is not near as good as that tea you sent us in the fall, our butter is almost out we can get it at the store but it is 40cts per pound. we have browned the last of our coffee. Give our regards to Mr & Mrs. P. no more at present but write soon. Yours truly Mrs. E.M. Boizard Miss Ettie Boizard

From Eleanor & Marietta to Oliver

Feb 21st/67

Dear Father
We received your letter dated the second of this month which we were very glad to get. We received the two dolls *{dollars}* also. Mama is a little better of her cold and my eye is a little better. The last money that you sent us I took and got some yarn to knit you some stocking It is only $2.40 a pound and not good at that. it is half dirt. I should have to take this two dolls that you sent and get some sugar and other things that we need about the house. shoe strings are only 5 cts per pair and every thing accordingly Ray is in the store and he sells every thing dearer than ever. Mama is knitting. The dog does nothing but bark. we are having very pleasant weather but it is very lonely here. I have attended but two parties this winter and there is not any church to go to we have not got any thing to read and so you see that time drags along very heavily. I have written all the news to you and so I shall close no more at present. Yours Truly Mrs E.M. Boizard Miss M.E. Boizard

PS I have to pay 20cts for a bottle of ink that I used to get for 5cts outside.

Glen Arbor
Feb 29th 1867

Dear Father,
We received your welcome letter dated the 9th of this month and $2 also
we are very glad to hear that you are well as this leaves us at present.
When you write let me know whether you will want any stockings before
you come home, if you do I shall try and send them by the first boat that
goes to chicago save your old ones for they will do to *{?foot or first}*
Your dream was true about us being ragged   we never wanted dresses as
bad in our lives as we do now.   You will have to get some muslin for
your shirts and Ettie some underclothes   I would like to have it so I
could make your shirts by the time you come home, you can get it either
bleached or unbleached which ever is the cheapest. Dont get it less than
a yard wide get it as much over a yd. wide as you want to   you will find
a sample in this letter. *{There is a sample sewn to the top margin of this
letter.}* We have had another snow storm   it snowed Saturday and
Sunday. We have two hens that lay every other day we are glad of it as
we can have some eggs to eat occasionally. Mama is knitting all your
socks   I have written all the news so I shall have to close. Write soon.
Yours Truly & c. Mrs. E.M. Boizard Miss M.E. Boizard

From Eleanor & Marietta to Oliver

Glen Arbor
March 8th 1867

Dear Father
We received your welcome letter dated the 16th of last month and two
dollars also. We were very glad to hear that you are getting better this
leaves us well at present. You wanted to know what we have to eat   we
have plenty of potatoes and flour and tea we have, good coffee enough
for one meal   we have had to buy butter sugar & meat - it just takes the
$2 for to get things for the table as everything is very high in here. I
gave Mrs. Tucker some tea for the use of the stove as I had the tea to
spare and not the money.   I suppose Mr Tucker will soon want the
money for cutting the wood. You must get a dog chain and send it in as
soon as navigation opens for we cannot have him following us
everywhere we go and fighting every dog that he meets. The chicks has
commenced to lay and we have some to eat occasionaly. The weather

155

is very mild at present and has been for quite a while back   it is thawing today.   Mama has got rid of all her biles *{boils}* but two.   I wish that the boats were running so that you could come home   We have never heard anything from Bridges and I presume you have not either.   will you send in some cabbage & cucumber seed as soon as navigation opens.   I guess that I have written about all the news as we have not any to write in here it so lonely   no more at present   write soon. Yours Truly
Mrs. E. M. Boizard
Marietta Boizard

From Emma Bridges to Marietta

Mary Cooper Wells *{Maricopa Wells}*

March 11 1867

dear Eta

i set down to write you at last after a long time but i no you will forgive me when you hear the reason i did not write sooner   dear Eta we have seen a great deal of hardships since i wrote you last   when your letter came to **fort grant** we were expecting everyday to leave so i thought i would not write to you until we herd where we going   we were at **fort grant** a little while when we got orders to leave for **camp reno**   then the order was countermanded in 2 weeks   we were ordered to **fort Macdowl** and we left and had a hard road to travel.   when we got Macdowl we were wore out and had to live in tents in the broiling hot sun for 3 weeks before we got a house to go in to   now dear friends i got something to tell you.   i was maried on the 27 of December   you will be surprised i supose   i was married in tuson *{Tucson}* my husband is solger *{soldier}* now but when his time is out i see citizen life to   dear friends i know you wish me a great deal of hapiness   my Mother told me to tell your Mother she did not let me throw myself away on a drunkerd   she says your mother knows what trubel *{trouble}* she has seen   she says i never will have such trubel   she says to tell your Mother that she has been very happy since i ben maried but she often thinks of her and cries to think she is not with her   my Mother is at **fort Macdowel** now and I am at Mary Cooper *{Maricopa}* Wells about 45 miels *{miles}* away from Macdowl   my husband is comasary Agent here   my Mother is comeing down to live with us   jenie has grown very big and so has tomy   he often speaks of your mother   you never say anything about dick how is he getting along   i suppose you had a pleasant time on chrismas day   we

156

had not anything but rations to cook   we are hundreds of miles away of civilaztion   out here amounst hostile apaches   all we ever see is two companys of solgiers   a couple of women. i hope you will never come to such a county of arizona   Eta i wish you would send me something to read   you cannot even get a newspaper   you promised to send me your photograph i wish you would   i will send mine and my husbands as soon as we get where we can get them taken   write often and i will write oftiner as well   i must say Mother told me when i wrote   to send her love to all   i give my love all and more   you try write to me soon i shall be anxious to hear from you   direct your letter   Mrs Emma Brown Mary Cooper Wells AR   i remain your own dear friend   Emma.

From Eleanor & Marietta to Oliver

Glen Arbor
March 15th 1867

Dear Father

We received two letters by the last mail   one was dated the 23rd & the other the 25th   one had $2 in it   we were very glad to hear that your health was improving   we are both well at present.   Our barrel of flour is half gone   it will last until the first of May   it begins to look like sugar making   I wish I had muslin so I could be making your shirts. I am working at the last pair of socks and have got them almost done. you might send us an almanac as we have none, and the Ledger, no 52   in 1867   will you get any bounty   I never heard you say any thing about one and I thought I would ask you   I have just had a letter from Austin Newman   and he wanted to know how you were. Mr Tucker has been here sawing wood today   he has {chilblarins ?} on his heels   when you write be sure and let us know whether you want me to send you your socks out or wait untill you come home   we got a paper also by mail   I shall have to get butter & coffee with the two dolls that you sent us. I wish that I could buy a beefsteak. There has been a tug running from South Manitou Island every week this winter   it will soon start for Chicago. The Dog still barks at the least noise that he hears   we have the best cat in the country   it will sit up tall like Tuckers dog. Charlie Fisher thinks that it is the best cat that he ever saw   he says it will do everything but talk. it is hard to get anything to write as we have not any

news and it is very lonely   we wish that you were at home. No more at present   write soon. Yours Truly & c. Mrs Eleanor M Boizard
Ettie Boizard

From Eleanor and Marietta to Oliver

Glen Arbor, Michigan
March 22 1867

Dear Father

We received your letter dated the second day of this month and two dollars enclosed. we are well and hope this will find you the same. You spoke of getting some dark calico dresses when you get them get eleven yd in each, and you spoke also about being almost out of debt. I am very glad of that   we must pay that bill of $7 at the store   if we don't they will begin to think that we are not going to pay them. if I should want anything on credit I would be ashamed to ask it. I am glad to hear that your eyes are better. If they should trouble you again take chamber **lye** and rain water take half and half   we have had three or four days of very cold weather but it is thawing today. Mr Fisher is not well at all this winter   they will soon commence to make sugar. when you have the money to spare I wish that you would get 3 or 4 yards of crush toweling as we are out of dishcloths and tea towels   do you think that you can come home soon   save all of your old clothes for carpet rags if nothing else. we cannot find anything to write as we don't have any news in here write soon. Yours truly & c. Mrs E M Boizard Miss M E Boziard

From Eleanor & Marietta to Oliver

Glen Arbor
March 29th

Dear Father

We received your letter dated the 9th of this month and the money also Mama is not well and has not been for about a week. she has done nothing ever since she has been so unwell but lie around. when navigation opens send her in some good brandy or whiskey as she wants to put some raisins in it and take it to strengthen her. She had a spell with her heart and she has had weak spells ever since and chills & fever but she is a great deal better today   it still keeps snowing   it seems as though we are never going to have any spring   we dont think that we will have any sugar making this year   I think that our flour will last - untill the first of May   I see by those papers that you sent us that every thing is a great deal cheaper out there then they are in here.   excuse this short letter as the mail goes out today and I have to take this down today   I could not leave mama very well during the week and so I had to go down today with the mail. I shall have to close now for I must hurry write soon. Yours Truly   Mrs. E.M. Boizard   Miss M E Boizard

From Eleanor & Marietta to Oliver

Glen Arbor
April 4th/67

Dear Father
We received your welcome letter and the $2 also which we were glad to get and 4 papers also two Republicans, Times and the Police we were glad to get them as we were lonesome. Mama is better but still she is not well enough to go around the house to do any work   if it not be asking to much I would like you to get me just a common wooden rocking chair as she is not strong enough to sit up all day   She wants a strong one. one that wont come all to pieces.   she feels like she did when we were in Newport she dont have any chills now but is very weak.
The snow is going off very fast   you ought not to have bought your stockings it costs more to buy the stockings than it does the yarn and after they are bought they are not worth anything   Mr Fisher has quit using tobacco   our hens dont lay as much as they used to they have stopped to rest a while   we write so often that we dont have any news to write there is a **grist mill** William Burdick owns it   it has been running since last fall. no more at present   write soon   Yours Truly
Mrs E M Boizard   Miss M E Boizard

Glen Arbor
April 12th 1867

Dear Father
We received your welcome letter the money and paper also which we
were glad to get Mama is a great deal better than she was but still she is
very weak. I was at the store and Mark Todd asked me about that seven
dollars he wants it by the first of May I cant pay him any out of that
two dolls that we get weekly as it takes all of that to get things for the
house. Mama has not been away from the house for about a month and
she dont know how soon she will be able to go away from it. The folks
are making sugar. Brothertons have made 182 lbs and they sugared off
twice in one day and made that much   the snow is going off very fast
we have had eight trees tapped and we are boiling the sap down for
vinegar. you spoke of calico being 18cts it is 25 in here and its hardly
worth picking up   muslin that is only three quarters of a yard wide is 45
50 & 55cts - butter is 40cts per lb. I am sorry that I had to send for that
bill of Marks if I had know that he would have been so particular   I
shall not have sent for the dresses   we have on just as little as we
possibly can. but we cant complain as there are people worse off than
we are. Mr Fisher has quit chewing tobacco and he is a great deal better
no more at present   I shall bring this letter to a close as it is nothing but a
grumbling letter   write soon. Yours Truly Mrs. E M Boizard
Ettie B

Glen Arbor
April 26th 1867

Dear Father
We received the letter by the last mail   one had a one dollar bill in it. we
were glad to hear that you were well. Mama is getting better very fast
she is almost well but she has nervous spells sometimes I am making
your shirts and I want you to tell me whether I shall send you a couple
when I get them made. I shall make you three shirts out of the muslin.
we could not get such muslin in here for 50cts a yd. It is time that we
had commenced to plant potatoes but I dont know whether I can plant
any or not as the ground is not plowed and it will be hard to work. I shall
have to take that dollar and pay for getting Etties shoes mended   I wish

that you had sent me a few spools of Coat cotton I use the numbers from 40 to 20 more than any other. Our hens lay very well now we get 4 eggs sometimes. I do wish that you would send us in a dog chain for I cant have Carlo following us everywhere he fights every dog he meets. I got some coffee down at the store and payed 50cts a pound for it and when it is made it tastes like old rotten wood. I shall have to close as I am in a hurry to go down town no more at present write soon. Yours Truly Mrs. E M Boizard   Miss M E Boizard

To Oliver from Eleanor and Marietta

Glen Arbor, Michigan
May 1st 1867

Dear Father

We received your welcome letter dated the 22 of last month and the money also. I made you a shirt last week and I cut another one this week. I am a great deal better I will make you three shirts and Ettie one under garment in your next letter, write and tell us whether we shall send you a couple of shirts. do you think that you could sell shirts if we could get the material to make them. if you think we could and we could get the stuff we could help get our clothing (Ettie & I) we have not got the barrel down from McCartys Dock yet as there are not any teams around that we could get as Fishers have sold all their teams. we have had three nice roses on our bush. Brothertons hogs trouble us very much, and Charlie the dog is so brave that he gets up on top of the house and barks at them. we have had quite a shower today but it has cleared off very fine have you heard anything of Bridges lately I am afraid the Indians have killed them all. No more at present write soon.
Yours & c.Eleanor M. Boziard   Marietta E Boizard

From Eleanor & Marietta to Oliver

Glen Arbor
May 10th 1867

Dear Father

We received the letter and two dollars also we did not get the provisions untill yesterday Mr Brothertons folks did not go up untill then. I will send you three shirts by Mr Newman and you may sell one if you can get

$3   do so and you can get more muslin and send it in. Dont send any
more provisions on any boat that will land at McCarty's Dock for they
might just as well be in Chicago as up there   for there are not any teams
here that we can get as the people are using their teams in plowing and
dragging. We did not get that book or letter from Captain Rosman as he
did not leave at Glen Arbor. I guess he must have forgotten to leave it at
the store. Mama is not very well today I guess that she has worked to
hard for a day or so. I guess that Carlo will have to be killed for he eats
all of the eggs. no more at present please write soon.

PS All the neighbors send their best respects. Mrs. E.M. Boziard   Miss
Ettie Boizard

From Eleanor and Marietta to Oliver

Glen Arbor, Michigan
May 17th 1867

Dear Father,
We received two letters one dated April 27th and May the 11th we
received $4 and the book and braid also. I feel a great deal better then I
did when Mr. Newman was here.   I hope that you will like your shirts.
The next lot of Provisions that you send in I wish that you would send
me in some kind of beef as I have a hankering for it. Brothertons does
my hauling and they want to know whether you can get any blue cotton
stocking yarn   see if you can and write and let us know in your next
letter   but you need not buy any untill we send you a sample. It don't
seem worth while for us to plant any potatoes for the pigs   there are five
or six pigs running   they are here most all the time and we have not got
any fence to keep them out   it just keeps one person another time to
watch them   I wish you would send me in some dried apples or some
kinds of dried fruit   be sure and send all the provisions on the **Young
America**. no more at present please write soon. I will take this down to
day and try to send it out to you by the Captain of the **Young America.**
Yours truly & c.   Eleanor M. Boizard   Mary E. Boizard

From Eleanor & Marietta to Oliver

Glen Arbor
May 27th 1867

Dear Father

I have good chance to send a letter out as far as Milwaukee by Mr.
Walker Cooke, as he is going out he can send it by mail or send it by the
Captain of the **Young America** or whatever boat he goes on.
Mama is well as usual   we had to have Carlo shot as he ate every egg
that the hens laid.   for about four weeks we did not get an egg but since
he was shot we have got over four dozen   he has been dead about a week
we would have had to pay a dollar taxes for him and he ate all our eggs.
when you send in anything more you must try and send us some more
flour as I owed part of that that you did send. I can't eat more than one
meal of corn-meal at a time as it sours on my stomach. I have not been
to Glen Arbor or down town for over four months. it is quite cold here
we have to have a fire most all the time   we have used all our wood up
that we had chopped   there is an exhibition down town tomorrow night
I dont know whether I shall go or not as I dont go anywhere much since
mama has been feeling so unwell. no more at present write soon.
Yours Truly   Mrs. E. M. Boizard

From Eleanor & Marietta to Oliver

Glen Arbor
June 7th 1867

Dear Father

We received your welcome letter the money and the papers also. mama
is not very well, she planted some potatoes and she could hardly get out
of bed she felt so stiff and old   the least bit of work that she does it
makes her sick it is hardly worth while to plant any thing   for there is
five of Brotherton's hogs here most all the time and it keeps one of us
running after them most all the time, as we have not any fence to keep
them out. I shall not try to plant any thing another year unless we have a
fence for it will just be labor lost. We had to borrow flour today as we
were all out of flour. Ettie received a letter from Mr Newman he arrived
home all right   we have two hens setting   eat a good lot of beef steak for
us both   I have been to town once since the eighth of March and it nearly
killed me. We would like very much to see you in here no more at
present write soon Yours Truly Eleanor M. Boizard Mary E Boizard

From Eleanor and Marietta to Oliver

Glen Arbor, Michigan
June 10/67

Dear Father
We received your welcome letter and two dolls also you did not say
anything about the yarn of Brothertons and they are on nettles about it   if
you don't soon send it we will have to pay them the money for the
hauling those things from McCarty;s Dock. They wanted cotton yarn
two pounds. Do you think that you will stay out where you are and have
the same employ as you have. cant we come out and stay this winter so
that Ettie can go to school as she is not getting any schooling here as the
snow is too deep in the winter and it is too warm in summer and for her
to walk six miles every day she can't stand it. you could rent a couple of
rooms somewhere in the city I don't think that It would cost any more to
do that than it would for you to pay your board pay your wash bill and
keep us beside   they have a school teacher here but she is not much older
then Ettie is herself and I don't know anything about her education   all
the girls are going or gone out to school even Louisa Goffert   she was
out all last winter and part of the young men and boys also. we would
not want to come untill almost the last boats for we would have the
potatoes to dig   we could bring what potatoes that we would want to use
while we were out there and they would not cost as much as they would
to buy them out there   we would not want to take anything with us
excepting our clothing and bedding   when you write let us know what
you think about it we are out of both lard and butter as I have to use
butter most everything. the weather is very warm we can hardly stay in
the house, no more at present please write soon. Yours truly
Mrs E M B
Miss M E B

PS I forgot to sign our names in the last letter EMB

From Eleanor & Marietta to Oliver

Glen Arbor
Augt 22nd 1867

Dear Oliver
Yours of the 5th of this month came to hand this mail which was last
Monday   there was $2 in the letter which we were very glad to get. I
have two very large boils on my arm but one of them are broke   they

164

must make me sick   the potatoes are now as large as good sized hickory nuts   we wont have our seed from them and the ground not being plowed makes it worse   we are not going to have any squashes this year and we wont have any bean for seed. if we dont go out we will have to have the house plastered I shall have to get a pair of shoes before very long for that pair that you got me when you were here are almost worn out.   they may last through blackberrying   you will have to send the money to me so that I can get them here   for you will not be able to send the right size to me. the wine is working very nice   I hope the butter and chickens feed will soon come. you spoke of getting a house in October but if we come we wont come much before the last of October. dont get more than two rooms.   no more at present   write soon
Yours & c.   E. M Boizard   M. E. Boizard

From Eleanor & Marietta to Oliver

Glen Arbor
Augt 30th 1867

Dear Oliver
I received the cornmeal & butter and then I got a letter with $1.75 in it. did you pay the Freight on the meal & butter it was 40cts   we paid that here   we had a shower here yesterday but it did not do much good as it did not lay the dust - the potatoes look worse then they did last fall when I dug them   I guess that it is because the ground has not been plowed and this dry weather too. Last Monday we got 18 quarts of blackberries and when they were dried we had over a gallon still. Wednesday we got 21 quarts. I was glad to get that bag that had the cornmeal in it   if we have any potatoes we will need some bags to put them in   when we come up to Chicago.   when you get the house dont get it down on the sand amongst the Irish   it may be such a thing that Charlie F will come out and go to school to this winter   but we are not certain   they talk some of him going when we go.   no more at present   write soon
Yours & c.   Mrs E M Boizard   M E Boizard

From Eleanor & Marietta to Oliver

Glen Arbor
Sept 12th /67

My Dear Oliver,
I received three letters by the last mail and one by boat   we got $8.00 in
three of them. We have picked over a hundred quarts and we are going
to pick some more blackberries tomorrow. Ettie got a letter from Emma
her Fathers time is out he has gone to California to reenlist - Mr Lloyd
cannot leave his homestead but we can nail this house up. we were very
sorry that you have been sick. I will write more next week as I have no
time I am very tired I have been berrying all day   write as soon as
possible. Yours Truly   E. M. Boizard

From Eleanor and Marietta to Oliver

Glen Arbor, Michigan
September 20th 1867

Dear Oliver,
Yours of the 9th came to hand in the due time. I was very glad to hear
that your health was improving   there was $2.50 in the letter and a
photograph. You spoke of getting a house for $10 a month we cannot
get ready to come before the last of October or the 1st of November   you
can get it if you can by that time. You spoke of selling this place that I
shall never do untill I have a better place to go to. I have got it   now I
intend to keep it as poor as it is. You spoke of bringing all our things and
everything we had but I won't for it would destroy the furniture more
than it is and it would cost more to pay the freight on it –then it would to
new   anyhow we want another bedstead and lounge. Get a house with
two good rooms anyhow but don't get less than two rooms when you do
get them get straw enough for two under beds and have it in the house
when we get there.   for what few chickens we have it would cost more
to feed them there then they are worth and we would have meat to buy
anyhow the hawks are carrying them all off. it has been very warm for
two or three day period. I don't know how many potatoes we will have
as soon as they are ripe I shall dig them. our flour is almost out but we
can buy a few pounds here and that will do untill we come up to chicago.
We were black-berrying the other day and picked 21 quarts I am going to
go once more and when we get them all dried I shall weigh them to see

how many I have. One of our little peach trees has three peaches on they are as yellow as can be. They look so nice and they are almost ripe. Fishers will have about 50 bushels of peaches & Tuckers will have about 12 bushels. you spoke of letting Todd have the wood off of the place   if we do it will only grow up to briars and weeds we had better let the wood stand. no more at present write soon. Yours Truly
E.M. Boziard   M E Boizard

From Eleanor and Marietta to Oliver

Glen Arbor, Michigan
Sept 24th /67

My Dear Husband,
I received your welcome letter dated the 19th of this month there was $3.00 in the letter & three newspapers also. Ettie and myself went blackberrying today and picked 24 quarts it is the last time that we shall go as we are both of us most sick from going a berrying. we have had quite a good rain here but it is too late for to do the potatoes any good. when we come up to Chicago you will be ashamed to walk the streets with us for we will look so rustic and shabby for we have not had any new clothing for almost three years. Dick O'Donald I presume that you have heard about him   he is an Irishman he got drunk and built up a fire and laid down and went to sleep the shanty took fire and they could not get him out before he was half burnt up   his head arm and the lower part of his limbs were burn off. The shanty was burned down to the ground he left a wife and five children the oldest is a girl about four months younger then Ettie   this happened last Tuesday. I will write more next time. I am very tired. Write soon Yours truly
E.M Boizard
M E Boizard

P.S. If you have any old clothing send it in to us for Mr. Lloyd. send me in three or four gunny bags to put our potatoes and if you can send me a pound tea and that will do me untill we go out. EMB   MEB

167

Glen Arbor
Sept 28th 1867

Mr Dear Oliver

We received your welcome letter yesterday and were somewhat surprised to hear that you had not got any from us as we always answer them as soon as we get them it will be impossible for us to come Chicago by the first of the month as the potatoes are greener now than they were a month ago and they are not fit to dig yet and if we were ready we have not got the money to come with when you do rent the rooms get room enough   for Charlie Fisher expects to come out to school and board with us this winter   when you do rent them get straw enough for two beds - by the time we get there and have it in the house we will not fetch anything excepting our winter clothing & bedding I paid $3.25 for 50 weight of flour today as we were out. I have to pay two dollars a pound for tea and it is not fit to drink   for chopping wood last winter we owed Mr Tucker $13 1/2 we have paid him $4.00 I suppose I shall have to pay him the rest before I go out. The nights are getting very cold no more at present   please write soon. Yours Truly
Eleanor M Boizard
Marie E. Boizard

Please send us a *{?}* large *{?}* we will want it very much before we come to Chicago

PS Since writing the above I have received $2 from Mr Ray.

From Eleanor & Marietta to Oliver

Glen Arbor
Oct 2nd 1867

My Dear Oliver

I received your letter yesterday by the Prop. **Brooklyn** you spoke of me bringing the stove I am afraid of getting it broken   perhaps we can find a stove   if we cant we can get a parlor cook stove as we need one any how to put in the room. I shall not bring any furniture with me as it will

168

cost more to get them to the boat and all than they are worth   we wont
need more than three or four chairs a bedstead lounge and a table. we
will have our potatoes to bring and they will cost a good deal. I don't
know who many I will have or anything about it when we do come we
want to come on the **Oswegatchie** so that we can leave this dock. it
would cost so much more to go to McCartys dock and I don't know
whether I can get a team or not   we will be ready about her second trip
you can let us know by that time what we are to do because if I have to
move I wont come for the expense and trouble will be more than it is
worth   we can not rent the house   we might get some perfect stranger in
it   we can nail the door & windows up and get Mr Fisher to look at it
once in a while   no more at present   write soon   Your & c.
E.M. Boizard

From Eleanor & Marietta to Oliver

Glen Arbor
Oct 13th 1867

Mr Dear Husband
Your letter came to hand in due time I was glad to hear that you were
well as this leaves us at present. You spoke of us bringing our furniture
I will bring our stove but not the table or chairs for they would not be fit
to be seen. The **Oswegatchie** will be here at this dock about the 27th of
this month. you need not buy the bedstead & lounge untill we come up
to Chicago for I want to buy them myself. I have no chairs to bring
except those cane seated ones and I would not take them as a gift by the
time they are taken to Chicago and back again   you may send the money
to pay our passage or buy the tickets and send to us just as you think
best   I can't write anymore as I have to hurry for Ettie & Charlie are
going up to the other dock and I want to send this up by them.
Ettie is going to have her tooth pulled. no more at present Yours Truly
E.M. Boizard
M. E. Boizard

From Marietta to Charlie

Glen Arbor
Thursday Morning
Oct 24th/67

Dear Charlie

You must not be surprised at me writing to you but I forgot to ask you if you would write to me every week and I will do the same and then we can hear from each other oftener if you should not come out this fall please come in the spring but I want you to come down to the boat and see us off. Yours forever Maitie E. Boizard

From Marietta to Charlie

Glen Arbor
Oct 24th 1867

My Dear Charlie

I received your note and was very glad to get. I guess that we will go out tomorrow some time. I feel so bad I dont know what do   I want to see you very much but I presume that you will not want to come clear up to the other dock to see us off but I should like to have you.   you may direct your letter to me in care of my Father, direct to No 93 South Canal Street Chicago Ill's

From Marietta to Charlie

Milwaukee
Oct 28th 1867

My Dear Charlie

I arrived safe in Milwaukee after a very pleasant trip. I was not a bit sea sick but I expected that I should be   some of the ladies were sick. I cried myself to sleep on the boat   I felt so lonely and I wanted to see you so much. did you see me cry when I was waving my handkerchief. We are visiting at Mrs Cookes the girls are all trying to find out who I am writing to but I will not tell them. Mrs Tator came home from Portage City yesterday. she said she saw Herbert McCarty on the cars   he talk some of attending Commercial College. He is in Milwaukee someplace. There was a couple of Mrs. Tators Friends call last evening to take us to the Theater. (Mrs Tator & I) but it was raining and I could not go and anyhow I did not care about going I would rather been where I could see you then go to the Theatre. I feel so home sick that I dont know what to do Today is Sunday and it seems a great deal lonelier then Glen Arbor because I am not acquainted with any person here and there I am I would give most anything to see you if you are as lonely as I am I feel sorry for you Well I presume that you think I had better write about something else by this time how did you get home that day after the boat left. I had a dream about you last night and the night before I guess that it will come to pass I presume that you will like to know so I guess I will have to tell you I thought that you came to Chicago and you were at our house and you were sitting down by a window and you were holding a young lady on your knee I shall judge that she was about 15 years of age I was not acquainted with her but perhaps you know her, but I dont you called her your (dear Little Wife) I have come to the conclusion that you know her I would like to have an introduction to her. remember I dreamed this all in two nights and if I dream it again tonight I shall begin to think that you are married or just about to be I hope that you will send me a piece of the wedding cake and the card also. I shall send a parcel by the Captain, the trimmings for your mother are in it. Give my respects to all inquiring Friends and tell them I will write them as soon as I can. remember what you said about writing to me. My Mother sends her love to all of her Friends she says she would like to see you all again well I can not think of anything more at present but perhaps I can before I go on the boat. no more at present please write soon. Yours until death parts us Maitie E. Boizard

P.S. Please excuse all mistakes and poor writing for I am very much confused the folks are talking and Kittie is playing on the Piano.

From Marietta to Charlie

Chicago
Nov 6th 1867

Mr Dear Charlie

I received your welcome letter the day that I arrived in the City I would have answered it before the later day but I had to help clean the house. I have not commenced to go to school yet but I expect to about Monday. I presume that you have rec'd my letter before this I am looking for an answer and waiting patiently. I do wish that you would come up and spend the Winter. I have attended the Theater once since I have been in the city and once while I was in Milwaukee and when I *{thought}* we were going home we went to a party and danced one **quadrille**, and then went home. I went with Miss May Cooke & Mr Anderson. I presume that you have attended several parties since I left Glen Arbor have you been down to Mr. Tucker's lately I wish that you would pet my Kittie and think it is me. I am so homesick that I feel like crying most all the time. My mother is not feeling very well. She has a bad cold she coughs some she looks almost as bad as she did when we went down to Glen Arbor four years ago. How do George & Charity get along do you think that they will get married. you must not think that I am inquisitive but you know that I am not in GA and I feel interested. I dont know what to make of you I dont know whether you are in earnest about that engagement. My Mr. Newman is here he has been here about two weeks he starts tomorrow for Pine Lake. when we came to the City he was at the House that my Father boarded at. My Pa says that we cannot board you any cheaper than Five Dollars a week and do your washing also. he had to pay this and pay for his washing also. Mr Newman is paying six for his board. we would board you as cheap as we possibly could everything is very dear. you ask me if I did not see you waving your handkerchief yes my Dear I did and it seemed like taking part of my life to see you standing on the Dock you looked so lonely Mr. Newman says that I am heartless but I told him that my Heart was in safe keeping and out of his reach am I right, my Dear Charlie My heart is in Glen Arbor. How are all my young Friends getting along and you especially I would like very much to see you again but if nothing happens I promise myself the pleasure of seeing you in the spring if you dont come up this winter. My ma sends her love to all the Family & all inquiring Friends Give my respects to all the young folks and receive my love please write soon Yours forever and ever Maitie E. Boizard

P.S. Please excuse all mistake and poor writing. Maitie

Direct to 195 South Canal Street Chicago Ills.

Chicago
Nov 13th 1867

My Dearest Charlie,

I rec'd your welcome letter last sunday morning   my Pa went out and
when he came home he brought me the letter   he tried to plague me   he
told me that he had none for me   My ma and I reached his pockets and
we found one. I am sorry that you are so lonely   but I am worse off than
you are as I am not acquainted with any one. you spoke about that party
that I attended in Milwaukee and though that it was not much like the
parties in Glen Arbor. I agree with you there as the dancing is not near
as good as the dancing in GA. You or I can dance a great deal better   it
was for the Benefit of a dancing school but it was not to be compared
with Mr. Kings school, I will say that much for old G_ A_. You were
right about me holding my head down and crying. My Dear (if you will
permit me to call you such endearing names) but I guess you will for I
will anyhow. you need not be afraid of me taking your dear head off as I
will not for I think to much of it for to do that. You were right about my
dream. You know what has passed between us and remember if you are
true to me I am to you. Mr. Newman has not gone home yet but he says
that he will go in two or three days.   we went to the Minstrelles
(Minstrels} last night they were not worth going to see. I am so mad at
him that I dont know what to do. Has Mrs Tucker come home yet   I
hope she enjoyed her visit   have you heard anything about that parcel yet
I hope that you have rec'd it ere this   I fixed your letter on the parcel
and I dont see how they would get separated unless the Captain took the
letter off of the parcel. you mentioned a party at Mr Decker's who got it
up I am glad to hear you say that you dont attend such parties   not that I
want you to stay away from them because I am not there   for of course
you can do as you like about that but I don't think such places are fit for
young men or girls that think anything of their honor or themselves   take
my advice and stay away from such places.   My mother sends her love
to your ma and all the Family. My love to all the Family and a good
share for yourself My Dear write soon   if you will permit me to sign my
self, Your own True Little Wife Ettie
to Charlie
P.S. Here is a note please hand it to Mrs. Dorsey dont get mad at me for
signing my name as I have Ettie

173

N.B. My Mother is not any better   she has a cold in her head and a bad cough   she had a spell with her heart the other night   I am afraid that she will not be as healthy as she was in Glen Arbor   I have not been very well, one day I was sick in bed but I am much better   excuse poor writing as I have to get dinner now.   Ettie

From Marietta to Charlie

Chicago
Nov 21st 1867

My Dearest Charlie

I rec'd your welcome letter dated the 9th of this month and was somewhat surprised to hear that you had not rec'd any letters from me, as I have answered every letter that you have written   when I read your last letter I had a good cry it made me feel so homesick. but if I could have had a good look at you I would not have felt so bad   when you spoke about my Poor Kittie I did not know what to do I hope that you will pet her for me. Is Mrs Ayres at Glen Arbor yet.   there are two letters on the road to you ahead of this. I shall be very sorry if you dont come up here this winter I have not commenced to go to school yet but I have been examined and the teacher says that she will send for me as soon as there is a vacancy. I am expecting a letter from you every day   it is just one month day after tomorrow since we left Glen Arbor. but it seems more like six months than one. but never mind if we dont have gay times when I come home it will be because we cannot   has there been any changes there since we left   how many young Ladies has come ther   I hope that none will steal my Dear Charlie's Heart away   if they should what would poor Ettie do she would cry and break her heart   you may think that I am in fun but I never was more in earnest in my life   please believe me Dear, your own through life. dont let any person see this Mr Dodge is in the City he was here yesterday. Mr Newman is here yet he is expecting a boat in every minute they have been looking for five for a week I am in hopes that he will start soon for I can hardly tolerate him well my dear I must close as it is near noon and I have to get dinner. Give our love to all the Family and friends and receive all my Love and that is just as much as the letter can carry and believe me your own Dear little Wife Ettie write soon   direct as before.My Pa's address is 167 Randolph Street that is where the store is it is a large Paint Oil and Glass establishment I thought I would give you his address also Maitie B

174

Chicago
Nov 23rd 1867

My Dear Charlie

I have not rec'd any letter from you for over a week   I thought I would write and see whether you had forgotten me and again I thought that you were not at home. I did not know but you had take a notion to go away some where I did not know. I thought I might have said something in some of my letters that would offend you. If I have I am very sorry as I did not do so intentionally. Mr. Newman has gone home   he went last week. We are having very stormy weather it has rained for two nights and a portion of the day   it is very muddy. I see more mud in one half day than I have seen in four years. I was out last night with my pa and it was raining so hard as it could pour. I feel so home sick that I don't know what to do. I never knew what it was to be homesick untill I came out here. If I ever get back to old Glen Arbor, I don't think that I shall leave it in a hurry. I have rec'd one letter from Sarah   she send her love to you & Frank, but I had ought to have got it before I left Glen Arbor. how many Ball's has there been in the place since I left. there will be a grand one in the city sometime during the month of December   only $20 a ticket   that is not very much. what would you think to have the tickets so high in Glen Arbor. I guess that it would be the grandest Ball that ever has been in G.A. I have been to the matinee they have them every Wednesday & Saturday afternoon. they are at **Woods Museum**   they are mostly for children but any person that wants to can go. I heard the Peg Factory was for sale, is it a mere rumor or is it a fact. you know that there are so many false reports that you cant tell anything about what you hear. I tell you news fly very rapidly   I heard that you were surely going up to Chicago, but Mr Dodge told me that and a lot more but I wont tell what. you know he has been a way from Glen Arbor most of the season but as soon as he landed at Mr McCartys Dock he commenced to take the news and what I have already told you amongst the rest. he needed to know if that was so I told him that I did not know for certain, what did you think about it.   how are all the young folks getting along. I presume they are getting along nicely and never miss any of their absent friends but absent ones do not forget them.   I hope that you will not forget Ettie B. for she is a true Friend if nothing more to you. don't be offended at me, I pray. I will enclose a note to Kate King will you be kind enough to hand it to her and I will try and do as much for you sometimes. Please give my Love to other inquiring Friends if there are any. our love to all

your Folks and please receive a good share for your own dear self.
Please write as soon as possible. From your Loving
Maitie

Direct to 195 South Canal please excuse all mistakes and poor writing
your own true Wife

but I hardly dare sign myself that for fear it will offend you if it does
please let me know Mattie

From Marietta to Charlie

Chicago
Dec 2nd 1867

My Dearest Charlie
I rec'd your Welcome letter dated the 16th of Nov and you may be sure
that I was glad to get it   I am expecting to get one either today or
tomorrow   I hope that you are not offended with me for writing to you as
I did in my last letter but I had the Blues so that day   I felt as though
every person despised me   I know that it is very wrong to entertain such
feelings but I could not help it. I am very sorry that you cannot come out
here this Winter as I shall be so lonely for I dont know any person. Mr
Dodge has gone down to Ogdensburgh   he has been gone about a week.
I have not commenced to go to school yet and I dont know when I shall
as there is not any vacancy but I am studying at Home   My Arithmetic
is the most that I care about and my Pa can learn me that   if I only knew
as much about it as he does I would do. I was quite surprised to hear
about the Weddings that took place in Glen Arbor I presume that when I
go back home that there wont be any person there but married Folk and I
will have to wear the {Willow?} what do you think about it   but you
must not get married untill I come home for I would like to be some
where where no one could see me and look on and see you kiss the
Bride. but you must not be like Tom Helm and forget to kiss the Bride
for if I should happen to be there I will kiss you to put you in the mind of
kissing her. please dont take my head off. Yes I guess that we will tell
the Glen Arbor People some news in a few years   I rather guess it will
make some of them open their Eyes dont you think it will My Darling
Chas. Yes I will take good care of your Heart and it will be the best of
care to   remember and take good care of mine   to tell you this candid
truth Charlie I never Loved any one as I do you nor ever shall. you

spoke about Mrs Tucker and getting her dress   I am very sorry but Tell
her if she dont get it we will make it right with her. How does my Pet
get along   you requested me to tell you what boat we came on from
Milwaukee   it was one of Goodriches Line the name of the boat was the
Orion. we left the Parcel for Capt Rosman and your Letter also   the
Letter was fastened on the outside of it I slipped the letter in under the
string that was around the parcel. My Ma says that she always knew that
you were mischievous and she says that she expects by the time we get
back you will be so roguish that we wont know it is Charlie Fisher.
You are quite excusable but I dont care how many questions you ask   if I
did not know you it would be different but as it is I dont care. yes I
know what a great Fellow you are to ask questions especially when you
asked me one question   I presume you can guess what one that was.
My Ma has not been well since we have been in the City she sends her
Love to all enquiring Friends here are some patterns for your ma   How
does Frank get along   poor boy I pity him since Angie has gone. but he
will soon forget her   My regards to all and My love to your own dear
self   please write soon I remain your own true Wife forever & ever
Ettie

please dont get mad I send two ledgers 37 and 39 we will get 38 as soon
as we can Please excuse all mistakes and poor writing as I dont feel very
well today

From Marietta to Charlie

Chicago
Dec 11th/67

My Dear Dear Charles
Yours of the twenty fifth is now before me   it was post marked Detroit
Dec. 9th you dont know how glad I was to hear from you as it has been
over two weeks since I heard from you last   I had almost given up as I
thought you had forgotten me but I presume that it could not be helped
for I know how long it takes a letter to come from G A to Chicago.
I hope it will be so that you can come up in the spring. I would like to
have you come I am very sorry it is so that you can not come this winter
as I thought that we would have such Gay Times   but you may Bet if we
both live to see each other again we will have just the Best of Times

You say that your Heart is mine   that I am most happy to hear and you rest assured that mine is yours as long as you wish for it   I dont think that there is any danger of any person winning my Heart as it is already given to you and I would sooner loose my Life then break the vows that I have given to you   although you may change your mind different from what it is now   I shall always remain true for it shall never be said that I broke my vows   not that I think you will and I hope that you will take no offense as I mean more, I will do as you said   I might in signing my name.   I hope that you will not go Crazy untill I come home and then after that I dont think that there will be any cause for you to   for I am as true to you as True can be.   I am not feeling near as well as I did when I was in Glen Arbor.   I feel dull and heavy all the time just as any person would when they were coming down with the Fever.   I must tell you how much I weigh   when I left Glen Arbor my weight was 112 pounds and now it is 102 lbs so you may see for yourself how the city agrees with me and as far as my ma   I dont believe she has been well a day since we left the shores of Mich.   I am very happy to hear that you are having such a good school   and that you are progressing so finely in your studies   as I have not commenced to go to school yet   but I am studying at home   I am getting along very rapidly with my Arithmetic   I understand it better now then I ever did before   for I could not see into it very well before but now I can   but it is coming to me just like all others to   I presume it will be about Christmas when you get this   so I will wish you a Merry Christmas   if you attend any parties please dance a set or two for me well I must draw this to a close as it is getting late and I shall have to write to Mrs Tucker yet tonight   Give my Love to Frank and all the Family and receive the greatest share for your own Dear Self   write soon and Believe me to be your Loving Little Wife   Ettie Boizard

PS   We will send two or three Ledgers   Tell your Ma that my Ma sent the beads in Mrs Tuckers parcel and she will make it right if you shall not get them   she sends her love to all   Ettie

Please excuse this poor writing as I am in a hurry

enclosed you will find a letter for Mrs Tucker   when you write please tell us how the House is and all around it.   You know what the color of this envelope denotes   please dont laugh at this letter I wanted to write all I could on it.   Ettie

178

Chicago
Jan 13th 1868

My Dear Charlie

Yours of the 4th of this month is now before me and you can not guess
what pleasure it gives me, to hear from you   but I was sorry to hear that
had such an accident but I hope that you will recover from it   I was glad
that it was not any worse than it is   I was very glad to hear that you had
such a Gay Time on Christmas and hope that you may enjoy your self at
all the Parties especially the Fourth of July but you had ought to take
some of the girls I request you to take some one to the next party if it is
not untill the Fourth of July please do take some one   for I know that
you can find plenty up there to take   as for me I dont expect to attend
any more parties in a very great hurry as there are not any here, that I
would care about attending and dear only knows when I shall ever see
any of my young Friends from Glen Arbor   as I dont expect that any of
them will come out here to see me unless you should take a notion to
come as I dont know when I shall come home.   I do wish that you would
try and come out or up   as it is so lonely that I dont know what to do   let
me know when you have concluded {who} to take to the next party if
you have made up your mind when you answer this   you must be careful
how you drive when you go out cutter riding but I am glad that you nor
Frank, either were hurt.   you spoke of the numbers that were cold at the
party it seems that there are more Folks at Glen Arbor then ever. you
say that you wish that I was there on account of the Grand Skating   I
wish that I was if it would do any good but alas it will not   one reason
is that I could not skate if I was there and there is not any likelihood of
me learning. I hope you Head is better   dont be offended at me or my
poor letter as I dont feel very well and I am so homesick that I dont know
what to do when I think of what gay times I have had. but I shall not
speak of it for it makes me feel worse. I hope that there is a good time
coming tho. {though} I came very near being run over today by an
express wagon   Tell Frank that there is a Little Boy here, that is as great
a hand to kiss as he is (not saying anything about Charlie) for I know that
he dont like to kiss the girls. I see that there is a blot on the paper   I did
not notice it untill I commenced to write on this side I hope that you will
excuse it. I rec'd a Letter from Mrs Tucker the same time I rec'd yours
when you write will you please tell us if the house is all there. today is
wash day and I will not be able to write much more. I will send your Ma
a list of prices. our love to your Folks and receive a good share for

179

yourself   please write soon   the weather is very strong and cold   it is snowing quite hard but the snow will not last more than a day or two and then the ground will be bare again.   Well I shall have to close as I have bread to bake and it is ready to mix up now   no more at present   but believe me your True Little Wife Ettie
to Charlie Fisher

From Austin Newman to Marietta

Pine River Mich
Jan 16th/68

Dearest Ettie

Yours of Dec 20th reached me day before yesterday and oh was I glad to hear from you - that is I was glad to get a letter from my Darling. but I think Ettie there was too much pepper in that letter; and I felt thankful that I was not near the writer when she wrote it -- But my Dear Little Girl you are not very mad at me are you. You dont think I have any right to lecture you. Why that is just what you have been doing to me.

But please Ettie let us be Friends. I agree with you them fellows are not worth talking to but if you make faces at them or look at them or give them the slightest chance they will take it. they would do the same to me - a man how much quicker to you a nice young girl as lovely and beautiful. I <u>was</u> angry at them fellows for staring in the Windows and calling out to us -- but we will not say any more about them and I am sorry for mentioning it at all. So please accept my apologies for doing so. In my other letter to you the principal subject was learning music and I have spoken to you so often or written rather, that you might be angry sometimes   but I do like music so much and you are a pretty good singer; that I desired very much to have you learn; but I guess it is as you and your Father say to big an expense. I shall tell you all the news Ettie or anything that will interest you or you will care to hear. The snow here is nearly 2 feet deep and the **Sleighing** is first rate   We have had some splendid skating too both before and since my last letter to you   Charlie and I and Harry too had great times on Pine Lake the water so clear as you know it is on those little Lakes. The water 3 or 4 feet deep some places where we skated it seemed as if there was nothing between us and the bottom -- come across trout or schools of herring and chase them until they got into deep water I wished very much you was there or here rather   It makes a person feel splendid to fly over the ice on water that

way. Please Ettie did we not have a pretty good time in Chicago last Fall
I wish we had taken some rides   I mean in a buggy or open Carriage to
go swift   it is some like skating -- well we will make it up some other
time if you will consent or say so and will permit and allow and order
and command –your very humble Servant -- please dont think me foolish
E for I would not like to have you labor under such a mistake.
There is a Steamer advertised to run from Traverse Bay to Manistee
touching at intermediate Ports   it will come to this place too and so forth
and soon -- and likewise etcetera -- the last is supposed to be Latin   I am
not in the enjoyment of the best of health   same as I hope you all are.
rheumatism bothers me some and sometimes low spirited -- untill I
begin to think of you then I feel better.   that last letter was a first rate
one; but Ettie there was only one leaf -- but then I know that it is hard
work writing letters - at least it is for me.   it <u>was</u> a very neatly written
letter.   You say my Bird is well   Oh Ettie I thought it was <u>your</u> bird - but
let me tell you please how we can manage it   You can get a Lady Bird
and your bird and mine can go to keeping House   Dont you think that is a
good idea Little One.   Please Dearest dont be offended with me for
calling you Little One for you know you are not very big or old either
We take the Traverse Eagle and I look over frequently to see if I can see
anything about G.A. but up to this have seen nothing of the people or the
place   Please excuse this poor letter   I will try and do better next time
With Love and respect Yours truly   Austin C Newman

From Marietta to Charlie

Chicago
Jan 22nd 1868

My Dearest Charlie
I rec'd your welcome letter dated the 11th of this month and you may be
sure that I was very happy to receive it   I was very happy to hear that you
were well as this leaves me at present.   I do wish that I could see you, as
I am very lonely.   Oh dear, my ink is so poor that I dont know what to
do.   you spoke of it being doubtful about your coming up here   I am
sorry and wish that it would be so that you could come.   you may look
for us on Capt. Rossmans Boat as we intend to come on the boat that he
runs if nothing happens more than I know of at present.   My Pa tries to
plague me by telling me that we will not go home this Summer but Ma
says that we will go home in the Spring on the Capt's boat if he run   but

I presume that he will   but please dont let any person know when we are coming as I want to surprise the Folks but when you hear the Propeller whistle you may think well that Ettie Boizard is on that Boat   she has come back to bother us all,   if you want to see me very much you will have to come down to the dock,   please excuse me for saying you must but you know that I dont mean it   but you can come down if you wish to. My Dear is your Grand Father still in Glen Arbor. I did not know whether he was or not   as you had not mentioned him. how is our house getting along or dont it get along   please let us know when you write as my Pa is uneasy about it   I rec'd a Letter from Charity and she says that Lottie Mason is a <u>Dear</u> <u>Good</u> <u>Girl</u>. I used to be a dear good girl once in their eyes but now I am a dreadfull girl I presume that you know what I mean   we will talk about skating when I get home. I will send you my picture as soon as I get it taken   I should have sent you one like {Remnies?} but I did not want to offend you with one, as they was not like me I just looked like a big Dutch Girl. You wished me to finish my dream well I will, I thought that I went up to Glen Arbor and we did not get off the boat in time so we were a way out in the Lake before we knew it and you were on the boat but we did not know it and then I thought that I was married to Austin Newman   I thought that he forced me to marry him but still he was not on the boat he got off at Glen Arbor and that was the last of him and then I saw you and commenced to cry and you wanted to know what was the matter and my Ma said that I married to Austin on the 10th of August   then you felt very sorry you kneeled down on the deck near me and put your arm around me and my arm was around your neck just then the part of the boat that we was on (you and I) sunk and you said it was better as that we should die together we were at the center of the Lake and the Sea was very thick all around us. I for my part dont know what to think of it. please excuse this poor Letter and writing but I am very busy and have not very much time   I dont think that you can read it   my ma sends her love to all. I can think of a great deal more to write but you see that I cant write any more as the paper is not large enough I guess that I shall have to get a foolscap sheet next time for I can think of enough to fill one. How does my Kitten get along. well I must close this Letter write soon
Your Little Wife Ettie B. to Charlie F.

you must excuse this sheet of paper as it is all that I have in the House. You said that you loved me more and more I will see about that when I

182

come home   dont be offended at any thing I say to you. Your
L____W_____ Maitie

From Marietta to Charlie

Chicago
Feb. 12th 1868
Wednesday Afternoon

My Dearest Charles
Your most kind and welcome Letter is now before me and you may be
sure that I am very happy to hear from you My Dear Chas. please dont
Laugh at my poor Letters. I hope that you will try to come up here this
Spring or in the Spring I should say. yes, we will start for home about
the middle of May if not before that if nothing happens. I must confess
that the Girls are rather high in your estimation. you say that you wished
I had been here last night as there was a party up to Brothertons I think
that they are going in on their nerves this Winter in having parties but let
them enjoy it while they may is all that I can say. I think that Glen
Arbor, is rather more lively than it was Last Winter at Least for the
young Folks. you spoke of me being so homesick and lonely I might
enjoy myself here if I could get acquainted with any young Gent's but I
dont want to now. I will not   you know what I have told you   there are
several young Gents that are trying their very best to get acquainted with
me, but I nix every ole ruse.   There are a whole Factory full of them
right next door to us   it is a Plowing Mill & Box Factory   everytime
that I go down stairs they can see me and I can see them   I guess you
know how it is with all these young fellows if there is any young girl
around   you say that you attended two parties   Both Dances or
whatever they are called   you have done better than I have for I have not
attended any   you know that I wont even attend any when I am at home
and therefore I dont know what they are called.   Oh I must tell you of a
very heavy crime I am guilty of and I do wish that you would tell me
how to get out of it   I have broke a couple of young Fellows Hearts as
they say   but I say that I have only bent them   they are both strangers to
me   but they told a young Lady that lives in the house that I had broken
their hearts   but I told her that I had only bent them. please tell me what
to do   I guess that they will get well when I am gone, dont you think so.
I pray that you will excuse this poorly written letter as I am not well and
dont feel like writing or doing any kind of work. My Mother and I am

both just about down sick, with colds. I know if you felt as I do you would not feel like writing but I dont want to let the week pass without writing to you My Dear. for that would be breaking my promise to you. Well I presume that Valentines Day will soon be along long before you receive this I will send one to Frank in your letter but you are not deserving of any as your dont write long enough letters you <u>scamp</u>. but I will see by the time I get another letter from you and if it is a good long Letter you may look for a Valentine but mind I would say who it will be from. I guess that by this time you are tired of trying to read my Letter or what ever you call it and I guess I shall draw it to a close. please write as soon as you can My Parents send their Love to all, and receive a good Share for your self from me. and believe me, your T____Little Wife Ettie

<u>From Austin Newman, family friend to Oliver</u>

Charlevoix
Feb 17th 1868

Mr J O Boizard

Dear Friend Yours of Jan 31st came to hand on the 14th. Harry got 3 letters at the same time and I got 2 yours and Etties. We are all in pretty good health here in the North Pole for it is almost too cold for comfort sometimes as you will see by the color of this Ink it has been froze and refrozen consequently makes it look "kinder" pale as the American says. As long as I get as good letters as this last my Dear Friend I shall be glad to correspond with you I began to think that you would not have much to write but I guess writing is what you are used to and you mix business and pleasure so easily; that a fellow don't feel any hesitation about haveing you write I certainly am much obliged to you for your kindness in doing that small favor for me Harry got a letter from one of the old hands of the 10th Harry wrote at a venture to Newport (the fellows home was close by there) calculating that it was about time for him to be out of money; the Gentleman wondered how Harry found out he was there; pretty well guessed wasnt it? You quite surprised me when I read that you were out of debt I really thought that it would take till spring to clear off the amount you owed the company your wages are so small. In a letter that I rec'd from Edward a short time ago he mentioned you and said that Army Clerks were hard to get so I wrote him 3 or 4 week ago and if there is any chance for better wages and enough to pay you to leave I will let you know for if you are to be absent from your home I should think the best way would be to go where you would get most wages We can wait and see what they will offer. Charlie has just got a letter from him (Edward) and he don't know wether he will come up here in the Spring or not but he says his wife wants to come and stay up here awhile; she has been here before He says she wants to come and set out a row grape vines About being pleased or looking forward to the time when navigation will open so I can go hunting you mean so that I can go to Glen Arbor for I believe I told you there was a Steamboat advertized to go there direct from here. I am afraid I shall not be able to go to Chicago in the Spring because it will put me back in my spring work same as it did last spring you see I want H & J to put in about 5 acres of Potatoes same of corn and 5 acres of other stuff good deal of work isn't it? Come to Chicago next Fall if living with a lot of stuff to sell My Dear Boz (that is **Dickens** -- by the way has he been in your little Village this winter) you did not tell me wether you was giving "Young America" lessons in French though I suppose you are so please don't be angry with me for mentioning it. I suppose Richard does 'make music all the day' and sometimes nearly deafen you I told Ettie she ought to get a mate for him and raise some canaries she could go into speculation. Does the shade of the Old Dog Troy ever trouble you now I don't want to hurt your feelings but he used to bark so often peace to his ashes I have a mind to write a letter to Mother; but I know she has both yours and Etties my love to her and best respects to yourself and all inquiring Friends yours Truly Austin C Newman

From Austin Newman to Marietta

Charlevoix
Feb 23rd/68

Dear Ettie
Yours of Jan 31st reached me on the 14th of Feb. when I got the envelope containing the Valentine I thought it was your letter I suppose I am in the enjoyment of as good health as most people -- but my dear little Girl I get very low spirited sometimes but that last letter Dear One made me feel very happy it was a real nice letter Ettie very neatly written and I do love you so for it. Darling and I have been four or five days not knowing how to answer it I will have to get down on my knees or in an attitude of prayer begging your pardon for not answering before you are or was so good to me when I was in Chicago last Fall and now this real

nice letter and Valentine makes me so love you that I dont know what to say -- and the very pretty verse that you wrote on the Valentine -- it is beautifull; Dearest both the verse and the Valentine Oh if I was only where you are would not I have some kisses! I think Beloved I missed happiness very much in not corresponding with you when I was in the Field -- but it always seemed so long whenever I would think of you till I would think next {of} you I mean that I thought of you as little as possible. That Valentine is very suggestive Darling the nice little church on one side and the nice little cottage on the other both embowered among the Trees and Flowers, and Lambs skipping around; When is all this to be realized? My Sweet One it seems so far away causes me to feel so low sometime and everything seems dark and distant. We have a book here, "Tempest & Sunshine" You are the Sunshine Dearest dont you know I always compared you to a sunbeam "bright and warm" Your letter is like a steel engraving very neat indeed. So you are going to make it all up by and by are you? For {?} now - well maybe I will have the happiness of being with you You know there is a preference for your Valentine in all dances and Parties for a year whoever the happy One may be -- but I dont suppose I need tell you anything about that for you know more of it than I do and you promise yourself or rather think there are good times coming for you   I hope so Darling and I hope you will permit me to make myself happy by doing all I can to please and make you happy. When I came to where you say (in your letter) that you intend to go to all the Dances for 10 miles around I thought it read for 10 night ahead you would be getting ahead of Time and no mistake Dearest! I do hope next winter to have a Horse of my own then when I want a Cutter ride I can have it and so can someone else I know of. Please Ettie will you permit me to tell you of some of the local news though there is not much room left so I guess I wont mind it -- but we had a Dance here at which there were 48 tickets sold there was twice as many as there ought to be - for comfort I really hope to see you and Mother here next summer and hope to make it a very pleasant visit I have some good times with Charleys little ones   I feel Dearest that I had ought to write you a longer letter than this but you will forgive me wont you? and I will try to make it right some other time. Please remember me to Mother. Beloved and kiss her for me please and Oh! Ettie have many kisses for your self Your most humble Servant and admirer
Austin C Newman

186

Written in Ettie's handwriting across the previous letter is "My Dear
Friend Charles   Glen Arbor Mich" *Apparently she forwarded the letter
on to him.*

From Marietta to Charlie

Chicago
Feb 24th 1868
Monday Afternoon

My Dear Fr. Charlie
Yours of the {?} of this month is now before me. I am most happy to
hear from you and that all were alive and well. I thought that you joined
in the Performances the night of the Masquerade Party   at least you had
ought to have done so   when I told you to save your Money I did not
mean that you should deny yourself the pleasures of Society for I am
perfectly willing that you should attend all the Parties but above all dont
deceive me. You spoke of sending me some kind of a present that was
what I meant when I told you to save your money and I told you what I
would rather that you should do with it but as matters stand at the present
time that can go with this {?}   you spoke of some large Fires in Chicago
there are Fires burning most of the time in some part of the city. last
Friday there was quite a large Fire a little over a Block from us on the
same street that we live on (Canal) from Friday Afternoon 4 oclock untill
Saturday Morning at six oclock there was no less than five Fires and so
you see that a Person is in danger of being burnt up alive   we often wish
that we were back in Glen Arbor as we are getting to be afraid for our
Lives on account of the Fires.   you say in your Letter that there are two
Boats going down to G.A. for Wood and then they are coming up to
Chicago if you can try to come up on them   that is if you are not
otherwise engaged   come up and go home with us as I have a Little Pet
Dog and I would like you to come up here and take care of   it is so large
that you can put it in your pocket   but that is not all that I want you to
come for   I want you to come so you will be company for us   that is if
you dont have any person that you have to take care of and keep
company with.   you say that would {not} let me go away again in a great
hurry if I do come   I dont know about that   I may come Back again and
learn to be a cigar Maker as I have had the offer of Learning the Tobacco
Trade.   Saturday last my Ma and Myself went up Town to get me a pair
of Shoes she caught cold in one of her eyes and she can hardly see to do

any kind of work. I agree with you that the Married Folks are having Gay Times also the young Unmarried Folks Oh! I almost forgot to mention that there was a very large fire this morning at four oclock A large Hotel and a stable that was attached to it and 24 horses the buildings were burned to the ground and everything that was in it but the Human Beings were burnt the Horses were all burned to death and there was another one this morning nine oclock. Your watch keeps splendid time I had to get it cleaned and regulated the Watch Maker said that it had not been cleaned for a great while. I had forgotten to mention it when ever I would write untill this time I meant to look what time it was and I saw it hanging up by the clock, the watchmaker showed me some silver chains and wanted me to buy one for the watch they are splendid chains for Five dollars if I had the money to spare just at that time I dont know but I would have got one that he showed me. I sent the ledgers and a Chicago paper no more at present write soon our regards to all. Yours sincerely Maitie Boizard

Excuse all my poor writing and mistakes as I am in a great hurry Ettie two more fires since I wrote my letter Ettie

From Marietta to Charlie

Chicago
March 2nd /68
Monday Afternoon

Dear Friend Charlie
I rec'd you wel. Letter dated the 20th of Last month I was very happy to hear that you were all well and enjoying yourselves as this leaves us at present you spoke of a man being shot over in Almira that is to bad I am sorry also Mr Tobin is Dead I pity his poor Family but misfortunes never come alone in this world. I presume that you all had a gay Time the 22nd of Last Month. It seems more like Winter today than it has since we have been here. it snowed all day yesterday and all night I guess that the Winter is just commencing you spoke of a Party over at Freemans I hope that you all enjoyed yourselves which you did I presume you say that you wished I had been there if I had been I should not have been in Attendance for I know that I should not have been welcomed and I never go where I am not welcome. you say that

this is **Leap year** and that the Young Ladies of Mich will engage their partners well I shall have leave that for Minnie to do as I dont know whether I shall be there or not. if I am I dont know what I shall but but I think that I shall be a Tobacconist or a Cigar Maker. I wonder why Mrs Tucker does not write I have written once to her and ever to Willie and have not rec'd an answer from either. I am glad that the House has not been disturbed and hope that nothing will be disturbed.

It is snowing again just as hard as it can snow but I like to see it snow I rec'd a letter from Sara Coggshell they are all well at present or were when she wrote her letter she is enjoying herself this winter excuse all mistakes as I am in a hurry and have to write fast I have rec'd Five very Pretty Valentines this year, but not one of them came from Glen Arbor. I know where they came from. I presume that the Valentines flew quite rapidly in Glen Arbor this year. Well I have nothing more to add at present My Parents send their Love to all enquiring Friends and to your Folks also My kind regards to all write at your leisure Yours respectfully Ettie

To Her Friend Chas.if permitted to call him so
please excuse all mistakes and poor writing.May B

From Marietta to Charlie

Chicago
March 14th/68
Saturday Eve.

Dear Friend Chas.
Your kind and welcome Letter dated the 27th of last month came to hand last Monday I must beg pardon for not answering it sooner but we have had company from Milwaukee for over a week. "Mrs Tator" she went up North last night to Menasha & Fond Du Lac Wis. I am very glad to hear that you are all well as this leaves us at present. I think instead of you apologizing for writing such poor Letters it ought to me for I never wrote so poorly in my life before. you say that I know that you never Hug or Kiss the Girls no I know that you never did but I dont know what you do this winter as I am not present to know I dont know about breaking any persons Heart if I should try to mend any of these young Gents Hearts for I am not sure it ever was mine to Break if I was sure I could tell a little better. you wished to know how my Pa's health was

this winter it has been quite well with the exception of colds and I rather
guess that is prevailing through-out the Country. My Ma is not near so
well she feels rather blue and wants to get home as she thinks her health
would improve if she were there   but I wont say when we will be home
as I dont know I for my part am as well as usual   but that is not so well.
I rec'd that Silver ring it was so large for me that I could not wear it so
my Ma wears it as it is just right for her. I presume that Frank got the
Valentine and note it is rather strange that your Ma has not rec'd those
collars that I sent I am quite sorry. I hear that it is reported around that
George Getchele is married to Miss Charity Brotherton I wish them
good luck and happiness I presume that you all had a Gay Time at the
Leap Year party at Mr Caleb Millers I attended a Sociable for the
Progressive Lyceum last week and had a splendid time   I will send you
the programme. I am a member of the **Lyceum** they are going to have a
Grand Ball on the Anniversary of the **Lyceum** which is the 31st of
March. I am not certain whether I shall attend or not it is just as I feel
on the occasion. The weather is quite warm here it is just like Summer it
is so pleasant. well every person has gone to bed or retired I should say
excepting myself and it is getting to be quite late. How are your Parents
this Winter Spring or whatever it is   for I dont know   well I guess that I
shall have to close My Folks send their kind regards my respects to all
write at your leisure Your Sincere & True Friend May B

My Pa sent your Pa a Paper

From Charlie to Marietta

Glen Arbor
Mar 18th 1868
Wednesday Evening

My Dearest Ettie
I received your Letter dated March 2nd and was glad to hear from you.
You say it seems more like winter there than it has before. I hope that
winter is not agoing to last much longer up there for it is more like
summer here than like winter   I saw four Robins today for the first this
spring that is a pretty shure sine *(sign)* of spring   the Folks are
beginning to make some sugar. it is not very plenty yet but I presume by
the time you get this there will be <u>gobs</u> of it (as Gramps says) gramp
often speaks of you and your mother   he often asks when you are

coming home I say Oh about next summer. he comes up to read the
Ledgers every week and he says Well Charly how is the gall *(gal)* I say
Oh she is well and lovely he says that is the kind. I talk of getting me
a suit of Broad Cloth and some think we are going to Be Married -shure-
in the spring when you get home I tell them of course we are agoing to
Be Married. So we are agoing to Be Married. aint we <u>my Dear Ettie</u>.
You spoke about the <u>girls</u> Engaging <u>partners</u> you said you would leave
that for Min to do now Dear E. you know that min freeman is my
Worst Enemy and I never would go with her. if it was to save her life.
My <u>Dear</u> Ettie I would like your company the fourth of July I thought I
would ask if we <u>were</u> engaged so no one could get you away from me
any way. <u>My Dear Ettie</u> you spoke of learning to make cigars. Please
dont think of staying at Chicago if you should learn the trade. Be shure
and come here in the spring I suppose you will begin to think about
starting for glen A. by the time you get this Letter.   Oh Ettie I had a
splendid Dream about you last night. I thought that we was married and
was haveing a gay time I dreamed that I was in Chicago three night
running and was with you Every time it must be that I am comeing up
to Chicago dont you think so I know that I would like to come up and
will try to come. My Dear Ettie I have bought me a gold Watch I
bought it today it is quite a nice one. My Dear you spoke about getting
some Valentines but not one of them came from Glen. I feel ashamed
for to ask you to Excuse me but there was not a Valentine to be got in the
County nor at Traverse so Chat. B says I tryed to get one to send to you
But never mind I will make it all right with some other presant you
wonder why Mrs Tucker dont write she says she has wrote and expects
an answer my Dear Ettie this is all at presant   look on the first page
My folks send their love to all. mother says that your *{house}* looks
splendid Please Write soon I remain your own Charley for ever <u>my</u>
<u>love to you my Dear From your true one Chas. Fisher   To My Dear</u>
<u>Little Wife Ettie</u>

Please Excuse all mistakes and Poor Writing.
Charles E. Fisher.

<u>From Marietta to Charlie</u>

Chicago
March 22nd/68
Monday Afternoon

My Dear Charlie

Your kind and welcome letter dated the 11th of this month came to hand
this morning and you may be sure that I was quite happy to hear from
you and that you were enjoying good health. so you can not tell whether
you will be up this Spring or not I shall give you our address it is 195 S
Canal Street Bet. *{between}* West Jackson and W VanBuren upstairs so
if you should come you would know exactly where to come. but come if
you can for I should like to see you and I want you to come and see what
a Fine City we are in. your Pa has been here and he can tell you all about
it. you think that you would put your arms around me and kiss me if
you were to see me and you say that we would have a good talk   what
kind of a talk is that   yes I know what it is in the spring especially in the
country   My Dear Charlie you may tell your Ma that my Mother has
had one of those spells with her Heart it was the worst one she ever had
I thought that she would not live until morning it was last Saturday night
that she was so sick My Pa was frightened more than I was   for he never
saw her in one of those spells   she says if she lives to get up to Glen
Arbor she would like you to save her a piece of Maple Sugar if you
please for she feels as though she could relish a small piece. you spoke
of a pet Dogy *{doggy}* that I had   he was stolen from the house a short
time ago a nasty old yaw yaw (Dutch woman) stole it and carried it off
and sold it before I knew it was gone. but I dont know but that I shall get
another one   his name was Pinky he was cream color and his fur was
curly he was just as pretty and hansome *{handsome}* as he could be.
There are not quite so many Fires as there were but still there are a few.
My Pa says that he will send us on the first or nearly the first Boat but if
any one should ask you tell them that you dont know   but remember
that the story will not rest on your head   I am willing it should rest on
mine   I have not been feeling very well for a few days back. I have had
to take care of a sick lady she has been sick going on three weeks and I
have had to take care of her   she has the *{?})* or Fever of the Lungs and
my Mother not being very well I have had to be doing the work in our
rooms and then in hers so you see that I have been between two fires and
now I dont feel so very well myself   I shall do well if I can stand it.
Dear only knows when she will get well   I hope that you will excuse this
poor writing as I have to write hurriedly hoping to hear from you soon.

192

I remain your True L.W.E
To Charles E. Fisher

That Lady is in rather poor circumstance and not able to hire a nurse and
we could not see her suffer they have been living in this house about
three weeks and she has been sick most ever since they moved.

From Charlie to Marietta

Glen Arbor
April 1st 1868
Wensday Eve.

My Dearest Ettie
I received your most kind and welcome letter which I have been so long
wating for. I am so glad that you overlooked those falsehoods. Oh My
Dear if I could only see you to tell you how I felt. I cant express my
feelings with a pen and ink *(Not signed, but from Charlie)*

From Marietta to Charlie

Chicago
April 7th/68
Monday Eve.

My Dearest Charlie
I rec'd your welcome Letter dated the 26th of March and you very be sure
that I was very happy to hear that you were all well as this leaves us at
present. I am so lonely here that I dont know what to do with myself but
hope that it wont be long before I can see you. I wish I had been there
when you sugared off but I dont thing that I should eat any You know
yourself that I dont care much for 'Sugar" but then I could see you Sugar
off. I am sorry to hear you speak as you do about coming up here but I
do realy hope that you will be able to come, for I want to see you very
much. Tell your Grampa that I am very much obliged to him for that
Kiss but I will tell you what you must do when ever you want to kiss any
one. you must kiss the one that you Love the best I will tell you who it
is if I only knew but you know that I dont and of course cannot tell I
will have to be like E- Ayres wait and see. you say that you often
dream that we are married and having Gay Times what put a thot in to
your Head pray tell I rather think that your Heart must be diseased a

193

Little Bit at Least with Love. If I was there I should sing the song to you of "<u>Oh</u>! <u>My Heart goes Pit-Pat Pit-Pat</u> " I dont think that I shall Learn the Trade of Cigar Making as it would take me at least six months to get so that I could make them good   if I were intending to stay in Chicago I think that I should learn as it is clean and easy work.   My Dear here are a couple pieces of Poetry "viz" "Two Brides" and "Wooing and Winning" I would like you to tell me which Bride is the Best   which one would suit your taste the best the 1st or 2nd I will tell you which one Suits me the best the last one. What do you think of the other Piece. Well I am Sleepy as it is getting quite late I hope you will excuse this Poor writing I know it is not very good any of it - but it is the best I can do My ma says that she wishes that she was at home for she misses her little home very much   although it is humble I dont know which misses it the most Ma or Me. well I can not think of any thing more just now I guess that I shall have to close for I can hardly see what I am writing My Folks send their Love to all   My Love to you My Dear C-.
Your Little Wife Ettie
From Ettie Boizard

To My dear Charlie Fisher

P.S. if you write again direct your Letter to Maitie E Boizard in care of my Pa at 167 Randolph Street for we may not be here then and if you direct it in care of my Pa he can send it to me for we may start the 20th of this month or the last.   Ettie

They are painting the Propellers and the **City of Boston** is most done I guess that they will all be ready to start soon. My Mothers eyes still keep sore and they will as long as we live near this mill. I rec'd a letter from Sarah Coggeshell. Maitie B.   May B.

<u>From Eleanor & Marietta to Oliver</u>

Glen Arbor
June 13th/68
Saturday Night

My Dear Oliver,
We are well and hope these few lines will find you the same. I dont know what to make of it for I don't receive any Letters   we have rec'd

but one since we came home and that is six weeks tonight. I will send this by Mrs. Clark, she is going to call at the Store. Will you please send us some Flour as we are allmost out   we were out but we borrowed some from Mr. Tucker. the weather has been quite favorable for the crops. you had better not put the letters on the N.T. for there is a regular Lake Shore Mail just put them in the Office and then we can get sooner no more at present write soon Yours truly E. M. Boizard

P.S. Ettie has not been so well for the last week   the last two nights I have been up untill 11 oClock

From Eleanor & Marietta to Oliver

Glen Arbor
June 23rd/68

My Dear Father
We rec'd your welcome Letter a few days ago and we were very sorry to hear that you were so unwell. but hope by the time these few lines reach you that you will be well. I rec'd that Parcel. I was pleased very much with the Shoes they were a very Good fit. I wish that you would try and send us in a Barrel of Flour if you could   for we have had to borrow twenty six pounds from Mrs Tucker. the Barrel that we did bring home was not near full and it was not packed any either. we want Butter & Lard also   we use more Bread stuff than we would if Potatoes were Plentifull   there are none that a person can buy as there was such a Failure of the Potatoe crop last season. I have not had a Spell with my Heart since we came home. Goods and Provisions are just as high here as they were during the War and any how they dont have any thing in the store. My Eyes are very weak yet   we will be here eight weeks next Saturday I thought that you were not going to write any more   we have just rec'd two letters since we have been here, if we had not heard from you when we did we would have sold out and come up to Chicago again tell Bertha and Mary Fink that I will write to them in my next or when I can get time tell Lizzie Hass also when you see her. I shall have to draw this to a close as it is getting late it is now ten oClock   no more at present write soon. Yours Truly E. M. Boizard M. E. Boizard

<u>From Eleanor and Marietta to Oliver</u>

Glen Arbor, Michigan
June 25th /68

My Dear Father

We rec'd a Letter and Box yesterday but I don't know how long they were at the Dock Mr Tucker brought them up from Town we were very glad to get the provisions as we were all out of everything but a Little Ham. we were glad to hear also that you are getting Better. you say that the weather has been quite warm in Chicago it has been quite warm here also and then again it has been quite cool nights and mornings it is quite chilly now. you must not worry about Ettie for she is feeling much Better than she was although it is true about spots in her cheeks when she first came back she commenced to get poor and she did not feel well either and every afternoon there would be a purplish red spot come in her cheeks but now she is beginning to eat more and feel better I did think that she was getting the consumption but I guess she is not it was because she did not feel well. Charity Brotherton will be married day after tomorrow to Mr. George Gettchels Ettie to be Bridesmad for her. Oh! Gracious what a pest the Mosquitoes and Gnats are they pester the Life out of a Person. if you should see Lizzie Haas tell her that Ettie rec'd that Parcel and she is very Much obliged to her that she will write as soon as she can get time as she is quite Busy now I wonder why she did not write a letter and send it when she sent the parcel. So Bertha is married when you see her congratulate her for us both and tell her Ettie will write a letter to her before long or after the Fourth we will not pay Mrs Tucker the Flour that we owe her out of this for it will take half of it. Give our Love to Mary Fink and tell her that I shall write after the Fourth of July and then I will have some news to write. we don't intend to sell this place unless we are compelled to as long as we can get anything to eat the lot is all growing up to Berry Bushes and I am not able to cut them down no more at present write soon. Your Truly
Eleanor M Boizard
Mary Etta Boizard

Chicago
October 29th 1868

Miss M. E. Boizard
By request of Mr Boizard, my old friend, I beg leave to inform you, that
he has been sick for the last two weeks and not been able to perform his
usual work, he has cough or very hard cold, and this in connection with a
slight fever made him unable to leave his room for 4-5 days. He is
getting better now however and will commence to work again next
Monday, when he will also tend to your request about Provisions &c.
You need not be anxious about him, because as I told you, he is all right
now, and if there is anything that he wants he is in good hands here.
I am Madam, very Respectfully
Your Obed't Servant
Philip Miduen

Glen Arbor
Nov. 3rd 1868

Mr Boizard   Dear Sir
As I have an opportunity to Send A Letter up to Chicago I thought I
would Write you A few Lines letting you know that I am well Also Mrs.
Boizard and Ettie is All well. Mr. Boizard Mrs Boizard Has not Heard
from you only what Mr Goffart told her, in over a month   she has
written rec'd no Answer. She Has Been Expecting a Box for some time
she did not Know But it had gone by on some other Boat Mrs. Boizard
says she is going to go out there if she don't hear from you in two weeks.
I tell her that she must stay here this winter any way or else leave Ettie
here this winter   I tell her we would take Good care of her. Well Mr.
Boizard I have not much time to write for the boat is most ready to start.
I hope this will find you well. Please excuse mistakes and poor writing,
Please Write soon. From your Friend   Charles E. Fisher

Please send A letter Back on this Boat if convenient.

From Eleanor and Marietta to Oliver

Glen Arbor, Michigan
Nov 3rd 1868

Dear Father

I shall hand this to the Capt as he is going off to Chicago, I would like you to let us know what we are to do   write and send a letter by him and let us know wether we will stay here this winter or come up to Chicago as we can not stand the suspense much longer   If I don't soon hear you may look for me. write as soon as you can and send it by the Capt no more at present Yours & c. E M Boizard   Ettie Boizard

From Eleanor and Marietta to Oliver

Glen Arbor, Michigan
Nov 15th 1868

My Dear Father

We rec'd the letter that Philip wrote and I was just answering it when I heard that there was some Freight up at the other Dock for us and I thought that I would not answer it untill we got it home   we got it yesterday and we were glad to receive it as we were just out of everything   my shoes suited me very much but they are rather large   I wish that Ettie had a pair of such good Leather as hers have got so that they leak badly   if you get her a pair get Lizzie Haas to try them on Ettie is going to send a letter to her in your letter and 50 cts to get an apron   hand the money to her if you can   you had better send her a pair and send her chain & pin whether they are mended or not, the apron is not for us   it is for one of the girls on the hill, we owe eighty lbs of Flour I would like to have you send us some cornmeal if you can before the Boats quit running, we were getting ready to come out as we were out of provisions   I was just going to sell the Furniture when the Freight came, we will have to buy some Potatoes, as we have only three bushels   there is three inches of snow and it very cold here all the time
no more at present write soon   Yours & c. E.M. Boizard
M.E. Boizard

From Eleanor and Marietta to Oliver

Glen Arbor, Michigan
November 18 1868

My Dear Father
We rec'd your welcome letter yesterday Charlie brought it over, I had answered your other one and sent it by Boat I am sorry to hear about your Cough you must try to get something for it.   if you don't get anything else get Licorice root and chew it, I shall look for a Letter every two weeks if I don't get one than I shall think that you are sick, we shall try to get along the best that we can   I am quilting a quilt for Mrs Brotherton   I guess it will be about two dollars. Ettie has a dreadfull time with her face last week it was swollen so that she could hardly see out her eyes, she has got her feet wet so much lately she could go out of the house hardly Why don't Mrs Fink write me. Old kittie and a kitten they all sleep together the Old Cat is larger than Pinky   he is playing with the kitten now   no more at present   write soon yours truly
E.M Boizard   M E Boizard

From Emma Bridges Brown to Marietta

Gila City AT
Nov 22 1868

my dear Eta
i set down to write you a few lines after so long a silence but dear Eta i am sure when you hear why i did not write you will excuse me. the last time i wrote i was in **fort Macdowl**   right after i had to go to **camp reno** and i was allways moving after that all the time   my baby was born the 11 of aprill and died 29 of August and dear Eta i felt so unhapy i could not write to you   dear Eta you could not tell how bad i felt   it was a litel *{little}* girl she was so pretty and i loved her so much but then you cannot tell a mothers feelings and i hope with all my heart dear Eta you will never have to go through the same trial of losing a child   her name was Emma Alice she had dark blue eyes and Auburn hair. we are discharged now and keep a store here and are doing well   in 3 years we will have a great deal of money and then we will go in Califorina to setel *{settle}* down. for life i hope. i supose you are married by this time   i do wish you would send your picture   i want to see how you look. i have asked so often and you have never sent it. my mother is in **fort yuma** yet   i am 18 miles from them. tell your Ma when ever we are together she is

allways talking about her and wishing she was with her. father is geting prety old now dear Eta i often wonder if we will ever meet again   i hope so. by the time you get this leter it be chrismas i wish you all a happy chrismas and many of them   i wish i was some where i could send you some token of my love for you. believe dear Eta i always regard you as a sister you know we allways opened our hearts to each other about our biter *{bitter}* troubels   dear Eta i want you to answer this leter and send a great long one   for you know how long it has since i herd from you. i will answer every leter you write for i am living all alone and nothing to do and there is no danger of me moving for the next 3 years. i wish you would write every 2 weeks. if you posibly can. i have got tommy living with *{me}* he is geting quite a big boy   he don't forget you yet   i have writen a long leter   i am sure you will be tired before you get to the end Eta if you think you could send me a mourning veil i wish you would   i canot get out here and i will pay you the price   i am in black for my baby give my love to your ma and pa and kiss them for me and dear Eta except my love Edwin sends his regards   direct your leter to Mrs Edwin A Brown **Gila City Arizona Teteritory** i remain your friend and sister Emma

dear Eta   acept this pencil as a chrismas gift Emma
never mind the veil

From Austin Newman to Oliver

Beaver Island
Nov 26th/68

Friend Boizard
As you will see by the date of this your humble Servant is on the Island known as "New Ireland" because of the great number of the Natives of that green Isle resident here   Whiskey is very plentifull so are Potatoes so are **Rows** and **ructions**. But that is enough of the "Greeks" (they speak their native Language it sounds beautifull) The Propeller Potomac being in here this morning I thought I would drop or write you a few lines I came over here with the Schooner "Burty Mac" she is 36 foot - keel She is a large open Sail Boat which Charley and I have bought for pleasure as well as profit. She is a very little Boat I came over with 25$ worth of freight and have been here 8 or 9 weeks and have made about 100$ would have made more but weather too stormy I got tired working

200

on the land and was wishing for some such business for a change and to get some cash for this Winter having been pretty well drained of the aforesaid commodity by payment of mortgage but as I said before the weather has not been very favorable. Concerning the "loved Ones" at Home I received a Letter from Ettie and returned an answer just before I left. The Young Lady did not say whether they were going to Chicago or not this Fall. I had a pretty good time at G.A. last 4th and when navigation closes I would like and will I think, pay the Folks a visit. I will try to be with them about Christmas and New Years. I hope youre enjoying yourself and have good health. I have been very busy the past Summer or season and so have you I suppose. My health has not been bad   Well the Steamer is going   I will write again soon   Please answer this   Goodbye   Austin C. Newman

From Eleanor & Marietta to Oliver

Glen Arbor
Jan 8th/1869

My Dear Father
Yours of the 20th and 26th of Dec. are now before me. we were glad to hear that you were well   we are well with the exception of cold but most - every person has that. we would not have known that it was Christmas here if we had not attend a party Christmas Eve. Charlie took Ettie and of course I went with them. I am glad to hear that you have found your Brother's name *{could possibly be 'home'}* you spoke of writing to him and sending Etties Picture I should not send it until you hear from him as he might not receive your letter. you wished to know the particulars I have got my wood paid for so far the hauling and cutting   I have earned 8 eight dollars by sewing for Brothertons. and the Boys cut my wood   we live as saving as we possibly can. you wished to know whether Austin was here spending the Holidays. he did not come. times are dull here as well as there. Ettie rec'd a letter from Emma Bridges or Brown and she sent Ettie some Gold Pencils I will send the letter in my next. She and her Husband are keeping Store at **Gila City** they are out of the army now. Mrs Bridges is at **Ft. Yuma** eighteen Miles from Emma. Ettie is going to send her Photograph to her. She has lost her Little girl she did not say what ailed it. What is the price of Print and Muslin a person can get eleven yds of Calico at Traverse City   no more at present   write soon

Yours Truly E.M. Boizard M.E. Boizard

Get me a mourning veil not a lace one. get Mary to box it.

From Eleanor & Marietta to Oliver

*The following letter is written on the bottom of Emma Brown's
November 22nd 1868 letter. Eleanor & Marietta sent Emma's letter out
to Oliver in order for him to read it and they wrote a note on the end of
it. Based on the contents of the following note, it was written, January
20, 1869.*

I have a very bad cold and I cough a great deal. provisions are very high
Sugar that is the color of Molasses they sell for 18cts a pound. Day
before yesterday was my birthday I was forty one the veils that I send
for are for Emma she lost her little girl and she is in mourning, you spoke
of Mary Fink getting married I think she is rather young to get married
she is not near as old as I am and I think that I am to young to get
married yet. we are getting along as well as we can you spoke of me
being a nice young Lady Charlie told me to tell you I am you imagined
just right I am getting poor just as I did last spring no more at present
write soon yours Truly E.M. Boizard M.E. Boizard

From Eleanor & Marietta to Oliver

Glen Arbor
Feb 4th 1869

My Dear Father
Yours of the 18th & 21st of last month are now before me we were glad
to hear from you and that you are well as this leaves us at present but
Ettie has been troubled with the Ear and Toothache a great deal here
lately for the last three days and nights she as be {has been?} so that she
could not sleep a great deal. but it is better now we rec'd the four
dollars also this week last Mail we rec'd the paper and shoe Laces and
we were glad to get them as were out of them they have the short cotton
ones down here at the Store they are very rotten I went to put one in my
Shoes and it broken in three places before I got my shoe tied. The snow

is very deep it is about three foot deep and last week the ground was bare in a great many places   up at the other dock they are drawing wood on wagons   the weather had been very fine for about three weeks but when it did commence to storm it stormed as hard as it could   you spoke of getting us a dress apiece and shoes if you get my dress *{?}* one get twelve yds of *{?}*   dark and an near plain as you can get   if it is figured get the figures small and Etties dress you *{ I can't read the writing as it is on a fold in the paper. There are about three words missing. }* it yourself   if you get her shoes get them high in the instep and as high the tops as you can   get twos   and you know my number 5 fives.   and you had ought to also get stuff for Shirts.   if you do get it   fine unbleached shirting yd wide and let me make them   where you buy them already made one costs as much as two would that I could make and then they are not near as good   and I would rather make them   I would rather make your pants vests and all but your coats   Who did Mary Marry   what has become of Betty & Morris   well I guess this is all that I can think of at present   this is my last sheet of paper and I can not write any more.   write soon and give our regards to all enquiring friends. E. M. Boizard   M. E. Boizard

Feb 9th

The snow was so deep that I could not go to town to get an envelope and have not seen any person that I could send   Ettie has been troubled with the tooth and ear ache for over a week and she could not go on account of the deep snow.
E. M. Boizard

From Eleanor & Marietta to Oliver

Glen Arbor
Feb. 18th 1869

My Dear Father
Yours of the 30th of Jan came to hand by this weeks Mail   also two dollars   we were glad to hear that you were well as this leaves us at present   The weather is rather changeable   one day the Sun shines the next it Snows and Blows and Thaws   the snow is quite deep   there was a time that it was all bare ground and those that were drawing wood had to quit.   There was a Grand Concert down at Todds Hall and a good party after the concert there were two cutters and a Stage Load come through from Traverse City   all went off nicely.   now I'll change the subject and

write more about home   the $2 that you sent this week we got $1 worth
of meat & 50 cts Sugar a quarter pound of tea at $2.00 a pound and you
see that took it all.   I wish that you would Send me money to get a
Barrel of Flour. it is $12.00 a Barrel and when we get it by the small
quantities it cost us about $14.00 we have bought seven doll's worth
I earned three dolls by quilting and took my pay in Flour and I paid $4.00
in money for some. we have to pay two dolls $2.00 for Tea that is not
fit to drink I will be glad when Spring comes so that we can get some
provisions in from outside   all the provisions that you sent in in the fall
are gone. I would give anything for a piece of beef we have not seen
any this winter. did you write to your Brother Pete. Charlie and Ettie
went to the concert he wanted me to go with them but I did not I did
not have anything decent to wear and beside I did not feel like going.This
is about all that I think of at present   write soon Give our regards to all
enquiring Friends. Yours as Ever E. M. Boizard Marietta Boizard

 To Mr. John O Boizard
93 South Canal St Chicago Ills

From Eleanor & Marietta to Oliver

Glen Arbor
Feb 25th 1869

My Dear Father
Yours of the 7th & 14th came in this weeks Mail. we rec'd the Veils and
three dollars Ettie rec'd a Letter from Mary Fink, it used to be. the
weather is very cold colder then it has been this winter and the snow is
very deep. you Said that you were dreaming about the House it was
very near true what you dreamt the plastering is all off and it is very
cold we can hardly keep warm with the cooking Stove you had ought to
try {as it is ?} coming on Spring to get a Heating Stove if it was
nothing but a Box Stove get a Second hand one and you will get it
much cheaper than you would get it next Fall anyhow we will have to
get one {?} Fall for we can not do with just the cooking Stove.
Mr Decker was burned out about four weeks ago they did not save any
thing one of the children a boy of five years was up stairs and he
found some Matches and got to playing with them and set the house on
fire. Mrs. Dorsey has a young daughter and the Family has got the
whooping cough. Flour is thirteen doll's per barrel and it is very poor

this has been a very hard winter on most every one. Rossman charges so high for what little he has in the store he has not got any thing in the store only as he goes through with the stage and brings it from Traverse he charges 20cts for lb of pork and it is all Fishy this is all at present Give our regards to all enquiring Friends write soon. Yours & c.
E. M. Boizard M. E. Boizard

From Eleanor & Marietta to Oliver

Glen Arbor
March 12th /69

My Dear Oliver
Yours of the 24th of last month came in this weeks Mail and we were glad to hear from you we rec'd the stationary and newspapers also two doll's. you spoke of the winter just commencing in Chicago it is about the same although for two days past it has been quite fair the snow is very deep the deepest it has been this winter I am in hopes that it will soon go off so that the Boats will run if not we will starve as there is nothing that we can get at the store I will get wood cut with part of the money that you sent me I have earned enough to get wood chopped until now   I wish that you would send us some provisions on the first boat and when you do send us some alcohol and camphor gum as we are out Ettie used a great deal on her Face. but I don't think she will be bothered with it any more for she had it pulled today Mr Perry was down at Mr. Tuckers and he came over and pulled it yesterday she was almost crazy with it and last night she did not sleep any with it
I presume when the snow does go off it will all go at once. send us some Butter & Lard the first chance that you can get as there is none to be got a dollars worth of meat when we can get it is not much larger then the dollar itself it is not very often that we can get meat there is none in the stores only as Rossman brings it from Traverse in the stage you spoke of getting us each a pair of Shoes get them pegged as they wear the best here in the Land. Mrs. Dorsey had a Little girl baby and it died with the whooping cough. the whole family had it Charlie has bought the Spring and five acres of land for sixty doll's he is going to build a house on it next spring coming if we don't get some new clothes we will have to {faint ?} and go naked. how do you stand with the firm no more at present write soon our regards to all enquiring friends

205

Yours Truly E.M. Boizard   M. E. Boizard

P.S. Burdicks Grist & Saw Mill was burned to the ground about two
weeks ago.

From Eleanor & Marietta to Oliver

Glen Arbor
March 18th/69

My Dear Oliver
Yours of Feb 24th and March 5th came in this weeks mail also a paper
the money $4. we were glad to hear that you were well as this leaves us.
The weather has moderated somewhat   I hope that we are going to have
a change in the weather now. Ettie went down town today and got some
tea and had to pay 18 shillings per lb   she wanted to get kerosene and
meat but they did not have any.   and they don't have any Flour to sell   if
they do sell any they wont sell more than 25 lbs and then it is not good
but the Flour at the Mill is cheaper and then it is good. when you send
in some provisions send three or four bars of Soap as soft soap hacks our
skin so to wash with it   you spoke of us coming to Chicago another
winter   we will have to get something to wear as we have nothing that is
fit   our clothing all gave out at once. Ettie and I have earned $18 this
winter in quilting   and out of it all we have got each of us an apron for
everything is so high. you spoke of Big Charlie and Little Frank it used
to be that but if it is anything it is Big Frank and Little Charlie for Frank
is Larger now then Charlie. Old Mr. Heeth is dead   he died with the
heart disease last week. he was Father in law to that Mr. Harrison that
was killed that I told you about   that was killed by a Tree. Well that is
all at present   Give our regards to all inquiring Friends   write soon
Yours & c. E.M. Boizard M. E. Boizard

Mr. John O. Boizard 93 S. Canal Street Chicago, Ill's

<u>From Eleanor & Marietta to Oliver</u>

Glen Arbor
April 2nd 1869

My Dear Oliver

Yours of the 14th & 20th of last month came in this weeks mail   the money also   we were glad to hear that you were well as this leaves us at present   the weather has moderated here   the snow is going off very fast last Saturday we could just see the top of a stump at the corner of the house and Monday we could see all the stumps in the clearing   some of our Neighbors are making sugar   I don't think that there will be very much made as the season will not be good for sugar   there have been two boats in this year   one from Chicago and I don't know   whether the other is from Chicago or Mil. and I believe they expect three or four every day. we rec'd a Letter from Emma Brown this week they are all well and she says they would all like to hear from you   they are at **Gila City** and her Fathers at **Fort Yuma.**   when you send in some thing send some factory for shirts so we can make them and don't go and buy shirts ready made for they are more expensive and then they are not half made. anyhow I would rather make them.   you Spoke of Charlie keeping **Bachelors Hall**   I asked Ettie about it she says that he is in about a year from her next birthday May 18th.   She says by that time you may expect a Son full grown about 21 years of age   as she will take pity on Charlie and help him to keep Bachelors Hall   She says that you must come home before his house is raised and help pick out the place that it will be built on and anyhow we want to see you.   how did it happen that the Family were Poisoned   was it done by Accident or did they take it themselves.   the next letter I write I will send you Emma's letter   send me in a paper of Lettuce and the long green cucumbers and also a paper of cabbage the Large Drum Head   don't get the early York as it will not amount to anything here. This is all at present   write soon
Yours until Death   E. M. Boizard   M. E. Boizard

Mr. John O. Boizard   93 S. Canal Street   Chicago Ill's

From J.E. Fisher to Oliver

Glen Arbor
April 3/69

Dear Sir

I take pleasure in introducing to you, the bearer of this note Mr. Henry Fisher. Mr Fisher lived for Several years at North Unity (Dutch Town) and carried on a Wood Dock there, but now lives in your City. he has been Spending the Winter here and now returns to Chicago I Send this to let you know that your Family and ourselves are all well– we have had a pleasant winter and good **Sleighing** for business in fact the Sleighing is good now, and we are beginning to grumble that we are having too much of a good thing, we wanted to See bare ground– Mr Fisher will return here in a few days if you wish to Send any communication by him he will bring it with pleasure Hopeing you are well and doing well I am your truly J.E. Fisher

From Eleanor and Marietta to Oliver

Glen Arbor, Michigan
Apr 15th 1869

My Dear Oliver

Yours of March 28th came in this weeks Mail and the money also we were glad to hear that you are well as this Leaves us at present. you spoke of sending us in some provisions I will be glad of that We have earned about $21 this winter by quilting but we took our pay in Flour and such as that and also in stove wood I quilted for Brothertons and the Boys cut some stove wood for Me you spoke of Etties shoes she stands in need of them if she had them now as it is damp under foot. Mr Lloyd has finished the rails and we must try to pay him as soon as we can he made a thousand and I don't know how much he charges a hundred but it is some over a dollar if you can not send it all at once try and send about five dollars at a time as I presume that he needs it for he is talking of sending his children to an Asylum We could not do without the rails for a fence any longer for we never could raise anything on account of the cattle & pigs, and anyhow we have Lived just as Saving as we could this Winter but the two dollars that you send us a week if we had not been able to earn a little as everything is so high I will send Emma's Letter to you no more at present write soon Yours & c.
E. M. Boizard M.E. Boizard

Glen Arbor
May 8th 1869

Dear Oliver,
Yours of April 30th came to hand yesterday   also the parcel of dry Goods
Gardening Seeds and spool thread   Ettie says she likes her dress very
much   but I don't like mine   if it had been most any other color or even
a calico I should have been better suited   you hadnt ought to have got
me a black dress for me.   if I had been in mourning it would have done.
the weather is very pleasant here and it begins to look like planting. I
should have to buy potatoes for such if I can get them. they are very
hard to get as they were so scarce last season. What have become of
Bertha and Mary.   I wish that you would get that butcher knife tempered
and sharpened and send it some time when you are sending a box in   as
we have not got any kind of a knife but a cane knife to cut meat with
when we have any to cut   we cant get any down here   our hens lay
some, but we have only four   our trees look nice none are winter killed.
I think they will bear this year if every thing is not killed with dry
weather   I have been making soap   I have made a half barrel full   that
will last all summer   Send me in some ether like that Mr Costan takes as
I need to take it occasionally   if you can get hold of any book or papers
send them to us as we don't have any thing to read.   have you written
home yet. I want you to try to come home this summer if you cant come
in this first part come when it will be so warm. Charlie has taken the
Saw Mill to run all Summer   he is head Sawyer & Boss in it   he gets
$40 or $45 per month   The Neighbors Send their kind regards to you.
remember us to all inquiring Friends   write all the news   Yours & c.
E.M. Boizard   M.E. Boizard

From Eleanor & Marietta to Oliver

Glen Arbor
May 14th 1869

My Dear Oliver,
Yours of the 8th is now before   we were glad to hear from you. I hope
ere this reaches you that you will be better   you had ought to be carefull
of yourself.   you spoke of Ettie helping me   she does all that she can,
but she is getting like she was last Spring   very thin and not feeling very

well. She weighs only 103 lbs and during the winter she weighed 109 lbs Ettie & I earn all that we can but that is not very much now that we are through quilting we intend to plant all that we can if the fence was only up I think that would help. I shall try to get some meat if they have any at the store as I would like to know how it tastes. I have sawed my own wood this three or four weeks. I could get Charlie to saw it but he is working in the Mill I wish that you would send me some glue as one of the bedsteads is coming all a part and I want to fix it. we are having a great deal of rain now do you still wear flannels you had ought to wear it and not take it off Ettie rec'd a letter from Emma B she says that her Ma and Pa were three hundred miles from her and there is not another woman near her white or black. the next time that you send any provisions send some cornmeal how much is flour per barrel. write soon Yours & c. E.M. Boizard M. E. Boizard

From Marietta to Charlie

Glen Arbor
June 5th 1869

My Dear Charlie
Will you come over early tomorrow as Mr. Lloyd would like to see you he was here yesterday and he left word that he would be here early in the fore-noon if you do not come over early you scamp I will give you a Scotch Blessing. No More at present Your L W___e
Ettie Draziob *{Boizard spelled backwards}*

From Eleanor and Marietta to Oliver

Glen Arbor, Michigan
June 29th 1869

My Dear Oliver
yours of June 25th is now before me and you may be sure that I was glad to hear from you as I was very anxious about you I have not heard since the 15th of May from you. in your last - you said that you would send us a Box of provision the next week but did not and didn't write either and of course we did not know what to make of it we did not have anything in the house to eat and Charlie got us some Flour and other things for which we owe him and Mrs. Tucker let us have some Butter on credit

Ettie is very mean sick and I worried myself nearly sick by not hearing from you   you had ought to have written or had some one write if you were not able to write yourself as were sorry to hear that you hurt yourself so badly   but hope as this reaches you that you will be well   I shall take part of this ten dolls to get something in the house to eat and the other part to pay some of my Debts. Ettie rec's a Letter from Emma Brown she says her Father has rec'd an **Ordinance** Appointment at **Camp Gaston Cal.** Dr. Traplers or Tarply has charge of the company she sends her regards to you. you had ought to have a light to go through the house with at night. buy yourself a candle if they don't give you one. it has rained very much lately most every other day through June   I have tried to earn all that I could but of course I did not have much time as planting took up most of my time and another thing there is not very much that I could get to do, this is all at present   write as soon as possible as we will be anxious to hear.Yours & c. E.M.Boizard M.E. Boizard

From Eleanor and Marietta to Oliver

Glen Arbor, Michigan
Aug't 6th 1869

My Dear Oliver
Yours of July 28th came to hand by this weeks mail and you may be sure that we were glad to hear from you   also to get the money $10. as we were out of everything to eat   we hardly knew what to get for breakfast the next morning   Ettie is better now but she was sick quite a while   you speak of it being so unhealthy in Chicago   I wish that you would try to come home   if you don't stay but a week   if you don't soon come Folks will talk about you not coming. anyhow I want you to come as I have something to tell you   Charlie says if you don't come he will come after you   he says it is so long since he has seen you that he has almost forgot how you look. you would hardly know him he has changed so   Frank has changed also   Mr & Mrs Fisher are both well and send their regards to you they often wish that they could see you.   the money that you sent I shall take some of it to pay some of my debts and the rest to get something to eat. I do wish that you would get us a Barrel of Flour as I owe over 50 lbs and of course must pay for it. send me a three quart pail also a two qt pan as all my tin ware is giving out   our pails leak and we have nothing to carry milk or anything   I wish you would send me

211

Alcohol for camphor as I have none   they have some down here at Frank
Todds but is more than half water. Charlie will put up the Fence after he
get through Harvesting if we can board him. yours as ever--
E.M. Boziard   M.E. Boizard

PS be sure to come home soon

From Eleanor and Marietta to Oliver

Glen Arbor, Michigan
Aug't 23 1869

My Dear Oliver
We have not rec'd any letter from you in nearly two weeks and we are
anxious somewhat. we are well I rec'd a letter from Emma Brown she
says that they are all well   they send their regards to you   she says they
have not had any rain since January. I wish you would send us some
Flour and provisions as we are very near out of Flour   there will be
enough for just one more Baking   we got Flour with the last money we
had   when this is done I don't know what we will do unless you send us
some   I went Whortle-berrying the other day and got 15 qts
Blackberries will soon be ripe. The neighbors are Harvesting now and
they are quite Busy. some of the wheat is quite rusty this season. Mr
Tuckers folk are out of Flour nearly and we owe them 50lbs and they
would like to get it if we had it for them   when Charlie & Ettie were up
at Frankfort they had their Photograph taken and he sends one to you   I
presume you will think he is somewhat changed   the Picture is very
good of them both they could not be much better. Ettie would have
looked Better if she had a dark Dress – Charlie is here working   he is
clearing to put up the Fence he is trying to get the Fence up   to put in
some wheat this Fall for another Winters Flour and we certainly had
ought to Board him while he is working for us. No More at present
Give our regards to all, write soon Yours & c. M.E. Boizard
Ettie Boizard

send us some postage stamps if you can   Ettie

From Eleanor & Marietta to Oliver

Glen Arbor
Sept 3rd 1869

My Dear Father
Yours of the 25th of Aug. came to hand in this weeks mail   we are sorry
to hear that you are out of employment as we are out of everything to eat
but potatoes   we cannot get any butter nor meat as we have no money
what was the cause of you not working for H & M any longer.   we have
gathered whortleberries as long as they lasted but they are gone now, but
we will have to get along the best that we can.   you were very foolish
not to take up with the offer that McCarty made you   the man they hired
is there yet and gets a thousand dolls a year.   our potatoes are splendid
what we have dug of them   if it were not for them I guess we would
starve.   I don't know what to do   I am near crazy.   if we had anything to
live on we could tell you to come home and stay   if there was anything
that you could do here   but we don't know of anything.   Charlie had to
quit working as we could not Board him   he wanted to get the place
ready to sow some wheat.   we don't know whether there will be many
Blackberries or not as we have not gone berrying yet.   we have been as
little expense as we could possible be as we have not had any provisions
from you since May and but very little money.   no more at present.
write soon   Yours & c. E.M. Boizard   M.E. Boizard

From Eleanor & Marietta to Oliver

Glen Arbor
Sept 8th 1869

My Dear Oliver
yours of the third came to hand last evening   M.D. Todd handed it to
some of Mr. Fishers Folks and Charlie brought it over last night   we are
sorry to hear that you are still out of employment but hope you will soon
succeed in finding work.   if it were not for our Potatoes I don't know
what we would do as that is all that we have   but they are splendid   we
cannot boil them   we have to steam them for they are so meaty   Charlie
says that we had ought to have twenty five or thirty bushels at the very
least and that had ought to last us all winter and furnish seeds for to plant
next season   that is if we can get anything else to use with them.

213

you spoke of Etties marriage to Charlie   they were intending to get
married next May   but Charlie wants to get Married this Fall   but she
has not got underclothing or anything that she could   she is not prepared
in any way   she had some money that she earned her self   but we had to
get the last flour that we had with it   she was intending to get some
muslin to make underclothing with it.   she has not had any clothing of
any kind in two years   as for calico dresses she has none.   and I don't
want her to get married and not have anything   if I can help it   but
Charlie says he wont wait any longer than her next Birthday.   He was
twenty the 29th of Aug't.   I have about eight or ten quarts of
whortleberries dried but I don't know about Blackberries as my shoes are
so badly worn that if I were to go berrying in them there would not be
much left of them   anyhow the briars would get into my feet.   I wish
that we had some tea or coffee. come home if you can when she is
married as they both want you to.   No more at present. Yours & c.
E. M. Boizard M.E. Boizard
P.S. we will let you know when it happens.

From Eleanor & Marietta to Oliver

Glen Arbor
Sept 28th 69

My Dear Oliver
yours of Sept 20th came last week also the Barrel of Groceries which we
were very glad to get as we were out of everything   but they were not
packed very good   all the bags were broke open   Flour Tea Sugar and
Coffee were all together.   Ettie was very much pleased with her cape
but if she had known what kind it was before you sent it   she would have
had you taken it to the Dyers and had it colored Scarlet   for we could not
color it so nicely and dress it as good as they   although we could color it
if we had the Dye.   if I could get it colored she could not buy it for less
than four or five dollars   it is too good a cape for us to spoil.   I hope you
will soon succeed in getting Employment   if we had our Winter
Provisions you could come home and stay all Winter.   My Shoes I like
very well   but they would have worn better had they been calfskin   that
kind of leather don't wear as well   I was glad to get the Tea & Coffee for
I had not had any for about three weeks.   Charlie has got the Fence half
way around the clearing and it looks real nice   More like a Farm

it is getting to be real wet and cold   and the house unless it is painted up will be very cold to live in this Winter and we have no lime and don't know of any in the place   I have just finished making a bed for Strawberries about five or six yds square   I am in hopes from this next Summer to have some fruit and that will help us a long some   no more at present   write soon. Charlie sends his regards to you. Yours truly E.M. Boizard   M.E. Boizard

P.S. Did you pay for this can full of Butter or not   I guess that there was about three lbs of Butter. the can holds six pounds and was just half full.

From Eleanor & Marietta to Oliver

Glen Arbor
Oct 12th 1869

My Dear Oliver
Yours of Oct 5th came in due season   we were glad to hear that you were well as these few lines leaves us   but we were sorry to hear that you were still out of employment   but we will have to do the best we can. the weather is getting quite cold   it makes a person think of winter. you spoke of Bertha having a Baby   is it a Girl or Boy. I wish that it was so that you could come home   but we have not got provisions nor clothing for the winter   if Rossmans would buy wood it was my intention to have some cut   we would get two shillings per cord and that would be some for us. I have but two calico dresses and one of them is of two kinds where I have mended it and Ettie has but one calico dress and that is all in rags   I have not had any underclothing since you were in Springfield and we are very near naked   our stockings I ravel out some to fix others. I can not get work enough to buy a half gallon of Kerosene   times are very dull for both men and Women   along the last of this month we will have to dig the potatoes   I don't know what we will do for our Winters wood if Charlie don't cut it for us   Mr. King that is Mrs Fishers brother in law has been here for the last year   he has been {?} all the time   he has a large Family to Keep   he's been out twice to get employment but did not succeed. you know just how we are situated   couldnt you work some place for your Board and not have your Boarding running up. we rec'd a letter from Emma B this last week   she says they are getting very tired of Arizona her Father & Mother are a Hundred Miles from them at a place called **Camp Gaston** she says that they wrote to her telling her

215

what kind of a place they lived in   it is an Oak Grove and they have a
cow and chickens and they have a Farm and are getting along finely.
they like it very much.   we see Mr & Mrs Dorsey yesterday they are
well and send their regards   they are getting along nicely since they
moved on their farm.   we rec'd the paper and was glad to get   we never
sit down to a meal but we wish that you were here. I hope it will not be
very long until you can come home and stay at home   when we get to
raising more and then we will be independent. No More at present
write soon Yours as ever E.M. Boizard   M.E. Boziard

P.S. Ettie says that she has such poor pens that she can not write good.
E.M.B.

From Emma Brown to Marietta

Gila City A T *{Arizona Territory}*
Nov 8 1869

My Dear Ettie
yours of Oct 12 came to hand last night   i was Glad to hear that you was
well and enjoying yourself.   we are all well and goying *{going}* along
the same as usual you bad girl you ought to be ashamed to say Glen
arbor is lonely   i am afraid if you was in Arizona you would go crazy for
want of company.   you seem allways to have some pleasure on hand   it
has been so long since i seen much pleasure i don't know what it is   i
tell Edwin i wont know how to act if i ever go in a church again   i
believe i would Stare my eyes out if i saw a theater   he says their not
much danger.   i received a letter from my father last night they are all
well and send their love to you and your ma   they say times are dull their
{there} and plenty of rain to make it worse   while we at **Gila city** aint
had no rain for over a year   what do you think of that.   there much
difference in your age and Mr Fisher is their   Edwin will be 26 the first
of next February   he is quite an old man you see.   we have very warm
wether here now in the middle of the day.   in the mornings it is quite
cold though i think we will have a cold winter this year   i think we
shall take your mothers advice about leaving Arizona if we can
i have not much news to write so you must not expect a long letter their
a great many soldiers camped her to day going up in to Arizona   there is
a little Girl here on a visit to me   and i really believe i would rather be a
lone she bothers me to death allmost   she comes from **fort yuma** 20

miles from here   i have not received any letters from newport for a long time   whatever is the reason i received the flower seeds   and i thank you very much i shall keep them until i go somewhere where i can grow them   but i don't think i shall plant them in this country   but i shall keep them till i go somewhere else.   i have written quite a long letter to you so i must stop for it is getting late and i have to write to my Father yet   Edwin send his love to your ma and your self.   give my love to your ma and pa and accept my warmest love   Dear Ettie give our regards to Mr. Fisher   write soon and believe me to be your sincere Friend and well wisher   good bye   write soon   Emma Brown

From Oliver to Eleanor & Marietta

Chicago Ill's
Nov 18th 1869

My Dear Wife
I Send you by the Pro. **"Lawrence"** Box containing 10# Lard 10# Sugar, 10# Butter, 5# Coffee, 2# Tea, 6 yds of Domestic, 4 Hanks yarn cost $12.50 all that I could possibly spare   I had to pay my Board, my washing & mending and bought a pair of Drawers and freight, which took all   I don't Know what to do, my job will run out about 2 weeks more and then I will be out of work   I will try to hold on to the job at the U.S. Circuit Court, till about the 1st Dec. and then if the Boats run till then and me out of a Job, I think I better try to come and See you all, and be present at Ettie's wedding, what do you think of it   do you think I could Sustain through the winter   Times are so dull in Chicago I am afraid I shall be thrown on the Public for Subsistance. I might do something up there at Glen Arbor and you might help me through the winter. I dread this winter in Chicago for people are working for their Board. I may be able to raise 20 dollars by the 1st Dec'r and then if the Boats don't stop running I may come to Glen arbor.   It is true I am not well fixed as I might be but I might be worse off – I will see about your pork as soon as they commence Packing. I may bring it up with me   If you can answer this   Send by Boat if possible in order that I can make Calculations. Your Husband "Oliver"

I rec'd Gus's Letter (or rather his) I could not get the Dresses yet Oliver

217

Chicago Ill
Dec 7 '69

My Dear Wife,

I send <u>Ettie</u> a Small Box containing Buttons and Silk trimmings. I got
<u>Bertha</u> to go and get them, but She only got the Buttons, so, I undertook
to get the Trimmings myself. I went to two or three places and I could
not get the Exact pattern, So, I thought I would take the nearest I could
find, in fact I could not run about much, as my feet hurts me very much.
I have had for the last <u>two</u> weeks <u>Rheumatism</u> in both feet, about the
<u>ankles</u>   so that I could Scarcely put my feet to the <u>Ground</u>. I had to use a
Stick to get along.   I Suppose the Court will End its <u>Term</u> this week, and
I do not think, they will put us on the next term, as it is not <u>Customary</u>. I
am very much worried to think I lost the Boat   I See the "**Allegheny**"
has returned from "<u>Traverse</u>"   we have been on one Case for 3 Days, it
may last 3 Days longer. If I possibly could get up this winter I would
risk it, as I am in <u>dread</u> of this <u>winter</u>. I think a great deal about Ettie's
marriage. it Seems to me, I can hear her in her <u>Childish</u> <u>talk</u>. However
all may go well with the Blessing of the "<u>Creator</u>" I have nothing more
to <u>add</u> at present, and as it is near 9 O'Clock (Court time) I must close.
Give my best wishes to Mr. <u>Fisher</u> and <u>Lady</u> not forgetting Mr & Mrs.
Tucker also <u>Dorsey</u> and <u>Lady</u> for truly I <u>esteem</u> them <u>Highly</u> and receive
a large Share for <u>yourself</u>   Kiss Ettie for me and tell <u>Charlie</u> to use her
gently. Bye the Bye, how is the little "**Keesick**"   you don't Say
anything about him– Farewell and using the language of the <u>Orientals</u>
"**May your Shadows never be less**"   Your Husband John O. Boizard

Glen Arbor
Jan. 2nd 1870

My Dear Oliver,

Yours of Dec. 21st came in the last mail   we were glad to hear that you
were well as this leaves us at present but were sorry that you could not
get home this winter. come in May if possible and then if we live we
will have a dinner and invite in the Family, Dorseys, Tuckers, Kings &
Fishers you wanted to know why Charlie & Ettie did not get married on
New Years. they could not get ready in time and as my Birthday comes
on the 19th they thought they would get married then. they will have it

put in the Traverse Herald and send you a copy   Ettie rec'd the
trimmings and handkerchief and was very much pleased with them.
Now I must tell you how I spend our Holidays   Christmas we went over
to Mr Fishers and took dinner   in the afternoon we went downtown to
Mrs Fishers Brother in law, Mr King and spent the afternoon & evening
then came home.   New Years Eve we went to a party at Todds   had a
very good time   Frank Todd did not sell a drop of Liquor and everything
went off nicely and quietly.   I was very glad to get the money for it just
Paid my Taxes as they were due.   if you see Lizzie Haas tell her I will
write soon to her   also show her Charlies & my Photographs.   I am glad
that you got some clothing for to keep yourself warm this winter.   we
have had a great deal of Snow but it does not stay on long enough to get
deep as the weather has not been very cold.   Charlie & Ettie will be
married between 12 & 1 o'clock.   Mr. Fisher will perform the ceremony
as he is Justice of the Peace.   if you have the means get a dinner of
Oysters on that day.   she says she would tell you to drink their Health but
she says she don't want any of the Family to drink any kind of Liquors
on that day.   Emma send Ettie Gold enough for a Heavy ring   that the
gold was dug a hundred yds from their door.   see if Gus could make it
she wants it a hoop ring carved.   she don't like to send it to Traverse to
have strangers make it.   This is all at present   write soon.   The neighbors
send their regards.   Charlie & Ettie their Love.   Yours as ever
E. M. Boizard M. E. Boizard

From Oliver to Eleanor & Marietta

Chicago Ill
Jan'y 12th 1870

My Dear Wife,
Your letter dated the Jan'y 2nd came to hand yesterday, and I am pleased
to hear that you Spent your Holidays, Cheerfully. I Spent Christmas with
Gus at our Washerwoman's house   her Husband invited us and we
furnished 2 cans of Oysters and She Fried some and Stewed Some and
with other nicknacks we made out a good Dinner and Supper   but Still I
was thinking about our Log house   I would have had a better appetite if I
could have Eaten it at home with you and Ettie.   I often wonder in my
own mind, if Ever I can live home again, for it seems to me that my good
fortune has declined for Ever – At present I am doing nothing but may
have Something to do after being brought down to the Extremity, Such is
a Poor Mans fate in this world.   One Week from today, I Suppose the

wedding will take place   I think this <u>Union</u> will be a Happy one, at least I hope so.   In regard of that ring that Ettie wants made for Emma   I spoke to Gus about it but he don't work in that line, but he referred me to Mr. Zepp a <u>Jeweler</u> whom, I Seen. he told me to make a good ring and Engrave or have it <u>chased</u> it would cost from $3.50 to $4.00 but it would be a good piece of work. So should you wish to have it done you must Send the Size of it up, So he can make it to fit. I did not understand, whether <u>Emma</u> wants it for herself or whether She wants you to have it. Either way, you must Send the Money down as I have no money   Should you Send it down, I think you might put in a newspaper with your marriage announced in it, otherwise Send it in a small <u>Box</u>. I have been Expecting to get on the Jury again, but there is a change among the Judges, hence the delay. It has been raining for the last 2 days and it is very disagreeable. it gives a person the Blues. I Enclosed 3 Handkerchiefs in <u>two</u> <u>newspapers</u> for your New Years gift, did you get them or not. Tell Charlie to write immediately after the 19th Jan'y. I will close   give my best regards to all my friends and accept my fervent wishes. "Oliver"

Mr. Graef & Morris Powers sends their respects. I will see Lizzie Haas shortly. J.O.B.

<u>From Eleanor and Marietta to Oliver</u>

Glen Arbor, Michigan
January 26 1870

My Dear Father

Yours of Jan 12th came to hand last Wednesday Morning and we were glad to hear from you that you were well. we wished for you to be at home and on that day as we were married. the ceremony was preformed by Mr Fisher at half past two oclock in the presence of Mr & Mrs Tucker, also Willie   Miss Allie Baldwin a Friend of mine was the Bridesmaid   Frank Fisher was Groomsman   Mrs Fisher was also present. we had a splendid day the Sun shone all Day and everything went off nicely. mother has gone off up to the upper Dock on Business we will write when she come home. I thought I would write now and then again when Mother is at home. I should have written before this but we have been invited out ever Since we were Married. We will give a dinner in May when you come home, then it will be warm weather and we can invite our Friends. I have saved you some Wedding Cake. I wish it was so that I could send it to you but I will keep it good untill you come home The weather is quite good now Mr & Mrs Dorsey were over a short time ago they were all well and send their regards to you. We rec'd the three Handkerchiefs and think they are quite pretty. Sunday we went **sleighing** That ring that I spoke of Emma made me a present of the gold for a ring and I thought that Gus could make it. You must be sure and come home in May if possible, well I shall have to close as Charlie will write some. write soon. Your Affectionate Daughter Ettie Fisher

P.S. I will not send the Gold at present as Charlie cannot get the money for it is rather scarce here and mother has none. No more at present yours as ever Ettie Fisher

Written on the bottom of Ettie's letter

Glen Arbor Mich
Jan 26th 1870

Mr Boizard
I am Happy to Address you as Father, we was Married just one Week ago today it was A splendid Day we all wished that you might have been here. we look for you in the Spring Ettie wrote you all the particulars about the Wedding. it will be Published in the Grand Traverse Herald I will send you a copy. There is no more news at present excuse this short letter I will write more next time
Yours Truly Chas. A Fisher

From Marietta to Oliver

Glen Arbor
Feb 14th 1870

My Dear Father
Yours of Feb 3rd came in Last weeks Mail, we were glad to hear that you were well as this leaves us at present. The weather is quite cold now but for a while back it has been quite warm and pleasant but it changes a good deal I presume that ere long the people will think of making preparations for Sugar Making. we are sorry to hear that you are still

221

out of employment. Mother says she was in hope that you did have as
she would like to pay Mr. Lloyd what she owes him as he needs it. She
says she can not get hold of money enough for postage. She is well with
the exception of her Ear, it is just the same. I hope you will be able to
be at home another winter. you Spoke of the Air of Glen Arbor
promoting Health Vigor and Fat Babies. I guess it is pretty much so
but I guess that I shall not bother with them for a while. Charlie says it
is rather poor property to invest in at the Commencement of Life
especially for poor Folks. I hear of one every Little while. There was a
Little Girl born today   A Family by the house of Lowery were the
happy Parents   they have five children now the oldest is about twelve
years of age. Charlie says he will write to you soon. No more at present
write soon. Mr Fishers Folks send their regards to you. Yours as ever
Ettie Fisher

From Eleanor & Marietta to Oliver

Glen Arbor
Feb 29 1870

My Dear Oliver
Yours of the 16th came in this last weeks mail. we were Glad to hear that
you were well as this leaves us at present but my Ear is not any better.
I hope that you will go back to Heath & Milligans in the spring also that
you can work there all Summer and be at home next Winter. we are
having fine weather now. you asked if we all lived in the House, yes we
do. I am going over to Mr. Dorseys tomorrow to visit Mrs. Dorsey.
You must look very much like a Clergy man with your Stove Pipe Hat
you had ought to get a white cravat. do the women all give you the wink
since you got to look so spruce. I guess that I shall get jealous. is your
Hat white. *{there is a change of ink right here. . indicating the rest of the
letter was written at a later time.}* the weather has changed it is now
snowing but {?} then it not. Mother has gone over to Mrs. Dorseys and
has not returned yet and I don't know when she will I just rec'd a letter
from Emma they are all well and intend to leave Arizona before long.
There is not any news of importance. Charlie says he will write before
long. No More at present. write soon. Yours as ever Eleanor M.
Boizard Ettie Fisher

John O Boizard
No's 48 & 50 Lasalle St. Chicago, Ill's Care of A. Graef

From Eleanor & Marietta to Oliver

Glen Arbor
April 14th 1870

My Dear Husband,
Yours of April 2nd came in this weeks mail we were glad to hear that you had employment again. I rec'd the money $10. part of which I will pay Mr. Lloyd as soon as I can see him I will give him half of it. when you are sending anything home, send what old clothing you have, we must try to work it so that you will be able to be in Glen Arbor this winter as you have not been at home in so long a time. I want you to come home this winter. we have a half Barrel of Vinegar made. about your old clothing I can mend what will need mending and the rest I can put in the carpet rags. If you possibly can send me a Shovel like the one I had. but I don't care about it being so large. when we went to Chicago we let Mr Tucker have our other one. there is none in the place. Don't forget my Lima Beans. My Ear don't get any better I am afraid that I am losing the hearing out of my other. The snow is all gone here but I expect there is some back in the woods it begins to look like planting time. No More this time. Charlie & Ettie send their love to you, the neighbors send their regards to you. write soon.Yours as ever,
E.M. Boizard M. E. Fisher

From Oliver to Charlie

Heath & Milligan
White Lead, Zinc and Colors
170 & 172 Randolph Street
Chicago, Apr 18 1870

Mr Dear Charlie
Your letter dated the 7th and post Marked the 13th came to hand this morning and as the **"Oswegatchee"** Starts out this Evening, it affords me Chance of Sending a Small Box containing 2 Dresses of Calico, one for your Wife and that other for your Mother in law also 20 yds of Domestic tell Ellen she must not make any Shirts for me, as I want her to use that Stuff for herself and Ettie. I can wear Flannell shirts with paper collars.

As regards the Pigeons, catch as many as you can and Keep them alive as they will bring from $2. to 2.50 per doz. as they are now Scarce Hurry them up as fast as you can as Mr. Milligan will see them disposed of. As regards packing them in Ice. I don't think that they will pay so well as if they were alive besides I think it would cost more trouble and perhaps wont pay you so well. If you can catch a large number, can't you coop them and Keep them and I can let you *{know}* when they will bring a better price. however don't lose no time now, if you can Send a few Hundred on the first Boat from Ogdensburgh do so, don't wait too long. I Send $10 to pay Mr. Lloyd did it arrive safe. Kiss Ettie for me, also Mrs. B I Sent Ettie ½ Doz Small Glass dishes to Eat her berries out of, also Pair of shears to cut carpet rags. I think to send shortly some old Clothes for Carpet Rags.
Yours Sincerely John O Boizard

Reply as soon as Possible

From Eleanor and Marietta to Oliver

Glen Arbor, Michigan
May 2nd 1870

My Dear Oliver
We rec'd the Box containing the prints and Factory also the Dishes and Shears we were pleased with all. I wish you would send me a half dozen just like them if you possibly can Ettie says she is very much pleased with them also very much obliged for them. tell us the price of the calico and Factory when you write I am pleased with them. I wish you had sent me some spool thread as I have none. If you send me some white and Black. Ettie send one dollar for you to send a Box of Pills **Dr. Cheesmans Female Pills** don't send any other kinds send them as soon as you get this letter you can send a Box or Parcels and put them inside of it. I wish you would send more Tea & coffee as there is none to be had at Rossmans at the N T Dock it is not worth Buying it tastes like hay. The weather is very warm here. I wish you would send the Tea & coffee as soon as possible as we are out of Both. also send that Butcher Knife when you send in any thing as we often need it. I have been working out in the lot and am very tired Charlie is not home he is working in the mill. but I expect he will be home before long to stay through Planting. if you should send lard or Butter don't send it in those

224

tin cans as we have so many   send jars as we need them   Charlie has a
young cow that will soon give Milk and we will need jars about for the
milk this is all at present write soon Yours as ever
E.M Boizard

From Mrs Fisher to Oliver

*There is no date on this letter; because Mrs Fisher refers to Charlie as
Oliver's son, and a reference is made to Mr Fisher farming the letter
presumably was written between spring & fall 1870*

Mr Boizard
Ettie has kindly allowed me to put a note to you in her letter. Will you in
your next letter give me the price per lb of **Pariswhite**. I have a recipe
for making **Kalsomine**, soak one fourth of a lb of glue over night in tepid
water, the next day put it into a tin vessel, with a quart of water, set the
pail in a kettle of water over the fire, untill it boils, stir constantly untill
the glue is dissolved, take from six to eight lbs **Paris white**, in another
vessel, pour on hot water and stir until it has the appearance of lime milk.
Add the sizing. Stir well, and apply to the wall while warm. Is the above
recipe the way **Kalsomine** is made in your establishment, Mrs Rosman
got hers of Milligan. one more question, can **Kalsomine** be put on to a
papered wall successfully. now friend Boziard if you will answer my
numerous questions I shall be greatly obliged. We are having very fine
weather, Mr. Fisher & Frank are farming. I presume you would hardly
know the boys, to see your son Charly with whiskers, weighing nearly
160 and Frank larger than his father, you must not stay away much
longer, or you will not know us, we are growing old so fast. Mr Fisher's
hair is quite grey and I have lost my teeth – well it is what we must
expect, time makes great changes, Mr Fisher & Frank send kind regards,
please accept the best wishes of your old neighbor and friend.
Harriett M. Fisher

From Oliver to Charlie

Dear Charlie

Your coop of Pigeons arrived on Saturday, on the "**Toledo**." I got your
letters about 2 o'clock. I then went down to look at them and found them
all right with the Exception that the Freight was not paid on them,
although you Stated in your letter that you would pay the Freight.
However, as before, I presume you did pay the freight on them and so
did I. If you paid the freight, you should rec'd a voucher for it. I enclose
you the receipt and also the **drayage**. I took them from the Boat about 4
o'clock on Saturday. It was too late. Consequently, I kept them until
this morning (Monday) and disposed of them as well as I could.
Some offered me $1.00. Some $1.25. However I persisted and got
$1.50. I sold them to a Commission Merchant on South Water St. I quit
H. & M. I can't get along there any more. He told me to hold on to them
till he saw his Pigeon man at the Stock Yards. He said they had some
11,000 more in Coops there to shoot them soon and I got tired of waiting.
Consequently I sold them I had to pay besides the freight 70cts. for
Drayages as I hauled them to Gus' shop and gave them water and feed
all day Sunday, and then I was obliged to haul them back to South Water
St. I send you by the "**Toledo**" the package of Dry Goods & c. with Bill
& c. You were quite lucky with the Birds as I found but one dead one. I
think now, as they are coming in such large numbers for shooting
purposes they wont bring so much at present. If you find that they are
plenty and you have the time to get them, pack them in Ice as before and
I will try to sell them for you at the Hotels. I hope Ettie will like her
Sheeting also her **Zephyrs** and Thread. Give my respects to your Father
& Mother, also Frank. Kiss Ettie and mother for me and receive my
regards. J.O.B.

I will send a letter to my wife about how I have been situated. The
Zephyrs cost 87 1/2

From Eleanor & Marietta to Oliver

Glen Arbor
July 18th 1870

My Dear Oliver

Yours of the 11th came to hand last week   we were glad to hear that you
were well, as this leaves us at present   I am very busy now as Berries are
ripe and of course I gather all that I can. yesterday Ettie cooked over
eleven quarts which I done up in cans and Bottles for winter use. I am
living alone now for Charlie & Ettie are living down in a house just the
other side of the Mill. they come and stay from Saturday until Monday
morning with me. You say you will get me a pair of shoes as soon as
you could   I should not ask you if I could get work to do. The ones that
I have I cant but just keep them on   I am sorry to hear that you have quit
H. & M. but am glad to hear that you have paid them the debt. I should
try to keep out of their debt if possible.   we all think you had better come
home and not stay there doing nothing.   this is all at present   write soon
the family all send love. Yours as ever E.M. Boizard

From Charlie to Oliver

Glen Arbor
July 18th

Dear Father

I rec'd your Letter and the parcel all right.   was well satisfied with the
price you got for them.   there is not any pigeons here now but I expect
they will be plenty after Harvest.   you say you have quit H. & M.
Business is Dull. we all think that you had better come Home. now
don't fail to come. we will look for you. if you have any freight I will
pay the freight when you come. I am now working for Mr. Grandy he is
building for a Grist Mill in addition to the old Saw Mill that Father used
to own. crops look well corn and Potatoes especially. I think I will
have 125 Bu. potatoes. 50 or 75 Bu. corn. 200 Heads cabbage,
cucumbers, Water Mellons, Tomatoes   Green Peas and string Beans
plenty. and there is any amount of berries. Whortle Berries Raspberries
and Black Berries. I have three live Red Foxes. Would they be saleable
there and much a price they are about ½ grown. No more at present
Ettie will write soon   From your Son In Law   Chas. Fisher

Glen Arbor, Michigan
Aug 30th 1870

My Dear Oliver
Your welcome Letter came to hand last week also the Shoes I am well
pleased with them but they are rather low in the instep for me, we are
sorry to hear of H & M's loss. Ettie rec'd a Letter from Emma Brown a
short time ago they have sold their place for twelve hundred dollars in
coins they think some of going to Texas to live. I am picking
Blackberries they are very nice this season we are having a great deal of
Rain. I believe I have never mentioned in any of my Letters that they are
Building a Bridge over across Glen Lake, the narrows they are cutting a
State road and the Bridge is in the Contract I believe the Bridge is nearly
completed. Charlie has been working on the State Road some. when
you come home, bring all your old clothing and if you can got hold of
any Bottles small just bring them also as they will answer to put Berries
in. no more write soon Yours & c. E.M.B.

Written on the back of the above letter

From Charles Fisher to Oliver

Glen Arbor
Aug 30th 1870

Dear Father Boizard
In regard to the freight on the last Pigeons I sent you. I payed the freight
on them before they went on the Boat. I took the Receipt you sent me
and showed it to the Agent. he then showed me a copy of the Bill he sent
to R. Diefendorf Agt, of N.T. co. and it was Marked Paid. The Mistake
is through R. Diefendorf. Now if you will go and see R. Diefendorf and
ask him to look over that Bill and he will see that it was paid, and make
him pay you Back what you paid him for freight. You spoke of coming
home come as soon as possible because we are all looking for you no
more at Present From Your Son In Law Chas. A Fisher

Glen Arbor Oct 8th 1870

Father Boizard

We rec'd your letter dated Sept. 22nd we were glad hear that you were
well. We are all quite smart. I was presented with A young Son Oct. 6th
12 O'clock in Day He weighed 7 ½ lbs. A bouncer both Etta and the
babie is quite Smart his name is John Edward Fisher. John is for you
and Edward for Father and Fisher for Etta and I. Mother B says it
makes her feel old to be called Grandma how is it with you. In regard
to sending those potatoes I will first send some Sitron {**citron**} about 2
bbls and then if you can dispose of them and send me 12 of those Gunny
Bags 2 Bu. Bags, I will amediately {*immediately*} send the Potatoes I
am preparing the sitron {**citron**} now   no more at present
We All Send Love Your Son In Law Chas. Fisher Glen Arbor Mich.

Will you let me know the market Price of cucumbers in the Brine Small
nice cucumbers. C.A.F. G.A. M. {*Charles A Fisher   Glen Arbor
Michigan*}

From Oliver to Charles Fisher

Chicago Ill
Nov 7 1870

Dear Charlie,

Your potatoes arrived last Friday the letter I got on Saturday but I had
Sold the potatoes the letter was <u>delayed</u>. The Market is flooded with
potatoes, they bring them in Car Loads   you Can buy them from 65 to 80
cts per Bushel, fine large peach Blows, larger than yours, however I Sold
yours to Heath as they had a quantity of Freight on the Champlain   it did
not cost me anything for **Drayage** he took them with his other freight I
sold them for 80 cts, and was pleased to get that for them.
I enquired the price of Flour, and they asked me $5.75 for ordinary
family flour and So I am at a stand what to do. I remit you $22 and if
you want Flour at that price, I can Send it before Navigation Closes.
The Bags I also Sold to Mr. Heath for 3 Dolls – he will pay me for them.
I will retain then 3 Dolls as I am in want of a few articles of Drawers,
stockings & c. The potatoes weight was 2000 pounds, by allowing 60
pounds bushel it would bring it about 33 Bushels, at 80 cts. $26.40
deduct f't 4.20 Bal - 22.20   I will get Etties nipple glasses I hope the
young mother will get over her trouble I am sorry that I cant See you all

this winter, as I think I can Still make a little this winter, by Staying with Graef and it may be occasionally I can Send my Wife a few dolls this winter   Ask my Wife if she will Send me a good Blanket, a dark one as I Sleep in the Shop, it Saves the cost of Lodging. I hope this letter will be Satisfactory to you and also my Wife – answer this letter by Boat pack up the Blanket, and give it to the Porter of the Boat accompanied with a letter. My best regards to all the family   My love to my wife and yours Yours with respect J.O. Boizard

I enquired about Pickles in Brine there is no sale this winter for them, they raised So many of them in Ill's that they Sold for 35cts per Bushel if you can keep them good until spring they will pay double from what they do now. J.O.B.

No other correspondence has been found written between Oliver and his family. It is assumed based on Eleanor's obituary and various other papers that Oliver died in November 1870. It is possible that he was struck with some type of paralysis. We do have a letter that was written to Marietta from a Doctor approximately 18 years after Oliver's death. This letter appears to be in reply to a letter that Marietta had written to him inquiring about receiving some type of financial aid or pension from the Government due to the circumstances surrounding Oliver's death. It does not seem likely that they ever received the requested aid.

To Marietta Fisher from Wm. Johnson M.D.

Newport KY
Sept. 25, '88

Mrs. E. Fisher

Your letter has been received and in reply to it. I have to state that so long a time has intervened that the circumstance of your Father's sickness has passed out of my memory. The question arises how to prove that he contracted the disease in the performance of his duty. There is no records at this place now consequently I cannot refresh my memory the reports of sick and wounded at the time generally stated the disease treated for and if for Paralysis you might establish a claim. It would be almost impossible to get witnesses for in the first place the Doctor that treated your Father is dead, and I am afraid the records which is now in Washington might not show the disease in your Mothers favor, but in the event your Mother makes any application and she thinks I can be of any help I will do so. Sometimes in reporting diseases the cause is reported and not the results of same. Your lawyer may make a beginning the whole thing will depend how the case is recorded I have forgotten dates, we know nothing of the Bridges family. My family joins me in sending kind regards to you all.

Respectfully Wm. Johnson M.D.

While stationed in Newport Barracks, Emma Bridges stayed some nights at a Mrs. Johnson's house and there is one mention of a Mr. Johnson. Could this be the same person?

231

Epilogue

Oliver's last letter to his family sheds no light on his deteriorating health nor does it foreshadow his impending death. Yet we are faced with a sudden and unwelcome end to their story. The end seems abrupt and leaves a longing in our hearts to know the rest of the story. I have asked my mom, "Are you sure you have given me **every** letter?" I am not looking for another letter from the middle of their story; I crave a letter that will put closure to their story. I want the explanation and the circumstances around his death. The letter from the Doctor that was written eighteen years after Oliver died creates more questions for me than it answers.

Was Oliver sick in Newport? Is that why he didn't re-enlist? In a December 1869 letter Oliver mentioned that he had rheumatism in both feet and ankles with a lot of swelling and he had to use a stick to walk with. Was that problem related to the 'paralysis' mentioned in the Dr.'s letter? Why would his family have waited eighteen years to write to the Doctor?

As with any research project, the questions never seem to end. Each attempt to solve one part of the mystery seems to expose several other riddles that warrant investigation. With time, maybe some of these unsolved parts of Oliver and Eleanor's lives will be known, but in the meantime, we must choose to focus on the wonderful treasury of knowledge that we do know.

Having read this book, it would be my desire that you would be inspired to journal or write more letters to your loved ones. Ask yourself "Who is preserving **my** family's history for the generations to come?"

We have this unusual and special collection of letters detailing the lives of a married couple who experienced the joys of companionship and the loneliness of separation as they tried their best to make a life for themselves and their daughter in a rugged and unsettled land. May each of us, treasure a little more dearly the gift of community that the early settlers across this country sacrificed for and left for us to inherit. **Jodie**

Time Line

Key

±Glen Arbor events

* National events

×Boizard /Fisher family events

1840 *1835-1842 The first of three campaigns against the Seminole Indians.

1841 ×John Fisher discharged from the US Army, April 17, 1841. He had served with Co. F., Eighth Infantry since April 17, 1838.

1842

1843

1844 *Telegraph system invented by Samuel F.B. Morse.

 *James K. Polk elected President

1845 *Annexation of Texas

1846 *Mexican War (1846-1848)

1847

1848±John LaRue moves to Leelanau Peninsula, making him the first Caucasian resident.

1849 *California Gold Rush

1850 ×Eleanor Melvina McGill marries James Magill

 *Railroad growth begins to mushroom from 1850-1860 and by the time the Civil War begins it is the most important means of transportation.

1851 ±John Dorsey moves to the mainland – Leelanau Peninsula.

1852 ×Marietta Magill born - May 18

1853

1854 ×John E. Fisher & family settle in Glen Arbor

1855 ±SS *Saginaw* lands in Glen Arbor with 14 settlers

 ×John Oliver & Eleanor Melvina Magill married July 16

1856 ×Oliver serving in 4th Artillery Company K - Fort Myers& Fort McRae during Seminole Indian Wars 1856 & 1857

1857 ""

1858   ×Oliver & Eleanor made a trip to Glen Arbor sometime during this year. The original paperwork for the Quit Claim Deed filed in 1859 was composed in October 1858.

1859×John Fisher builds a saw mill on Crystal River. It was capable of sawing 5,000 feet per day.

×Oliver - Private 4th Reg. U.S. Army Fort Ridgely, MN June 30, 1859-November 17, 1859

×40 acres of property were purchased in Glen Arbor for $40.00 from George & Anna Thayer (Traverse City Clerk, Quit Claim Deed 561) The deed was received for record on August 6 in Traverse City.

Oliver, Eleanor & Marietta move to Glen Arbor after Oliver receives a furlough or discharge from the Army in November.

*John Brown's attack on Harpers Ferry

1860   ×Oliver, Eleanor & Marietta live in Glen Arbor during this time. They may have fallen on tough times as, they move sometime prior to November of 1861 when we learn that Oliver has enlisted in the army again.

*Election of Abraham Lincoln

1861   *Civil War begins. April 15 President Lincoln issues his first proclamation asking for 75,000 men to serve for three months. In May he asks for 42,000 volunteers to serve for three years.

×Oliver joins the US Army again and is stationed at Newport Barracks, KY.

1862   *Homestead Act passed

×Stationed at Newport Barracks

1863   *Emancipation Proclamation

×Stationed at Newport Barracks

1864   ×In January or February, Oliver relocates to Chicago, he is employed by Col. Pomeroy, in the Quartermasters office.

×In May, Eleanor & Marietta, probably for health reasons, relocate to Glen Arbor. They rent a house from the Fishers until they are able to build a log house on a 10 acre piece of property they buy from John & Harriet Fisher. They move into their log house in August.

1865 *President Lincoln is assassinated in April.

*Civil war ends.

×Oliver stays in Chicago is employed in mustering out the troops, until October, when he moves to Springfield, IL to work for the U.S. Mustering and Disbursing Office.

1866 ×Discharged from the U.S. Mustering and Disbursing Office in June. Oliver returns to Chicago, works for Heath & Milligan.

1867 ×Eleanor & Marietta travel to Chicago in October to stay with Oliver for the winter.

1868 ×Eleanor & Marietta return to Glen Arbor in May.

1869 *First transcontinental railroad completed

×Oliver quits his job with Heath & Milligan in August.

×Marietta & Charlie get engaged.

×Oliver works for a short time for the US Circuit Court in the month of December. He misses the last boat out to Michigan.

1870 ×Marietta & Charlie Fisher are married on Eleanor's birthday, January 19, by John E. Fisher.

×Oliver takes a job with Heath & Milligan again.

×The last letter received from Oliver was dated November 7, in which Oliver asks for a warm blanket.

1871 ±The bridge is completed across the Narrows of Glen Lake.

1872

Photos and Memorabilia

Eleanor Boizard

John Oliver
Boizard

Eleanor
Boizard

Eleanor Boizard

Grandma Eleanor
Boizard

Marietta
Boizard
16 years old

1868

Charles and
Marietta
Boizard

Charles and
Marietta Boizard
married January
19, 1870

Charles and Marietta in their later years. Charlies died in 1909 at the age of 60.

John Edward Fisher son of Charles and Marietta Fisher. Born October 6, 1870

Sarah (McCarty)
King and sister
Harriet (McCarty)
Fisher 1860

Harriet Fisher 1865

John and Harriet
Fisher

Frank Fisher
Charlies brother
born in 1851

243

Frank & Charlotte
Fisher
Married in 1874

Emma Bridge
Brown married
Edwin Brown
December 1866.
Killed by
Indians on their
way to
California –
sometime after
1870

Edwin Brown,
Married to Emma
Bridges 1866

Edwin and Emma
Brown's baby

245

Possibly Oliver's
Army buddy
Wm. Bridges

Mrs. Tator – school
teacher
in Glen Arbor

Charity Brotherton
and George
Getchel married June
1868

Sarah Tucker

Genealogy Charts

Boizard

	__John Oliver	
	1820- November, 1870	**Marietta**
	m. July 16, 1855	----May 18, 1852
	Eleanor Melvina Magill	*m.* Jan. 19, 1870
	Jan. 19, 1828 - Mar. 29, 1911	Charles A. Fisher
		1849-1909

Mr. Boizard
m.
Catherine
b. Aug.3, 1787
(possible mom-
1860 Census
living in Phila.
is about the right
age.)

__ Catherine (Kate)
b. Dec. 2, 1830
m.   ------   Phineas
Christopher (C.C.) Dow
In 1860 census - living in Philadelphia

__Jacob
b. 1809
In 1850 & 1860 census living in Philadelphia

__ Elizabeth (Libby)
b. 1811   d. 1871 at the age of 60
There is an Elizabeth Boizard buried in the Old
Chester PA cemetery, next to Catherine Boizard.
This is possibly Oliver's sister.

__ Lewis Pierre (Pete)
b. 1815
m. Caroline   Caroline (Cally) b. 1849
b.1813   Charles (Charley) b. 1850
In 1860 Census living in Philadelphia.

__Mary-married a Doctor and traveled to California in a
covered wagon in 1856. Last heard from in 1858.

Fisher

John Edward Fisher
1817 -1900
m. April 1843
Harriet M. McCarty
1826-1914

—— **Charles A.**
Aug. 29, 1849-May 1909
m. January 19, 1870
Marietta Boizard
March 18,1852- 1935

—— **John Edward**
1870-1937
m.
Amanda Carlson

—— **Etta May**
1872-1958
m.
1. John Westcott
2. Dr. Charles Todd

—— **Charles Fredrick**
May 1874 - 1915
m.
Lottie Lowrie

—— **Francis (Frank)**
1851 - 1933
m.
Charlotte Atkinson
1858-1934

—— **Eugene**

—— **Clinton**

—— **Maude**

—— **Pearl**

—— **Myrtle**

249

Pages from Family Bible

The following images are scans taken from a Fisher family Bible that is on display at the Empire Museum in Empire, Michigan.

PARENTS' RECORD

MOTHER

Elenor Melvina McGill was born January the 19th in the year of our lord 1828

MARRIAGES.

Mr. John O. Boyard to Mrs.
Eleanor M. Magill on the 16th
day of July, A. D. 1855.

Mr. Charles A. Fisher To
Miss Marretta Boyard
On the 19th Day January 1870.

By John E. Fisher
Justice of Piece.

John Westcott To Ettie May Fisher
on The 17th day of March 1892 by
Chas. A. Fisher
Justice of the Peace

John Edward Fisher to
Miss Amanda Carlson

Charles Frederick Fisher to
Miss Lottie Lowrey (Lowrie)

BIRTHS.

Marietta Magill born in May 18th, A.D. 1852

John Edward Fisher. Son of Charles A. Fisher and Marietta Fisher. Was born October 6th 1870. 12 O'clock. M.

Etta May Fisher. Daughter of Charles A. Fisher and Marietta Fisher was Born March 30th 1872. 4 O'clock A.M.

Charles Fredrick Fisher Son of Charles A. Fisher and Marietta Fisher was Born May 6th 1874 12 o'clock night

Deaths

Memorabilia Photos

The following images are taken from the inside pages of Eleanor's Bible. This Bible is owned by Eleanor's great, great, great, granddaughter, Michele Pattan.

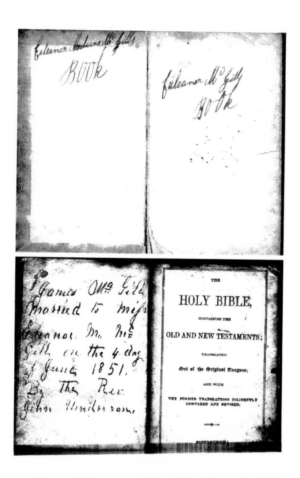

Eleanor Melvina McGills Book (top photo)
James MaGill married to Miss Eleanor M. McGill on the 4 day of June, 1851, by the Rev. John Henderson. (bottom photo)

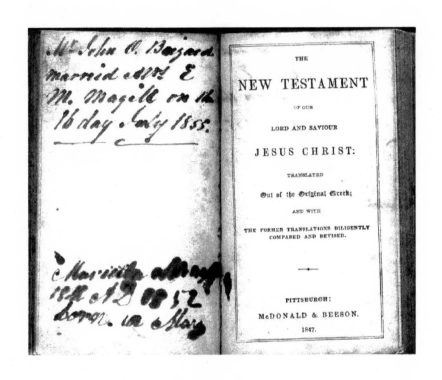

Mr. John O. Boizard married Mrs. E M. Magill on the 16 day
of July 1855.

Marietta Magill 18th AD 1852 born in May

The following photos contain some of the articles that were found in Etta May Westcott Todd's home in 1974.

One of several baby gowns.

Pencil box, medicine bottle and some cast iron toys.

Miscelleneous pins

Lipstick and make-up compact

Thimbles, marbles (some wooden),

sewing kits, beads, boot hook, etc.

Head vase, glass doll and hand woven baby rattle with
the name "Fred" on it with the date "1880"

Handcarved headboard (footboard also)

Artifacts from the Westcott house that are currently on display in the EmpireMuseum.

This little tea cup and saucer are heirlooms that have been preserved by the family. This cup has a note on the bottom of it that says "Wedding gift to Grandma Fisher in 1818." This would be John Fisher's mom, not his wife Harriet. There are also a few pieces of silverware that were given as wedding gifts.

This little 'jar' is an heirloom passed on through the family from HarrietFisher. It has a note on the bottom that says "Given to Grandma Fisher in 1853."

Crystal dishes that have been passed on from the Fishers.

Marriage announcement of Charlie and Marietta that was published in the Traverse City newspaper.

Obituaries & Death Notices

Charlie Fisher, May 9, 1909

Another Tribute to Charles A. Fisher.
For The Herald.

Charles A. Fisher, who had been ailing for several months was obliged to take to his bed three weeks ago, although a great sufferer, his family was not aware that he was dangerously ill until the last, and his death, which occurred last Sunday morning, was a terrible shock to them all. His funeral on Tuesday was held at his home and conducted by the Maccabees, as he was a charter member of that order. His remains were placed beside his father's, on the old homestead, where he lived. Charles A. Fisher, who was the son of John E. and Harriet Fisher, was born August 29, 1849, in Fon DuLac, Wisconsin. His parents with their family moved to Sleeping Bear Bay, now called Glen Arbor, in August 1854, where he has since resided. January 19, 1878 he was united in marriage to Miss Mary Etta Boyard, who survives him. They are the parents of two sons, John Edward and Charles Frederick, and one daughter, Mrs. May Prescott, and six grandchildren. He also leaves an aged mother and one sister, F. E. Fisher, and a large circle of friends to mourn their loss, as was evidenced by the great number of people that came to pay respect and take a last look at their friend, and by the tears that coursed down the cheeks of many as they left the side of the casket. Mrs. Fisher and the family feel grateful to those that rendered assistance and for the beautiful floral gifts, and to the choir, and to the Maccabees, and wished to give them their sincere thanks.

Eugene Fisher, who has been a very great sufferer, with an awful felon on his right hand, the swelling going to his elbow, is getting better, since it has been lanced on his thumb, hand and arm.

H. M. FISHER.

Death of Charles E. Fisher.
For the Herald.

May 9th, at the hour of 7 a. m., Charles E. Fisher, aged fifty-nine, passed the Great Divide. Tuesday at 10 a. m. several hundred of Leelanau's citizens witnessed his interment on the beautiful hill where, inland lake looks like a bit if Italy's blue water while in the other hand the tortuous ribbon of Crystal river winds and turns on its way to Lake Michigan. Here, beside his pioneer father, the man who has long served his town as supervisor, clerk, justice, was laid to rest by members of the Knights of Maccabees, the which lodge he belonged, and in which he carried an insurance of two thousand dollars. Deepest sympathy is felt for the wife, daughter and two sons of the deceased. His aged mother, Mrs. Harriet Fisher, his brother Frank, business man, two daughter-in-laws, several grand children, three nephews, two nephews and many connections by marriage formed a large gathering. Glen Arbor is indebted to Mr. Fisher for his active interest in securing the bridge across the narrows of Glen Lake. His public spirit, kindness of heart and sincerity won for him a host of friends. His demise is a distinct loss to the neighborhood and county.

PIONEER IS DEAD.

Charles Fisher, one of the early and highly esteemed residents of Leelanau county, died last Sunday morning at his home in Glen Arbor. For several months Mr. Fisher has been failing in health, owing to kidney trouble. He came to this county when a child 5 years old, having lived here 55 years, he has always been noted for his disposition to take an active interest in the welfare of the county. We and the entire community extend our sympathy to the surviving wife and sons in the loss of an old friend and old settler whom all knew so well.

The funeral services were held last Tuesday.

It is sad that one we cherish
Should be taken from our home,
But the joys that do not perish
Live in memory alone.

All the years we've spent together,
All the happy golden hours
Shall be cherished in remembrance,
Fragrance sweet from memory's flowers.

Not now but in the coming years,
It may be in the better land,
We'll read the meaning of our tears,
And there sometime, we'll understand.

	Name of Deceased.	No. of Tent	Name of Tent.	Location.	Date of Death.				Cause of Death.	Amount Assessment paid.	To Whom Payable.	Amt. Benefit Certificate.
					Day	Month	Year					
	K O T M M			Transfer to Death								
	Louis Larsen		Washington	Ballard							Widow	
	Chas A Fisher		Sleeping Bear	Glen Arbor							Widow	
	Oscar A Emmel		Au Sable	Au Sable							Children	
	Oscar A Emmel		Au Sable	Au Sable								
	Thomas V Henan		Lincoln	Saginaw								
	Thomas V Henan		Lincoln									
	Matilda Turner		Kvart							Brother & sisters		
	Wm J Brenner		Concordia	Evart								
	Fred W Stochel		Concordia	Saginaw							Widow	
	Lafayette Weldon		Lansing	Lansing							Widow	
	Alphonso Carter		Cassopolis	Lansing							Widow	
	Mark T Chappel		Stevens	Cassopolis							Widow	
	Wm H Simpson		Newport	Detroit							Widow	
	Chas Lafleure		Newport	Newport							Widow	
	Lyman Munroe		Harmony	Port Huron							Widow	

(Continued on page M.)

Eleanor Boizard's Obituary

GLEN ARBOR.

The mail boat from South Manitou was over today.

At the town meeting today the following ticket was elected:
Supervisor—Mark Randall.
Town Clerk—N. B. Sheridan.
Treasurer—Charles Ehle.
Highway Commissioner—John Westcott.
Justice of the Peace—Lansing
Member Board of Review—Raderick Dunn.
Constables—Fred Fisher, William Bennett, Charles Riggs, Herbert N. Sheridan.

Mr. and Mrs. Edward Fisher went to Leland, last week to attend the funeral of Mrs. Margaret Neilson, who was Mrs. Fisher's grandmother.

Eugene Fisher and his grandmother who came here from Maple City Saturday to attend the funeral of Mrs. Bozzard, will return Tuesday.

Another pioneer gone, Grandma Bozzard, who has been sick and a great sufferer, passed away March 29th, at the home of her daughter, Mrs. Charles A. Fisher, by whom she was tenderly cared for during her long illness. The funeral was held at the house on Sunday, Rev. Gliddon officiated. The casket was covered with flowers, the gifts of loving friends. The selections by the choir were well rendered. Her remains were laid to rest in the Fisher cemetery. Elenor M. McGill was born January 29th, 1828, in Wheeling, W. Virginia. At the age of four her mother died and she went to live with a Quaker family in Winan Town, Penn., where she was kindly cared for until her marriage in 1850, in Pittsburg, Penn., to John O. Bozzard. Mr. Bozzard was an Indian war soldier, was also in the Mexican and Civil war, served United States 25 years. He died 40 years ago. They came here in 1858, and she has lived here ever since. Mrs. Fisher and family wish me to thank the choir for their kindness, also Mrs. Shea, Mrs. Earl, Mrs. Burgess and all the ladies that so kindly rendered assistance during her sickness. They have our sympathy in this their hour of sorrow.

April 4, 1911.

264

Etta May Fisher Westcott Todd's house where the Boizard Letters were found in 1974

Glossary

Anaconda folds: This term was used to describe the strangle hold that the Union was exacting upon the southern states, through their use of a seaboard blockade which would prevent importing and exporting of their goods. The Anaconda plan also called for the Union to gain control of the Mississippi River in order to divide the South. The plan as it was proposed was designed to isolate the south and bring about a quicker surrender with minimum bloodshed. The Anaconda Plan was never officially accepted by the Government, but several of its key components were implemented .
(http://encarta.msn.com/encyclopedia_761567354_5/Civil_War.html#p9
0) accessed 30 December 2008

Arizona Territory: From 1863 - 1912 this was an organized Territory of the United States that encompasses our current Arizona and New Mexico states. From 1861 - 1863, the Confederate States also claimed a portion of the land. This territory played an important role in the Civil War on the western frontier.
(http://encarta.msn.com/encyclopedia_761570033_11/Arizona.html#p67
accessed 30 December 2008

Ague: Fever, sometimes accompanied by shivering and shaking. It was often indicative of the onset of malaria.

Allegheny: No information was found about this particular propeller.

Bachelors Hall: I have found many references to these words in writings around the mid 1800's, but nothing that gave me a specific definition or explanation of the phrase. In researching this phrase online, I even ran across a song written about keeping bachelors hall. The context of the words seems to point to young men when they would move out of their parents house and set up their own house. In some instances, a marriage was forthcoming.

Bee: This term is used to describe a large group of people that have joined their work force to accomplish a task together.

Beechnuts: The American Beech tree produces a small triangular shaped nut that falls to the ground in the fall. Many people have described them as being bitter. They are not highly valued as a food because of their small size and the difficulty in peeling the nut.

Bigler, John: The third Governor of California. He was in office from January 1852 - January 1856. At the time that he is mentioned in this book, April of 1856, he would no longer have been the actual Governor, which probably explains why he and his 'top ten' were staying in a boarding house. Bigler, remained active in politics and held many appointed offices before his death in 1871 at the age of 66. (http://www.californiagovernors.ca.gov/h/biography/governor_3.html) accessed 30 December 2008

Bilious: Nauseated, sick feeling to the stomach

Bitter Aloes: A laxative made from the leaves of aloe.

Boils: An inflamation of the skin, generally pus filled.

Bonar: Possibly a French word meaning 'gentle & mannerly.'

Booth, J. Wilkes: The infamous American actor who shot and killed President Abraham Lincoln on April 14, 1865. This assassination occurred just five days after the confederate south had surrendered. Booth himself was shot and killed on April 26. He was an outspoken sympathizer of the south. (http://encarta.msn.com/encyclopedia_761573391/John_Wilkes_Booth.html) accessed 30 December 2008

Bounty: A reward offered by the government to encourage men to enlist or re-enlist in the military.

Brevet: A temporary military promotion that does not include a pay raise.

Brooklyn: In 1866 this propeller was built in Cleveland by the yard of Ira Lafrinier for the Northern Transportation Company. http://www.hhpl.on.ca/GreatLakes/Extracts/Details.asp?ID=5429&n=2) 10 October 2007

Brownsville: There is a Brownsville, PA which is near McClellandtown (where Eleanor was raised) and there is an old military fort in that town, but I have not been able to determine if a company from the 4th Artillery occupied it during the years around 1855. There is also a Fort Brown in Texas. The 4th Artillery was stationed there for a time also during the Mexican war. (http://encarta.msn.com/encyclopedia_761578313/Brownsville.html) accessed 30 December 2008

Camp Reno: An outpost of Fort McDowell. It was occupied by the US Army, 1st Calvary from 1867-1870. Its purpose was to allow the Army to keep steady watch on the activity of the Apache Indians and to curtail the raiding that had been plaguing the farmers. (http://www.ghosttowns.com/states/az/campreno.html) accessed 10 October 2007

Camp Gaston California: This camp was located about 45 miles north of Fort Yuma and served as an outpost to the Fort. It was founded in 1859 and was intermittently occupied by soldiers through 1867. (http://www.militarymuseum.org/CpGaston.html) accessed 10 October 2007

Camphor germ: Camphor is a substance that comes from the wood and bark of the Camphor tree. It has a unique smell and is used medicinally as a topical substance to aid in healing infections and to stop itching. I could not find any reference to 'camphor germ,' although a lot of resources did state that camphor was good for killing germs.

Carbuncle: A painful inflamed area of infection in the skin. The infection is deep and the inflamed area may have several openings which ooze pus.

Castile soap: A hard white soap made with vegetable oil and sodium hydroxide.

Chicago Marine List: A record of ships at port, their destinations and schedules.

Citron: This may be referring to a small round watermelon. I couldn't find any word spelled 'sitron' as it is spelled in the letters.

City of Boston: This propeller was launched in 1863 for the Northern Transportation Company. It was built at Steven and Presley's yard. (http://www.hhpl.on.ca/GreatLakes/Extracts/Details.asp?ID=5557&n=16

City of New York: This propeller was built in Cleveland, Ohio and her home port was Chicago. She was launched in August of 1863 for the Northern Transportation Company. (http://www.hhpl.on.ca/GreatLakes/Extracts/Details.asp?ID=1207&n=2)

Clarks Grammar: A grammar textbook first published in 1847.

Cleveland: A propeller (boat) built for the Vermont Central Railway, by Moses and Quale at Cleveland, Ohio. (Julia Dickenson & Dorothy Bolton, *The Boizard Letters* (Empire, MI: Empire Area Heritage Group) pg. 145)

Cosey: Possibly – chatty; talkative; sociable

Cotillion: A formal dance or ball

Cypher: This term was used in reference to completing mathematic calculations.

Day School Bell: In the letters this clearly looks like the word 'bell,' however, it is unclear what that would refer to. If instead it were the word 'bill,' than it would probably refer to the school tax bill that was sent out twice a year.

De oldest of de wimmins: This quote is used three times by Oliver in reference to either Eleanor or Marietta. Its' meaning is not known, possibly a French Creole saying.

Dickens, Charles: Arrived for his second visit to America in November 1867, he stayed for five months. Initially his plan was to travel as far west as St. Louis, but due to poor health, he stayed on the East Coast. (http://charlesdickenspage.com/america.html) 30 December 2008

Dr Hooflands German bitters: A medicine formulated from vegetable products that guaranteed to cure problems ranging from 'disgust of food', 'liver ailments', 'nausea', 'constipation' etc. (http://www.whilbr.com/itemdetail.aspx?idEntry=898) 30 December 2008

Dr. Cheesmans Female Pills: A pill that was touted as being able to regulate a women's monthly cycle, as well as curing headaches, hysterics, disturbed sleep etc. (www.thomasgenweb.com/1859_scranton_republican.html) 10 October 2007

Drayage: a charge for hauling cargo

Drilling: A heavy linen fabric generally used for work clothes.

Dropsey (on the Brain): edema - swelling

Dutch Stews: Possibly a combination of root vegetables (carrots, beets, potatoes, turnips etc.) simmered in a liquid.

Empire: A propeller merchant steamer, built in Cleveland, Ohio in 1861. Its home port was Detroit, Michigan. (Julia Dickenson & Dorothy Bolton, *The Boizard Letters* (Empire, MI: Empire Area Heritage Group) pg. 145)

Epicurean: A person who loves and seeks out pleasure in life.

Erysipelas: A severe skin infection, accompanied by vomiting, caused by the streptococcal bacterium. (http://encarta.msn.com/dictionary_/erysipelas.html) 30 December 2008

Felon: A pus filled inflamation around a finger or toenail.

Fools cap: A term for a large piece of writing paper that was approximately 13" x 17".

(http://encarta.msn.com/dictionary_1861612760/foolscap.html) 30
December 2008

Forage: Food that comes from plant sources.

Fort Denaud: A Seminole Indian War fort, it was located about 20 miles
north of Fort Myers. In 1857, its location was moved two miles from its
original post. http://www.geocities.com/naforts/flsouth.html#seminole
10 October 2007

Fort Grant: Located in Arizona Territory, it was established as a Fort to
scout out hostile Apache Indians. The soldiers were often sick with fever
and ague. (GrahamCountyArizona/apacheconflictii.msnw) 10 October
2007

Fort Jupiter: Orginally this was a settler's fort, but it was later used as a
POW camp for the Seminole Indians.
(http://www.geocities.com/naforts/flsouth.html#seminole) 10 October
2007

Fort Kearny: This military post originally called Fort Clark was
renamed in 1848 after General Stephen Kearny. It was a post established
to protect emigrants as they traveled to Oregon. This was never a walled
fortification, but it served as a supply depot and sentinel post. The fort
was never under direct attack, but it served to outfit several companies of
soldiers that were on Indian campaigns.
(http://www.esu3.org/nebraska/ftkearny/ftkear.html) 10 October 2007

Fort Keis: A Seminole Indian fort located ten miles south of Immokalee.
It was used during the years of 1838-1857.
(http://www.geocities.com/naforts/flsouth.html#seminole) 10 October
2007

Fort Lauderdale: Located on the East coast of Florida. Used in the
early part of the Seminole Indian War. It was abandoned in later years.
Settlers did not arrive until around 1890.
(http://www.geocities.com/naforts/flsouth.html#seminole) 10 October
2007

Fort MacDowl: 1865-1891 – This fort was established in 1865 in Maricopa County, on the west bank of the Rio Verde. It was initially called Camp Verde but was renamed Fort MacDowl. It was created to combat hostile Apache Indians. In 1890 it became an Indian Reservation. (http://jeff.scott.tripod.com/ftmcdowell.html) 10 October 2007

Fort McRae: This fort was occupied during the years of 1838 and 1857 during the Seminole Indian Wars in Florida. It is on the eastern shore of Lake Okeechobee, it was a stockaded depot. (http://www.geocities.com/naforts/flsouth.html#seminole) 10 October 2007

Fort Myers: Fort Myers was Seminole Indian Fort that was occupied during the years of 1850 - 1858 & 1863 - 1865. It was a large stockade with four barracks, eight Officers' quarters, administration building, hospital, laundry, blacksmith, bake house, sutler, storehouses, and wharf. I visited the city of Fort Myers and the local musuem in January of 2008. There are no remains of the fort left to see, as the city of Fort Myers has been built over top of the actual site. Occasionally as street repair work is done, artifacts are discovered and placed in the musuem. (http://www.geocities.com/naforts/flsouth.html#seminole) 10 October 2007

Fort Ridgeley: In 1853 the military began building Fort Ridgely. Its purpose was to be a police post to keep peace for all the settlers moving into the land. In August of 1862, after nine years of tension, the U.S.-Dakota war began. The Dakota Indians attacked the fort directly on August 20 and August 22. The fort that had been training soldiers for the Civil War suddenly found itself under a direct assault. Army reinforcements were sent in to end the conflict. (http://www.mnhs.org/places/sites/fr/) 10 October 2007

Fort Yuma: First established in 1850 as a post along the Colorado river, its purpose was to provide protection, from the Yuma Indians, to emigrants that were traveling west along the southern route. The soldiers also maintained a ferry and they helped transport emigrants over the river. The fort saw sporadic use throughout the years, in 1864 it was used by the Quartermasters Corp. to establish a supply depot. In 1883 due to the extension of the railroads, the supply depot was not needed and the fort was abandoned. (http://www.militarymuseum.org/FtYuma.html) accessed 30 December 2008

Fort Randall: Constructed in 1856 in the Dakota Plains along the Missouri River. The fort was important in its day, strategically located as the Army's central supply depot. (https://www.nwo.usace.army.mil/html/Lake_Proj/fortrandall/military.ht ml) 10 October 2007

Garrison: A fortified military post that stationed soldiers.

Gellots 303: A metal tipped utensil dipped in ink and used for writing. The designation '303' refers to the style of the tip. The '303' is a stiff point that can be used to make fine lines.

Gila City: In 1857 gold was discovered upstream from Yuma on the Arizona side of the Colorado River. This began a gold rush to Arizona and Gila City was the boom town. The town had saloons, stores, a jail and church but by 1864, Gila City had become a ghost town. (http://www.ghosttowns.com/states/az/gilacity.html) accessed 30 December 2008

Governor's Island: From 1783 - 1966 Governor's Island was an Army post. After the Revolutionary War, two forts were built on the Island, Fort Clinton and Fort Jay. During the Civil War, Fort Clinton was used as a Confederate soldier prison and Fort Jay was used as a prison for Confederate officers. (http://encarta.msn.com/encyclopedia_761574939/Governors_Island.htm l) accessed 30 December 2008

Granite State: A wooden steamer that was built in 1852 for the Vermont Central Railway, by Moses and Quale at Cleveland, Ohio. (Julia Dickenson & Dorothy Bolton, *The Boizard Letters* (Empire, MI: Empire Area Heritage Group) pg. 145)

Grist mill: A building that was used to grind grains into flour that could be used for cooking.

Hickory Shirts: A work shirt made of a heavy material.

History of the United States: Probably the textbook entitled *History of the United States, from Their First Settlement as Colonies, to the Close of the War with Great Britain, in 1815.* It was published in Cincinnati, Ohio by Morgan & Sanxay in 1837.

Jackson: Probably Jackson, Michigan. The soldier's had just been drafted. They may have had to report to Jackson Michigan to muster in and receive their orders.

Jaconet: A light weight cotton cloth used for clothing.

Jessee: old word possibly meaning a severe scolding or beating

Kalsomine: An inexpensive water based paint for walls and ceilings. It contained zinc oxide, water, glue and sometimes a tint.

Keesick: I could not find anything about this word. In context, Oliver seems to be referring to a child.

Lager: A beer brewed by a slow fermentation process.

Lawn: A lightweight, sheer cotton or linen fabric.

Lawrence: This propeller is part of the Northern Transportation Co. fleet of boats. It was built in 1868 in Cleveland, OH. The propeller cost $50,000 to build.
(http://www.hhpl.on.ca/GreatLakes/Extracts/Details.asp?ID=2618&n=5)
10 October 2007

Leap Year: One common leap year tradition relating to courtship and marriage is that women can propose on February 29.

Lye: A strong soap consisting of sodium hydroxide.

Lyceum: A hall or auditorium that was used for lectures or philosophical discussions. The Progressive Lyceum of the Spiritualist movement was analogous to the orthodox Sunday School program.

Maine: A propeller that was built in 1852 in Black River Ohio. Its'

home port was Chicago. It was part of the Northern Transporation Company. (Julia Dickenson & Dorothy Bolton, *The Boizard Letters* (Empire, MI: Empire Area Heritage Group) pg. 145)

Maricopa Wells: The post was established in 1865 and was used intermittently until 1867. Maricopa became a station for the stage in 1868. . (http://www.geocities.com/naforts/az2.html#maricopa) 10 October 2007

McClellandtown : A small town in western Pennsylvania. It is believed that this is the town that Eleanor McGill was raised in by the Quaker family that took her in after the death of her mother.

McNallys Geography: A textbook by Francis McNally called "An Improved 'System of Geography."

Melodeon: A small parlor size organ.

Merrimack: In 1861 when the Confederate Army took over the Norfolk Navy Yard they discovered the burned out shell of the *USS Merrimack*. This hull was revamped and covered with iron. A steel ramming bow was also added. The *Merrimack* was then re-commissioned as the *CSS Virginia*. She is most famous for her engagement with the Union's ironclad ship the *Monitor*. Neither ship delivered a mortal blow to the other, the battle ended in a draw. (http://www.history.navy.mil/photos/sh-us-cs/csa-sh/csash-sz/virginia.htm) 10 October 2007

Miller, Leo: A spiritualist leader who taught that when a body died, the soul came back and communicated with children.

Minstrels: a troupe of performers. Sometimes they were known to sing Negro songs, they often had their faces painted black. http://www.thefreedictionary.com/Minstrels) 30 December 2008

Newport Barracks, KY: Even though Kentucky was a slave state and many of its residents were divided about the war, Kentucky remained in the Union. During the Civil War, the sick and dying were brought to the hospital at the Barracks. Confederate prisoners were also held here. The Barracks experienced many floods throughout its existence and in 1895 it was abandoned for military purposes and turned over to the city of Newport. (http://www.nkyviews.com/campbell/newport_barracks.htm) 30 December 2008

New Salem: A small town in western Pennsylvania, south of Pittsburgh.

North Port: A small town north of Glen Arbor. It was the first county seat, and John Fisher traveled there to register the Boizard's deed as well as for other official business.

Ordnance Appointment: The ordnance department in the Army would oversee the procuring, safe keeping and distribution of the weapons, ammunition, tools etc.

Oswegatchie: A merchant steam vessel built in 1867 in Ogdensburg, NY. Her home port was Port Huron, Michigan. (Julia Dickenson & Dorothy Bolton, The Boizard Letters (Empire, MI: Empire Area Heritage Group) pg. 145)

Paper cambric: Cambric was a densely woven fabric with a smooth finish. It was widely used from clothing to shoes. It was available in many different weights and grades. Paper cambric was not washable.

Paris white: Crushed chalk that is used as a pigment in paint to make putty or filler.

Peterson's Lady Magazine: A magazine that discussed ladies fashions in great detail. The November 1863 issue discusses the latest styles for: gloves, dressing coats, petticoats, hair, morning caps, morning wear, chemisettes, collars, cuffs bonnets etc. Other issues discuss recipes, review books and offer timely advice.

Pinky: In the early mentions of 'Pinky' I believe they are referring to a cat. After 1867, 'Pinky' is the name given to a small dog. The first dog was stolen, but Marietta talked about getting another one.

Pomatum: A perfumed oil or ointment for the hair.

Preempted: The right given to settlers to purchase public land.

Quadrille: A dance of French origins in which four couples dance a series of five sections.
(http://encarta.msn.com/dictionary_/quadrille.html) 30 December 2008

Quartermasters Department: The Quartermasters Department in the Army was responsible for providing the soldiers with supplies, food, equipment, clothing, artillery. Sometimes civilian help was employed to help accomplish these tasks.
(http://encarta.msn.com/dictionary_/quartermaster.html) 30 December 2008

Quinine Pills: A medicinal substance used to fight malaria that is extracted from the chinchona bark.

Row: brawl

Ructions: a noisy fight, disturbance, uproar

Rural New Yorker: A newspaper that was published weekly in Rochester, NY from 1850 - 1878 called Moore's Rural New Yorker.

Sanders New Series Spelling Book: This was the title of a spelling book written by Charles W. Sanders.

Secessia: A name used in reference to the southern states that had decided to secede from the Union.
(http://www.sonofthesouth.net/leefoundation/civil-war/1862/may/lincoln -slavery.htm) 30 December 2008

Sect'y Seward: Seward was the Secretary of State during Lincoln's presidential administration. An assassination attempt was made on Secretary Seward's life at the same time Lincoln was shot. Seward was stabbed, but he survived.
(http://www.archive.org/stream/assassinationdea00gard/assassinationdea 00gard_djvu.txt) 30 December 2008

Senna oil: This oil was used to relieve the symptoms of constipation. When combined with other substances such as pumpkin seeds, it was effective in the removal of parasites.

Skeleton hoops: lightweight, circular hoops that helped give a skirt, a round, full appearance.

Sleighing: The act of riding in a sleigh along the snow covered ground. In this time period, the sleigh would have been like a wagon, with skis instead of wheels and it would have been drawn by a team of horses.

Sloughs: lowlands or depressions that are filled with mud or mire, could also refer to bogs, or marshes.

Slush: May be referring to slop or mud along the streets, or possibly to the greasy nature of the food that he was eating.

Soldier's Rest: This refers to buildings that were built for the purpose of housing and feeding army regiments that were passing through. There is an article about a place called Soldier's Rest in Chicago. That building was fairly large with four rooms in it. There was a kitchen/dining room and the other three rooms were sleeping quarters. The dining room held twenty tables and each table could sit twenty men. It was decorated with streamers and stars and stripes. I have also seen an online picture of a kitchen in 'Soldier's Rest' Virginia. I am assuming that there was a building of this type in Michigan that Dorsey and Parker stayed at before they headed to Jackson to be mustered in, or receive their orders. (http://www.51illinois.org/page4.html)

Spirit of hartshorn: A solution of ammonia in water.

St. Louis Arsenal: This was a major supply depot for the states fighting the Civil war on the Western front. Oliver was working in Springfield at an arsenal in 1866, they cleared out all of their extra supplies and shipped them to the St. Louis Arsenal. (http://www.civilwarstlouis.com/arsenal/appendixC.htm) 30 December 2008

Subsistence Department: This department was responsible to secure contracts with suppliers to provide the needs of the army.

Sutler: A civilian storekeeper who had permission to operate a general store either on or nearby a military post. (http://www.thefreedictionary.com/sutler) 30 December 2008

Toledo: Actually called "The City of Toledo" this steamer received all new upper cabins and a fresh coat of paint in 1866.
(http://www.hhpl.on.ca/GreatLakes/Extracts/Details.asp?ID=5422&n=3)
10 October 2007

Typhoid Fever: An illness caused by the bacterium Salmonella Typhi. It is common worldwide. It is ingested through contaminated food or water. Left untreated it can last for three - four weeks. It causes symptoms like: fever, headache, chills, and constipation. In severe cases death can occur.
(http://encarta.msn.com/encyclopedia_761563010/Typhoid_Fever.html)
30 December 2008

Woods Museum: Colonel Woods Museum, Randolf Street (between Clark and Dearborn) in Chicago, Illinois.

Young America: The propeller was built in 1853 in Buffalo, NY. She was originally part of the Cape Vincent Line, later she belonged to the Northern Transportation Company. During the winter of 1859-1860, the Young America had many improvements made in order to accommodate first class passengers and to improve the comfort and convenience of its passengers. The Young America was rebuilt from the waters edge up in 1864.
(http://www.hhpl.on.ca/GreatLakes/Extracts/Details.asp?ID=7418&n=8)
10 October 2007

Zephyrs: A light weight fabric.

Index

269

281